Wealth creation or redistribution

How a select group profit at the expense of the rest.

Peter Kralj
10/21/2013

CONTENTS

PREFACE

The idea that I should first write a book about practical economics and finance came to me when I first started to question why our governments regularly manipulated interest rates. The lowering and raising of interest rates was clearly a transfer of wealth or purchasing power from one sector – savers - to another – borrowers. It seemed clear that the underlying theory of these wealth transfers was that some people spend money more sensibly than others and that if only the government could get the money into the right hands our economy would grow and grow and we would all get richer and richer for ever.

Yet no economists, politicians or academics ever addressed or questioned the premise that spending by one sector of our economy was more conducive to economic growth than spending by another.

There was also the assumption that lower interest rates were good for all despite the obvious harm they did to the wealth of savers. The simple theory seemed to be that since borrowers will spend their money whilst savers did not and since spending resulted at least theoretical in economic growth because it resulted in consumption then it is better for borrowers to have spending power than savers. Whether this theory makes sense or not I leave others to decide after reading this book. The injustice to say nothing of the legality of merely taking money from one sector to give to another outside the democratic process instead of using the taxation process is another matter and concerned me.

I also questioned the indiscriminate nature of these redistributions which helped borrowers who were struggling as well as borrowers who were earning vast sums of money and needed no help at the expense of savers who were extremely wealthy and could afford the redistribution of wealth as well as

1

savers who were barely getting by and could not afford the drop in their incomes.

Enquiries from those in authority and from journalists got me nowhere. They did not seem to have even considered the questions that I was raising and were unwilling to do so. Everybody knows I was told, by one well known journalist, that lowering interest rates is good for an economy. Clearly I was the only one who did not know.

I also noticed with alarm and concern the vast increases in salaries of bankers, executives, sports personalities and celebrities of various kinds that started in the 1980s and goes on to this day. I failed to understand why it was that these people were receiving massive increases in their incomes for doing what was essentially the same job that their predecessors did before for a fraction of their income. I also could not understand how it was that nobody in authority questioned whether this vast increase in wealth could be accomplished without any adverse consequences.

This book shows how where some person accumulates wealth without creating any new wealth somebody somewhere sooner or later gets to pay the corresponding price. That person need not even be in the same country. The loser will probably never have met or be aware of the existence of the person who made the corresponding profit. Indeed through the borrowing process the corresponding loss could be suffered many years after the profit was made when the connection between the profit of one and the loss of another will have been lost or at least become obscure.

The inevitable conclusion is that in advanced economies an increasing amount of economic activity results in a zero sum gain which is obscured in time through the process of borrowing.

Governments refuse to even acknowledge that this phenomenon exists. They assume that where any person becomes wealthy it must follow that that person is creating wealth for the economy.

They even assume that the new wealth created is invariably greater than the wealth that those who profit have accumulated. Logically this is nonsense. This book exposes these faulty assumptions.

It became clear that our economic managers were running our economy on the basis of a number of assumptions rather than on the basis of actual consideration of the facts as they existed.

These assumptions led me to a more critical analysis of what all perceived to be the new economic miracle, the new industrial revolution, the PC and the internet. For 30 years economists, businessmen and financiers have marvelled like small children in a candy shop at the new electronic toys that keep appearing before us under the guise of "technology". We are led to believe that the PC and the internet would revolutionise our lives, make us all wealthier. More and more of us would be able to afford more and more holidays, many would be able to afford second homes, that second car, the boat and many other luxuries that until recently were unthinkable for most of us.

Based on this belief or assumption I witnessed with scepticism the large number of people on modest wages buying homes abroad, buying boats and taking luxurious vacations. A new phenomenon overtook the young. After leaving school most of them – at least in the UK – took a "year abroad". Their parents paid.

How could they afford all this luxury? The answer at least in the short term was by borrowing on the ever increasing nominal value of their homes, where inflation had taken off in an apparently never ending spiral.

Yet nobody performed an analysis of how the new technology would make us all richer. Nobody analysed the difference between the use of this new technology for leisure and for business. So mesmerised were the business people by the new electronic instruments and the ease with which they could

3

reproduce images from far away that they assumed that this must make us all wealthier.

My own analysis of the widespread use of technology is that by far the greatest use of it was for social or leisure purposes rather than for business and to the extent that it was used for business it did not result in any increase in the end product of which it forms merely a part of the process of production. This book explains the mirage of new technology as the economic saviour of the world.

One feature of the social aspect of the new technology that concerned me is how it is free at the point of delivery – that old socialist phrase. Yet those who deliver this "free" service are fabulously rich. As I write Twitter is being sold to the public for $1 Billion. Those who spend time on Facebook, Google and Twitter do not pay for their fun. Payment is done collectively by those who happen to buy the goods that are advertised there, whether they use these IT products or not. I suspect that if these services were to be charged for usage they would not survive for long, or at least their owners would not profit so much. This phenomenon is generally ignored. The collective payment by others many of whom do not use a service for the entertainment of those who do is reminiscent of the worst aspects of socialism. Yet nobody in the US, where the government is brought to a stop from time to time because of the opposition to universal health care, complains, or even notices the contradictions.

The reality is that in an advanced industrialised society the interaction and interdependence on all of us on one another makes assessing our relative worth difficult if not impossible. Claims that we are rewarded on the basis of market forces seem hollow when there are more doctors and lawyers than we need but not enough plumbers, yet the former are considerably better paid.

I deal with the unemployment problem and how high pay has been sustained contrary to the principles of a market economy, in what is claimed – wrongly – to be a capitalist society. The manipulation of market prices for labour so as to sustain unrealistic and undeserved high salaries is a scandal with consequences for all of us. The way in which the market is manipulated to suit those who are overpaid for doing something that most can do is explained in the book.

Whereas economists and politicians all agree that inflation in consumer prices is a bad thing they seem to have come to an agreement that inflation in durable assets such as real estate and investments is a good thing. That is part of the reason why interest rates are kept artificially low. I explain the errors and faults of valuers of companies and real estate and how such errors can be avoided and how they led to the problems that we now face. I explain the interaction of inflation, interest rates, valuations and loans and how serious errors were made by ignoring these interactions.

In 2007 the financial crisis hit us and we discovered that our debts were overwhelming. The prosperity of the past 30 years had been largely built on a sea of debt. The authorities foundered. They continued to believe in the old policies that led to the disaster. They reacted in the only way that they know how. They forced interest rates as low as they possibly could and printed money. The patient that was taken ill from a drug overdose was prescribed an increased dosage of that drug.

The last chapter of this crisis has not been written but the Euro came in for special criticism, which I found to be unwarranted. The printing of money is seen as a panacea, a get out of jail free card. The Euro zone cannot indulge in this activity as easily as a national government and this is said to be damaging. Nobody needs to suffer if the government can just print money. That is the policy of the Western governments. This policy has been tried before and has catastrophic results. I deal with both these issues in the book.

The British government and many British experts have been amongst those most viscerally opposed to the Euro. It cannot work, they said, because the Euro zone economies are not identical. Yet the British government operated the largest and most widespread single currency – the Sterling area – the world has ever known. It covered economies that were so different it would make the Euro zone differences look insignificant. I deal with this duplicity in the book.

The authorities have been so focussed on the mountains of debt that they failed to notice that for every $ borrowed there is $ lent or saved. Governments talk about imbalances but do not explain what they mean. The real imbalance is that whilst some are burdened with more debt others must be revelling in more surpluses. I address this issue in the book and show how these imbalances occurred and how the problem of excess debt can be avoided.

The crisis brought into focus the many winners from this unbridled borrowing binge. It was obvious to me that what happened was the first phase of a vast redistribution of wealth. This started with the probably unwarranted rewards of vast sums to a large minority. Needless to say these winners did not complain. The crisis brought us to the second phase, deciding who would suffer the corresponding loss for these – in many cases – unlawful redistributions of wealth. Nobody was volunteering to suffer the losses. The government – the taxpayer – with its printing presses was naturally the first to step forward. The process is now taking place of allocating losses that correspond to the profits made by those who became wealthier during the past 30 years. Use of the printing presses means that the losers will be indiscriminately selected. Most will probably not deserve to suffer to pay for the profits of those who made the spectacular gains. They did nothing wrong. Yet they do not see the connection. This book attempts to expose what is really going on.

I concluded that unless and until our political masters learn that the modern developed western economy consists largely of wealth redistributors rather than wealth creators they will be unable to make the right decisions as to how to get out of the current catastrophic situation. How could they after all even consider that redistribution of wealth was what caused the problem when their basic premise was that all those who had profited had in fact not only created the wealth that they received but created wealth that exceeded what they themselves received and therefore benefited the rest of us. The theory – or rather assumption - is that those who have become vastly wealthy over the past 30 years are benevolent individuals who create more wealth than they keep for themselves and thereby benefit the rest of us. If my theory was right then those who enriched themselves were really taking it from and impoverishing the rest, without creating anything new. Certainly my theory was alarming, but it at least explained how and why we are in such a mess financially.

If our politicians really understood the difference between wealth creation and wealth redistribution through the banking and private sector their policies would be different. They might not be so afraid of high taxation driving what they believe to be the wealth creators, but who in reality are wealth redistributors out of the country. They might decide that new IT at a time when we have large number of unemployed is not necessarily a good thing unless it results in more end products being produced.

One of the popular myths is that the government cannot afford to pay its pensioners because government and science has been so successful that we are living longer. The inability to pay us is the result of our success. Nobody did the maths. They just assumed that it must be right that if we are living longer we cannot afford to receive pensions. I did the maths and found that this is untrue and misleading. The only reason why governments and employers cannot afford pensions is because of redistribution of wealth to the lucky minority.

The vast and clearly excessive salaries that bankers and executives have earned have been a scandal but the response of our economic managers has been that the matter should be handled by the shareholders. What none of them seem to realise is that the majority of shareholders are not enfranchised. The real shareholders are members of pension funds and investors in funds. These investors are not allowed to vote in the companies in which the fund invests. Only the fund managers can do so and the fund managers are amongst those who have profited from the vast increased in incomes during the past 30 years. They are not willing to control the excesses of the companies in which they invest their clients' money.

Nobody cared. Nobody noticed. Nobody listened. Of greater concern was the fact that the disenfranchised real owners of the companies were unaware of the power that they potentially possessed and how that power was being usurped by the fund managers, for their own advantage. Those in power had done very well and liked things as they were. They did not want to be told that what had happened was wrong and that their premises were wrong. They continued to pray and hope for growth. If only they could defer the evil day by more debt, economic growth would miraculously appear. They knew that the created real wealth and therefore the problems must be as a result of some other cause, some other person's misfeasance, possibly some structural problem with the economy. The thought that they were the cause of the debt problem by redistributing wealth to themselves never occurred to them. It still does not, and more worryingly governments are unwilling to even contemplate the possibility that this might be the case.

I wondered why our leaders seemed to consider that economic growth was as natural as a human right – an entitlement. They seemed to believe that economic growth will occur so long as we restructure our economy, so long as we pay less tax, so long as we have lower interest rates, so long as we are more educated. If only the government will do something. None of the pundits considered the possibility that it might actually be their fault, our fault. All the arguments and supplications are self serving and amount to nothing more than the claim by whoever is making the statement that if only the government would give him more money we would all be better off. This nonsense continues to be argued in all economic forums. There is of course no natural right to economic growth. Every athlete or performer peaks and so do economies. Ours may have peaked. Yet our politicians will not countenance that possibility. It would be political suicide to do so. How could a government get elected without promising its voters indefinite increases in prosperity. Telling the truth simply is not an option.

It was clear that economic management was based entirely on assumptions and hope rather than proper consideration of events as they really are. It was clear to me also that unless the authorities changed their thinking we would continue to stumble from one catastrophe to another, hoping that somehow by some miracle we would "recover". After all we "always have done". This itself is a questionable assumption.

I decided that my views had to be expressed in a book. The book explains in layman's terms how finance including some special techniques works, how money is created, how banks work. It explains the foreign exchange markets and interest rates, pensions and private equity or leveraged buy outs. It deals with corporate governance and real estate and the dangers of inflation even in real estate. It has no references like an academic book. It merely shows my experience in these areas and explains it like it is and not how those who work in those businesses would like us to believe that it is.

I invite readers to read selected chapters, all of which stand alone, like a number of essays on different topics. Hopefully reading one chapter might lead to reading others.

I encourage all students of economics or finance to read this book. It might give them a different insight into their subject and lead them to question what they are being taught.

This book should be read by those who listen to the news and are perplexed by the finance and economic reports. Hopefully it will enable them to be more critical of what they politicians say and do and lead to them being better informed when they vote in an election for a party that promises one form of economic management or another.

1. ECONOMICS AND POLITICS

Nearly all people wish to improve their living standards. This desire also existed in primitive times.

Economics is the study of the creation and distribution of wealth within a society. Modern economic discussion is all about growth, or the creation of wealth that did not previously exist. There is little discussion about distribution of wealth or the acquisition of wealth by appropriation, except by government through taxation. Yet the real economic problem in any advanced society is not so much how to create wealth but how to distribute the wealth that is created collectively. This is as much a political question as an economic one because it involves subjective judgments as to who contributed most, how to maintain peace and stability within a society and how, if possible, to encourage more wealth creation.

The modern so called capitalist economies distribute wealth through what are said to be market forces. The wealth that is distributed in this way is claimed to be the best measurement of the value of the contributions of those who received it towards creating the wealth of that society. The result is that anybody who receives payment for his services claims that such payment accurately reflects the wealth that he has created. That may have been true in primitive economies but this book will show that this is not really the case any more and that when wealth is created in advanced industrialized economies it is usually by means of a complex combination of effort by several persons whose relative contribution to the end product cannot properly be valued. It will also show that with advancing mechanization together with the operation of modern lending and creation of money by banks and governments it became possible for large

11

sums of money to be accumulated without any new wealth being created.

For political reasons governments find it helpful to flatter their electorates by saying that they all work hard for their money. They tell their electorates that the money that they earn accurately reflects the value of new wealth that they have created. The reality is somewhat different. It is now possible to become fabulously rich without creating any additional new wealth. Indeed the more advanced an economy is the more likely it is that those who participate in it are not required to produce any new wealth.

Governments are unwilling to even consider the possibility that modern economic activity involves mainly redistribution of wealth rather than wealth creation because to do so would imply that somebody else will sooner or later have to suffer the corresponding loss of wealth that a redistribution of wealth without wealth creation implies. It would also mean that the redistributions are from poor to rich. Yet the recent financial crisis shows that that is exactly what has been occurring.

It is not until governments and the financial regulators acknowledge the existence of this phenomenon, instead of talking blithely about economic growth as if it was a human right, that the present crisis of debt will begin to be solved.

The history of increases of wealth is primarily one of appropriation of wealth by one party from another, and not one of economic growth or real wealth creation.

Ancient societies achieved increases in living standards not through human innovation but by acquisition, through war and domination of other societies. European history until the 20th century was dominated by a series of wars the end purpose of which was frequently the acquisition of wealth from other countries. These wars did not result in the aggregate amount of wealth of the winner and loser being increased but in a transfer of wealth from loser to winner. The loser got poorer, many of its members were killed or became slaves, and the winner appropriated property that previously belonged to the loser. This was classic redistribution of wealth, or appropriation. Civil wars had the same result except that the redistributions of wealth were within the same country.

When the New World was discovered by Spain, Britain and France this proved to be a source for increased wealth – or real economic growth – in those countries. The East India Company also provided Britain with increased wealth from the East. However the East India Company was a trading company and although spices and silk from the East became available in Europe it did not necessarily involve any real wealth creation. When gold was discovered in South America it was transported back to Spain. That represented real economic growth. The British with their superior maritime power were able to frequently redistribute this wealth simply by attacking the Spanish ships laden with gold. This was of course nothing more than warfare at sea and it achieved the same objective as land wars achieved, except that it was more focused and not so destructive to property and persons.

The history of economics is therefore one of new wealth being discovered and being redistributed. Two important principles emerge from this history of economics that are important. Firstly that new wealth tended to come from the discovery of new colonies, and secondly that such wealth tended to be redistributed through wars and state sponsored theft or piracy.

The principle of improvement in living standards through wealth redistribution therefore has a long history and it is often a bloody and violent one.

Those ancient tribes and societies that were small and often itinerant and therefore owned no land shared the burdens and benefits of their existence. There was little opportunity to accumulate material wealth. They lived practically from hand to mouth and shared the good times and the bad in the same way as a small family does today. These itinerant tribes had little in the form of capital.

When societies became settled and land came to be owned tensions arose as to how the goods and services of the society were to be distributed amongst its members. These societies were no longer like large families. They did not share the consumable wealth that they produced. Land was the main form of capital wealth. Certainly ancient itinerant tribes had cattle and other livestock that are properly described as capital but land had the distinctive feature that it was permanent. Moreover so long as people lived on land the owner of land had a considerable degree of control over those who sought to make their living from the land.

The leaders of the settled societies made sure that they controlled as much land as possible. Here we see the beginning of serfdom. The serfs lived on and worked the land. The lords owned the land and charged the serfs for what they produced.

This is the start of the capitalist system. The owner of the capital – the Lord – extracted a return on his capital. The worker who produced food from the land was allowed to keep the minimum necessary. There was no question who controlled the reins of economic power.

Within these settled societies there was little opportunity to redistribute wealth in the way that nation states, except by theft, and that was punished most severely. Indeed in Norman times in England theft was punished more severely than the taking of a life.

These settled societies saw the powerful getting richer and richer as they accumulated not only large areas of land but buildings that lasted indefinitely. The poor had little opportunity to acquire buildings or land.

During this period of social development there was little improvement in living standards of the poor. There is no evidence of economic "growth" as the economists call it. Those who controlled the wealth, were the ruling class and they were able to increase their wealth by going to war against other countries. The poor were only able to participate in such wealth generating activities by joining the army and pillaging if they were successful. The price they paid for these opportunities was a high one since they had no guarantee of success. Of course the ruling classes also took a risk when they went to war.

There is some evidence of craftsmen introducing new instruments to make their work easier but these improvements were minimal and it is fair to say that there probably were little improvements in living standards as a result of what today we call economic growth in the middle ages, indeed until the industrial revolution. Certainly we see the development of the wheel and of more advanced forms of transport such as carriages, the use of animals to plough fields, houses replacing caves or tents and boats and ships with sails. However these developments and increases in living standards were modest. They were certainly not widespread.

In the 18th and 19th century the world experienced a revolution the likes of which have never been seen before and are unlikely to be seen again. This was the industrial revolution. Almost every aspect of life was to benefit as a result of the introduction of machines and electricity. These machines not only made life easier for all but they were able to manufacture better goods, in vastly larger numbers. They also enabled more land to be cultivated. Everybody benefited.

It was indeed fortuitous that the industrial revolution occurred at a time when the world had been fully discovered, mapped and colonized. There was no opportunity for the old world to acquire new wealth from the new.

The new machines paid for themselves many times over. The benefits to mankind were and are immeasurable. There were some disadvantages as people who before were employed in cottage industries were displaced by machines which did their work better and more accurately, and with greater ease and speed. Gradually these unemployed or their children came to be employed either in producing or maintain the new machines and factories or in providing better living conditions for those who were at work. However and over a very long period the vast majority came to be employed in office. A modern advanced industrialized society nowadays has considerably more people working in offices than in making the goods and providing the services – transport, health and such like – that increase the living standards of all.

There is no question that this period gave rise to substantial increases in real wealth. The goods and services that were produced as a result of the industrial revolution was far greater than any of the gold discovered in South America. It was a period of real increases in wealth. More importantly it did not occur as a result of wars and appropriation and therefore at the expense of the impoverishment of others. The new wealth was created as a result of human ingenuity and endeavour. It was real wealth creation, or real economic growth.

The move of the labour force from fields and factories into offices took many generations. It accelerated in the 20th century. At this time the world discovered that wars were not longer to be tolerated. Europe and the developed Western world entered a period of relative peace, with few exceptions. It was no longer possible to redistribute wealth in the old ways. The industrial revolution meant that unlimited wealth could be created without the ravages of war. The process goes on today with China and India now gradually emerging from a primitive economic state with the introduction of mechanization.

The regular improvements in living standards during this period of industrialization and peace have resulted in a level of complacency by economists towards the causes and effects of industrialization. There is a general assumption that economic growth will go on for ever. It is a natural right of modern democratic countries. Sooner or later we will all grow richer. Poverty will be eradicated. This is a mistake. A more critical examination of the state and trend of modern economics and in particular the movement of workers from factory and farm into offices requires careful examination.

What were the reasons for and the effects of this change in human activities. That should be the foundation of any analysis of modern economics. Before we address this extraordinary and substantial change of human activity from producers of goods and services into office workers we must mention

The rise in office workers was necessitated by the displacement of workers in farms and factories. People had to do something. Whether the office workers were necessary is something that was never examined. Office workers came to be referred to as bureaucrats, a rather disparaging term that implies that their work is useless and indeed a burden to those who produce the goods and services that we consume.

That these office workers were able to justify their existence by acquiring higher living standards than their parents who worked in fields and factories is not in doubt. Whether they were necessary to the economy is a question that has never been addressed.

To the office worker his employment was a means of participating in the wealth produced increasingly by machines. To the factory and farm owner the question whether the services produced by the office workers were of any incremental benefit to his business had never been addressed.

An appreciation of modern economics cannot be complete without addressing these questions in a modern context. Can the economy afford this army of office workers. Are they being paid the right price. What is the real value of what they produce. Can their continued employment at their current rates of pay be sustained. Indeed is there room for more of them. These questions are generally ignored but must be addressed in modern economies that are creaking at the seams and where unemployment is an increasing concern.

The new army of office workers used their newly acquired skills to persuade the factory owners – the entrepreneurs – that their services would enhance their profits or prevent them being depleted for example through competition. Their job was also to show the entrepreneurs how they could become more and more efficient, frequently by cutting costs, which often meant more job losses. Their function to this extent is therefore protective rather than to increase production of wealth. They helped one entrepreneur from losing business to another. They helped entrepreneurs to calculate their wealth and sometimes to make objective decisions as to whether a particular activity was profitable or not.

In general it is reasonable to conclude that office workers were able to participate in the wealth produced by the entrepreneurs but did not themselves create any new wealth.

The government also assisted in redeploying those who had been displaced by the new machines. It introduced increasing amounts of new laws and regulations that are commonly called red tape. Many of these rules are of no assistance to the production of wealth – indeed they are deleterious - but the entrepreneurs were required to adhere to them and therefore to employ more office workers as a result. Many of these regulations were beneficial for example to working conditions, but they did not result in any increase in wealth creation.

The absence of the ability to redistribute wealth through warfare or state sponsored piracy gave rise to another activity for office workers. Taxation has been around for ever. It was mainly a way of financing wars. It now came to be used to redistribute wealth domestically.

Government came to take a more active part in providing services. It operated and employed people in hospitals and

18

schools and in most cases made the lives of all better. There was also universal provision for the poor and economically inactive. There was sufficient wealth produced for a minimum standard of living to be achieved by all.

The new wealth created as a result of the industrial revolution was not spread evenly amongst the members of the society. Much depended upon the way in which the society was organized. Where the new wealth continued to be appropriated largely by the rich and powerful the result was revolution. This occurred in France in 1789 – 1799. A similar event revolution occurred in Russia in 1917. In both these cases the despised heads of state and many of their acolytes were brutally executed. The underlying cause was undoubtedly the inequitable sharing of the goods and services of the society.

The next important economic event occurred in 1929. It was known as the Great Depression. It started at different times in different countries and arguably had different causes. It lasted until 1939 or beyond in many cases and was terminated only by Word War 2.

Prior to the Great Depression there were no records regarding economic growth – referred to now as Gross Domestic Product ("GDP"). The undoubted, widespread and consistent increases in wealth that arose as a result of the industrial revolution were reversed as a result of the Great Depression. Unemployment became widespread, in some cases reaching 50% of the working population. People grew poorer.

Following the war there were firstly fewer people and lots of rebuilding which kept people employed for a considerable period. Secondly there were many fewer mouths to feed. This resulted in the prosperity of most nations apparently increasing.

There are two significant factors that occurred during the Great Depression. One was massive inflation in the US stock market. This led many who bought stocks to think that they could grow rich by just getting into the market. There was also massive and general inflation in Germany leading to the collapse of the currency.

This inflation, whether of the stock market or of ordinary goods resulted in massive redistribution of wealth.

Inflation came to be regarded as the curse of the modern economy – to be avoided at all costs.

Inflation is an increase in the price of goods or services in an economy. It has generally been regarded as harmful because it enables wealth to be transferred from one sector of an economy to another without anything being done by the transferees or transferors to deserve their profits or losses. During periods of inflation borrowers can profit at the expense of lenders or savers, home owners can profit at the expense of those who rent properties, workers can profit at the expense of pensioners. Inflation is indiscriminate. It can affect one item more than another. Those who are in business producing oil might profit at the cost of those who produce rice. Where there is inflation there is instability and it is a principle tenet of economics that a good economy is a stable economy. Inflation produces instability and one cannot tell what will happen.

A good economy is a stable economy. This is not appreciated often enough. Indeed instability for example in property prices has come to be regarded as a benefit, simply because it makes home owners feel good. They feel richer. Their homes have increased in value. Yet what they possess is the same land that existed many centuries before and its use value is exactly the same as it was then.

Inflation did not of course exist in times of barter. It is therefore necessary to examine the role played by money in economics.

Money has been around as a means of exchanging goods and services within an economy for a very long time.

Barter was cumbersome and inflexible. It was moreover impossible to be able to denominate every single item in a market in terms of all the other items. Money overcame these problems. It enabled large items to be exchanged for smaller ones. Exchanges of goods in a barter system generally occurred simultaneously. Money made this unnecessary. Goods could be sold one day and exchanged for other goods some time – often years – later. This is the start of the savings and credit systems.

Although the terms "savings" and "borrowings" are familiar to most it is helpful to redefine them in economic terms for reasons that will be clear later. Saving is the result of producing more than one consumes. Borrowing is the result of consuming more than one produces. Although it was theoretically possible to borrow in a barter economy the process was complicated and very limited. Money made borrowing and lending possible. There was lending and borrowing as far back as Roman times. Even governments got into debt and the history books show that the British government was regularly in debt.

The circumstances that lead to savings and borrowings are meant to be temporary. Thus the borrower, who has consumed more than he has produced has sooner or later to reverse the process. Likewise the saver who has produced more than he has consumed does so because sooner or later he will reverse the process and consume more than he produces. The reversal of the process wipes out the original debt.

This is an important aspect of modern economics that is insufficiently appreciated or even avoided and it is worth addressing it now. There are two ways in which a borrower who has consumed more than he has produced can reverse the process in the future, thereby repaying his debts. He can either produce more than he did when he borrowed and hand over the fruits of that additional production to the lender. Alternatively if he cannot produce more than he did before he has to reduce consumption below the level he did or would have done before.

Reducing consumption in absolute terms is difficult. It is easy for individuals to increase their living standards by consuming more than before. Reversing the process is painful and stressful. It is far easier to assume that the individual who has borrowed can at some time after he has borrowed increase his production by hard work or innovation. These assumptions depend to a large extent on what the individual does. In many cases increasing production is simply not possible. Nevertheless bankers, economists and politicians have tended to assume, without any evidence that this is possible, that we are all capable of increasing our production indefinitely. This is a serious mistake.

The ability to exchange goods freely through the intermediation of money also facilitated specialization. A farmer for example was able to devote all his efforts to growing one item of food that could later be exchanged for all the farmer's other needs. This enabled him to take advantage of the economies of scale and increased efficiency, productivity and quality.

Money has another vital and necessary function. It is a measure of value. Whereas in a barter economy a pig might have been equal in value to 2 sheep it might be very difficult to value a pig in terms of items of clothing or the value of a new house. Money overcame that problem so that all goods were measured in terms of their equivalent value in money. No matter how small or big each item had a value determined in money terms – its price.

The introduction of money into an economy was not without disadvantages. We are still discovering today many of the dangers and problems that would not have occurred in a barter economy.

The first and most obvious disadvantage was that theft became easier. Not only was it easier to steal money and buy a table or a pig with the stolen money than it was to steal the table or the pig but money is homogeneous so that tracing stolen money was far more difficult than tracing a stolen pig or table.

Another problem was that money is an unstable measurement. Whereas a temperature of 25C will remain the same in 200 years time and a mile was exactly the same length 500 years ago the same is not true of money. Money changes its value constantly with inflation or deflation. It is thus only a temporary and relative measurement of value at any time. A loaf of bread might change its price but it is still the same loaf of bread. It is no more valuable than before. If it changes price by more than, for example the price of a kilo of tomatoes the result is that value will be transferred from the owner of tomatoes to the owner of bread or vice versa. In a barter economy it would have been very difficult to say that the exchange rate of bread and tomatoes had changed. Consumers would notice and laugh at the obvious mistake. By using money as the intermediate means of exchanging of these two items it became possible for the relative wealth of the owners or producers of any two items in a market to change. The same principle applies to any other items within an economy. Money therefore could be a camouflage for wealth transfer to the producer or owner of one item profited at the cost of the owner or producer of another item.

For a long time the amount of money available was reasonably fixed as it depended upon the amount of gold held by the country's central bank. Prior to the introduction of paper money actual gold was used as money. In the 20th century this link between the amount of paper money and gold was abandoned and the amount of money in circulation was left to market forces. Nowadays all money is intrinsically worthless and its value depends upon the amount of goods circulating in an economy. It is known as Fiat money.

Money these days is created by banks. Whenever a bank makes a loan money is created. Put simply the bank creates an asset in its books – the loan to the borrower - and at the same time creates a deposit from which the borrower can draw. This deposit is new money created. When a loan is repaid the process is reversed and money is destroyed or cancelled. When the amount of money grows quicker than the goods and services available the result is inflation – rising prices. When inflation occurs savings are depleted without any money changing hands. Those who hold goods whose price increases, gain at the expense of those who hold money or the right to receive a fixed sum of money. Wealth is thereby redistributed from one party to another often without the parties doing anything. This dangerous and damaging process was not possible in times of barter. Neither was it possible to any realistic extent when the amount of money – and therefore loans – was controlled by the amount of gold which was largely finite.

It is important to dwell for some time on this subject because the risks are potentially catastrophic. An increase in the supply of money is similar to the increase by a company of its share capital by issuing bonus shares. This is not an uncommon event. Companies frequently issue bonus share – shares that do not require the payment to the company of any consideration by the recipient of these bonus shares. When free shares are issued to some shareholders but not to all the result is what is called "dilution" in the shares of the original shareholders. Dilution is another word for "redistribution". The value of the original shares falls and the result is a transfer of value from those who did not receive the new bonus shares to those who did.

An example will make this clearer. A company has share capital of £100 in nominal value and assets of £100. It issues 100 new bonus (free of charge) shares of £1 each in nominal value to a new shareholder. The share capital is now 200, £1 shares but the value of these share is still £100 because the assets remain the same. The new shares are now worth only 50p each. The result is that those who receive the new bonus shares have received £50 of value and those who previously owned shares worth £100 have shares worth £50. This is precisely what happens when money is created. Pending repayment, when the position is reversed, value – or purchasing power - is transferred from the holders of money before the creation of the new money to those who received the new money.

This process of dilution is regarded as so wrong that it is prohibited by law. Any bonus shares must be issued to the existing shareholders in proportion to their shareholdings. The money in an economy is therefore like shares in a company. It represents the right of its owner to a share of the company's assets and production.

Where new money is created for the purposes, for example, of building a new house or factory that new factory or house represents new wealth. It is the equivalent of paying for shares in the example above. In such circumstances so long as the value of the new asset is equal to the new money created no damage occurs. No inflation occurs and no transference of wealth occurs either.

Unfortunately not all loans result or are made for the purpose of creating of new wealth the value of which is equal to the new money created. Many loans are made to pay for existing assets such as existing property for example. When no new wealth is created the creation of new money is the equivalent of issuing bonus shares for no consideration. The result is exactly the same as in the example above. Wealth is redistributed as a result.

Inflation emerged again as a serious problem in the 1970s in many developed Western countries leading to a series of economic recessions in various countries.

Politicians and many economists consider that only general inflation is a danger. This is a serious mistake. Whether general or limited, inflation results in value being transferred from one person to another without any action by either party. That is its major danger.

Inflation in one sector of the economy tends sooner or later to be followed by inflation in other sectors as equilibrium is restored. Thus for example if there is inflation in property rents sooner or later the baker will have to increase the price at which he sells his bread in order to meet his rental obligations.

This redistribution of wealth – whether through inflation or otherwise - is dangerous to an economy because money represents purchasing power. The holder of money has the right to claim delivery of goods (and services) in an economy up to the value of that money. It is dangerous to allow too much money to be accumulated in a few hands because that gives those who have the money the ability to dictate how the labour force is employed. It might for example result in a reduction in the production of goods required by the majority and the production instead of luxuries for the small exclusive minority. Land that could be used to grow food for a whole country might for example be used for the amusement of the few wealthy individuals. They might choose for example to convert valuable agricultural land for golf courses. The wealthy might just choose to buy land and leave it lying fallow. The result could be starvation for the masses.

Politicians should be forever wary of such imbalances. Any government that ignores the widening gap between rich and poor is failing in its primary duty to maintain the peace.

Finally in advanced economies where co-operation was required in the production process money enabled vast sums of purchasing power to be redistributed by stealth leading to the impoverishment of innocent parties and the unjust enrichment of others. In all its functions, whether as a facilitator of exchange of goods and services, a store of wealth or as a measure of value money was intended to be the servant of the real economy. Money was only intended to change hands if there were exchanges of goods and services and then only to the extent of the real value of such goods and services.

Following the abandonment of the gold standard money came to have a life of its own. More and more ways were found of redistributing money without any corresponding real economic activity. Borrowing was a primary source for redistribution of wealth without the creation of any wealth simply through the process of overpricing. The introduction of money as a means of exchange did not and does not alter the substance of economic activity. This is the production and exchange of goods and services. Indeed it is still reasonable to regard all economies as substantively barter economies because money is merely an intermediate step in the process of exchanging goods and services. In a barter economy however transfers of wealth were obvious, understood by all and for that reason controlled. It was not possible to become wealthy without creating something of value. Process involved in the production of goods and services were simple and the effort involved in their creation was known and understood. The consumer was often able to say "I could do it myself more cheaply" and that alternative set the price of any goods.

The real value of a tomato was well known and understood. If the manufacturer of a shirt wanted the farmer of tomatoes to supply him with 100 tons of tomatoes for a year he would be the subject of ridicule.

When the goods being sold became more complex the possibility of paying more for goods and services than they were truly worth became greater. The manufacturer of a car or a train might ask for the equivalent of a lamb to be delivered to him every week for 30 years. How was the farmer who sold the lamb expected to understand the real value of the car that he was buying. Perhaps he merely decided that he could spare the one lamb per week.

Within the factories the situation became more difficult. The proceeds received for the sale of a car was to be distributed by the entrepreneur amongst not only his work force but the – forever increasing – army of office workers who provided services to him in marketing, finance, law and other areas the value of which he was unable to determine easily. The result was that he distributed the proceeds in a very subjective way. He used his discretion. Certainly there was some competition by these service providers but they had an interest in paying themselves as much as they could. The vital control by the consumer, who was buying a car was lost. The consumer could not say that he was not paying for advertising costs. He had no say in determining how his money was shared. That was done initially entirely subjectively by the entrepreneur.

This subjectivism in distributing the proceeds for sale of a complicated product meant that it became possible for persons to acquire vast sums of wealth without creating anything of value. How does one for example value a footballer. The football club receives revenue from viewers. They decide what they are willing to play to attend a match. However a TV company pays for the right to show a match. It gets paid by viewers, many of whom might never want to watch the match. The TV company sells advertising. Many of the viewers might never buy the product. The process is extremely complex. If a TV company or the trader who paid for the advertising goes bankrupt who is to blame. Who was paid too much. Was it the footballer. Did the TV viewer pay too little. It is impossible to say. Many will have profited, some receiving far more than they deserve. Money made this possible.

Redistribution of wealth should never be confused with wealth creation. That is a mistake that all modern governments and politicians make. They assume that if anybody acquires more money it must be because he has created something of value – new wealth. This is demonstrably a false premise and this mistake lies at the bottom of all the economic problems of today. Until politicians and economists accept the principle that accumulating increasing amounts of money does not mean that wealth has been created they will be unable to manage their economies properly and they will continue to lurch from crisis to crisis.

It is worth repeating this mantra. New economic wealth is only created if new goods and services are created. If a person acquires additional money without creating some new goods or services equal in value to that additional money then the additional money or some of it has been merely redistributed and somebody else will sooner or later have to pay the price by becoming poorer as a result.

Politicians are far too keen to acquire the support of their electorates by complementing them on their hard work. Everybody, no matter how little new wealth he or she creates is told that they "work very hard" for their money. This may indeed be so. However in many cases their money has merely been redistributed at the expense of someone else who will suffer the consequences. Debt, particularly long term debt enables this link between the gainers and the loser to be lost in time.

Many reading this will look around to see who amongst them has not created new wealth. It cannot be them of course because they "work hard for their money" so it must be somebody else. All are able to identify those on social security or unemployment benefit as being the beneficiaries of wealth redistribution. Few who work for a living will regard themselves in the same position. Sadly in an advanced industrialized society the redistributions of wealth that occur through the tax system are trifling amounts compared to the redistributions that occur in the private sector.

This is not the place to examine particular activities that produce no wealth or which produce wealth that is of far less value than the money they accumulate. I will however identify a few of these activities in general terms. All those involved in the sale or redistribution of existing assets, whether homes or financial securities are involved in redistributing wealth. Nothing new is created as a result of their activities. Yet they profit as a result. The sale of any such existing assets at a profit or a loss are redistributive and not wealth creating activities. All those involved in the process, whether lawyers, estate agents or bankers are likewise involved in redistribution of wealth for which someone else will sooner or later have to suffer the cost. Gambling in financial instruments is a similar large scale redistributive activity. Those involved in bureaucracy and red tape whether in government employment or the private sector are involved in redistribution. Professionals who charge too much for their services are involved in redistribution even if they are involved in bringing into existence some new asset, such as a ship or plan or factory. Marketing executives involved in maintaining market share are involved in redistribution and so are accountants who provide useless information on businesses that nobody reads. The list is practically endless. It is easy to see that the numbers involved are enormous. Indeed it is only those who are involved directly or indirectly in the creation of new assets that can be genuinely called wealth creating.

As far as the service sector is concerned this is generally thought to represent all those not involved in production. That is a mistake. Retailers for example are part of the manufacturing process and these activities are truly wealth creating. The service sector is only those involved in delivering services to the public. They include for example health practitioners including, administrators.

Entertainers, journalists, authors, and broadcasters to mention but a few are wealth creative because they enhance the quality of life of the rest of us. Bankers could be wealth creative or redistributive. They are wealth creative when they lend money for the purposes of building something new. They are redistributive when they become involved in re-circulating something that already existed. Thus most bankers are not wealth creators, they are merely redistributors of wealth. They have been disparagingly referred to as casino banks or as doing something that is socially useless. In most cases that is a fair description particularly as banking and investment activity grows and grows. Estate agents also could be wealth creative when for example they are involved in selling a new development but redistributive when changing ownership of existing properties.

It is not an easy task to identify those who are wealth distributive or wealth creators but the principles will be clear.

Just because one does work that is wealth creative does not mean that he is not involved in redistribution of wealth. Much will depend upon whether the wealth or money that they make for themselves is the correct value. No problem arises when the services of particular individuals is delivered to the end users. That is the right value.

When payment for services is made not by the end user but by some intermediate business the question of value becomes more confused. A banker might for example charge tens of millions of dollars to raise capital for some new business. That new business is valued at $1Bn so the bankers' charges are easily lost as part of the capital cost. However the valuation is based upon an assumption that the profits of the business will grow and grow. In fact the forecasts are hugely optimistic and the new venture is only worth $50mm. The bankers, lawyers and all others involved have redistributed vast sums of money from savers to themselves and the promoters of the business.

Another common error made by economists and politicians is that innovative new products are always wealth creative. This is naïve. New products should be divided between consumer and producer products. A new consumer product – such as the Iphone - undoubtedly represents new economic wealth. Unfortunately it is wrong to assume that it represents an increase in our living standards. We have to pay for new consumer products no matter how attractive and alluring they are. There is no doubt that the new IT products on the market over the past 30 years have not only given us a lot of pleasure but have been useful in numerous ways. The production by one small sector of an economy of a consumer item is only part of an exchange upon which all economies from time immemorial depend. What is the producer to receive in return for this new invention. I am not aware of any politician or economist who has analysed or even questioned the process. They have merely assumed that if the consumer pays money for the new product then we are all better off. This is a serious mistake.

All new goods and services are either wealth creating or replacing. The new café chains may be regarded as new activities and therefore wealth creating. However they probably replaced the pub as a source of leisure entertainment. To the economy they probably represent a zero sum gain. Economists should be forever wary about regarding a new business as incremental wealth. New businesses are either new incremental wealth or replacements for old businesses. Music shops on the high street have been replaced by internet sales. The latter are therefore not incremental. Yet economists think that the internet always represents incremental wealth. That is a mistake.

Certainly there is a time lag between the new business being created and the old dying out. During that period there appears to be economic growth. It is soon followed by the demise of the old business, or by more debt.

Economists make this mistake because of the experience of the industrial revolution, when the whole economy increased its productive capacity by introducing machines. Thus the maker of a car was able to sell his cars to people involved in the production of TV sets, travel companies and washing machines, each of whom was involved in producing more and more as a result of industrialization. That widespread ability to increase production does not exist today. We assume that IT will produce these efficiencies and make us all more wealth but this is an illusion. It is merely an assumption that has led to vast redistributions of wealth and will therefore sooner or later result in vast debts being incurred and sever reductions in living standards to compensate for the redistributions in wealth.

This is the principle of reciprocity. If the manufacturer of the Iphone or some other new popular product sells it to consumers there is no doubt that new wealth has been produced. However one has to consider how the consumer is going to pay for that new product. Unless the consumer is in a position to produce more goods or services – homes, cars, travel, clothing, food in return the new product can only be paid for by the consumer reducing his expenditure on other products. Wealth will be redistributed from old products to new. Alternatively the new product will be sold in return for a promise that the consumer will be able to reduce his consumption of other products in the future. If the consumer is not able to do so the new product will effectively be a gift. That will only happen once.

Now that by far the largest part of an advanced industrial economy is employed in offices the assumption has been made that the introduction of efficiencies in such services are wealth productive. That is a serious mistake based on the failure to properly analyse what occurs when such efficiencies occur.

Administration and accounting systems are part of the production line – when they are wealth creative – that produces an end product. It is the end product in the production of which all those on the production line participate that constitutes new wealth. The production line cannot move at a speed that is faster than the slowest part of the process. It is thus only if the efficiency produced by some new process or electronic tool results in more of the end product being produced that the "efficiency" results in wealth creation.

Whereas it is clearly true that when efficiencies are introduced into office work the amount of time spent in that part of the production process is reduced the costs of production should be reduced the economic benefit of such efficiencies is illusory.

Any industrial process is a production line. It moves at the speed of the slowest step in the process. It is only if the speed of the slowest step in the process is increased that more end products will be produced. This simple and basic business fact has been ignored in modern industrial societies.

Office work is part of the production process. Unless office work is an essential part and it is slowing down the production of the end product nothing will be achieved by making that step in the process quicker.

It is practically unknown that office work slows down the production process or is instrumental in speeding it up. It follows that we should treat efficiencies in office work with great caution before we assume that they will result in greater wealth for all of us. Generally the effect of introducing efficiencies in office work is to increase unemployment without any benefit to the economy. Wealth is merely redistributed from those who lose their jobs to others who might be the entrepreneur or other workers on the production line including perhaps other office workers.

This simple and logical principle is ignored by economists. It is a serious mistake. Office work is treated by economists not as part of the production process but as an end in itself. It is treated as a service. Improvements in office efficiency are regarded as increased productivity and therefore as creating additional wealth. They do not. It is of course questionable whether office work, or much of it adds any real value to the production process.

Another example will make these misconceptions clear. Assume that a factory is making televisions sets. It produces 100 sets a year and there are 10 workers each of whom is paid by receiving 10 TV sets every year. The 10 workers include 2 office workers who work at the factory full time. The two office workers devise a computer programme that results in their work being done in half the time they previously took. The number of TV sets produced remains the same. Yet as a result of their increased efficiency the office workers ask for an receive two extra TVs per year. They spend the rest of their time producing more

34

management information that also results in no additional TVs being produced. The foolishness of this approach is clear for all to see. Yet this is the approach adopted every day when technological improvements in office work have been introduced. Of course the efficiency improvements are usually produced by outside parties. The result is the same even if the outsiders receive 2 additional TVs.

It is pointless increasing the efficiency of a part of a process that does not result in any increase in the end product, and it is detrimental to reward those who create efficiency in such a process by giving them a larger share in the end product. The only sensible reward that should have been given to those office workers in the above example is additional time off. Yet instead of giving workers who produce efficiencies in a process that has no effect upon the end product more time off they are rewarded with more purchasing power. This is a fundamental flaw in the thinking of modern economists and politicians.

Of course if we accept that most office work is red tape and of no value except that it enables those who work there to participate in the proceeds from sale of the end product then the exercise of making office work more efficient is absurd. How can one make an intrinsically worthless activity efficient?

Modern economists assume without thinking about it that any efficiency in any part of a production process must automatically produce additional new wealth and that those who create that efficiency are entitled as a result to receive a greater share of the wealth produced by an economy. The inevitable result of such muddled thinking is that new wealth is assumed to have been created whereas it is often merely existing wealth that is redistributed. The use of money as a reward for these "efficiencies" enables this redistribution to be camouflaged. Sooner or later however somebody will have to suffer the corresponding loss.

The process of redistributing wealth by buying and selling property or financial instruments at changing prices whether the asset in question was increasing in value or decreasing came to employ larger and larger numbers. Innovative financial instruments came to be employed so as to make the process of wealth redistribution easier. These instruments enabled bets to be taken and money redistributed without any new wealth being created even by those who did not own assets that were notionally being traded. Indeed instruments were created that only had a synthetic value. The gambling business is now vast. It is not limited to horse racing and football matches. The stock market and the other exchanges are vast with trillions of dollars at risk and changing hands daily. The sole purpose of these activities is redistribution of wealth. No new wealth is created. All trades are in existing assets whose underlying value does not change as a result of these trades.

How were these vast overvaluations sustained for such long periods. Unfortunately governments were complicit in the process. Most overvaluations were sustained through the involvement of borrowed money. Whether it was stocks or real estate the value of an asset is based upon its future sustainable profits. In order to arrive at the value of such long term assets it is merely necessary to see what amount of money, invested at the "going rate" will produce that income – rent for real estate, and profits for companies. As interest rates fall the "going rate" on particular investments rises. Thus fund managers and real estate professionals always put pressure on governments to lower interest rates. Keeping interest rate low has another benefit for borrowers. It reduces their costs. Companies that are borrowers thus make greater profits. Home buyers have less to pay to their lenders.

It is impossible to over emphasize the principle that real wealth creation only occurs when new goods are manufactured. Wealth creation and wealth redistribution are two totally different things. Accumulation of money should be but in modern economies is often not the result of wealth creation. This principle is ignored by commentators, economists and politicians alike. They merely assume that wealth accumulation is the result of wealth creation. They assume that the only redistribution of wealth is carried out by the government when they raise taxes and pay those who are economically inactive. This is a very serious mistake.

One other significant change that contributed to the process of wealth redistribution was to occur in the way in which businesses were owned.

The entrepreneur had previously used his own money. He was able – within the limits of his profitability – to control the wages that were paid directly or indirectly by him to the new army of office workers. However his profits came to be reduced substantially not only because of the ever increasing cost of the office workers that he had to support but also through competition. In effect he came to consider that the available profits were not worth the risk.

The entrepreneur was a manager investor. He risked his own money backing and managing his investment.

He was soon to be replaced by fund managers who provided collective funds of savers to take the financial risks and managed the investment risk taking without risking a penny of their own money in the process. The business managers also came to be remunerated without having to take any risk. Here we see the emergence of the professional managers and the collective ownership of businesses. This is a major step in the departure from classical capitalism and towards collective ownership. The savers did not know how to manage a business. That function was taken over by the professional managers with – frequently - academic qualifications. Thus companies came to be owned by small investors most of whom had – and still have - no direct say in how the business was carried on and even if they did so would not have been able to understand what was involved. More importantly they were unable – and still are – to decide except collectively, how their money is to be used or how profits are to be distributed. The professional managers had nothing to risk. Thus whereas the entrepreneur took responsibility for his actions because he risked his own capital and reaped the rewards or suffered any losses the new business model split the two functions. All the risks fell upon the individual collective savers who could not say how their money was used. The decisions, including how profits were to be distributed were taken by the managers. Not unnaturally the managers awarded themselves the lion's share of profits in the form of bonuses.

The fact that they took no risk with their own money did not stop the managers – essentially part of the labour force – comparing themselves with the entrepreneurs of old and to demand rewards for their labour that were equivalent to or greater than those that the old entrepreneurs earned. They called themselves - and continue to do – capitalists, as if they were taking risks with their own money. In fact they were and are nothing of the sort. They are part of the labour force.

How were they to achieve the large rewards that they considered they were entitled to receive. The process was achieved and continues to be by means of the camouflage of money, borrowing and an inability of the real risk takers – the savers – to have any say in how their money is shared with the managers.

Like the trade union bosses of old the collective investors had and do not have any real say. There is no process in place to enable their collective views to be obtained and reflected in the way in which the companies that they beneficially own are run.

Politicians, either negligently or complicitly, have come to accept that the real owners of the companies are not those who beneficially own the shares but the managers who manage the pension and other funds. These pension and other fund managers are on the side of high rewards for the managers of the businesses because they too want to earn the large rewards that exceed what the entrepreneurs of old would have earned.

Whereas in the past any managers were paid the minimum amount that the entrepreneur considered appropriate and any super profits belonged to him this principle was reversed. Now with the new collectivization of business ownership the managers paid the investors the minimum return and paid themselves super profits in terms of bonuses. These bonuses could be massive and the managers took no risks.

The principle of the bonus is or should be that one is paid a bonus for supererogatory performance. Soon managers demanded – from other managers – bonuses for doing their jobs. Their job, indeed their duty according to law, was to do the best possible for their shareholders so in theory no bonus was required. It was after all their duty to do a good or the best job possible. Yet they demanded bonuses and got them.   They operated the system on the basis that their remuneration was controlled by "market forces". That was untrue. If there was a market it was rigged and exclusive. Their remuneration was never fixed by those whose capital was at stake in the businesses. They were not determined by ordinary people who bought the end product. They were determined by small and exclusive "remuneration committees" made up of other managers.

The individual investors were largely disenfranchised. They had as much control as an individual voter has over politicians. Indeed in most cases the control he had was worse because any investment a saver has through a fund does not entitle him to a vote. It is the fund manager who is entitled to vote and he does so depending on his own best interests. Frequently this coincides with the best interests of the managers of the companies whose shares are held by the funds.

That problem is that if one man's profit is not matched by new wealth created of at least equal value then sooner or later somebody will have to pay the price. The process always starts with overpayment. There are rarely complaints when that occurs. The overpayment is camouflaged by an overvaluation of some large capital asset. At some time in the future that large capital asset is found to have been overvalued and losses have to be suffered by others. At that stage there are no volunteers to take the burden. Those who have profited have long since taken their money and want to keep it. Those who are asked to bear the burden do not know why they are being singled out. They protest. They march. They riot.

Accordingly any government that fails to make the distinction between people or sectors becoming rich and creating real wealth and that allows massive redistributions of wealth without wealth creation is failing in its primary duty to keep the peace.

The Blair government was famous for stating that they had no problem with anybody becoming "filthy rich". They should have said that they had no problem with anybody becoming filthy rich by creating new wealth of at least equal value. Anybody who became filthy rich without creating any new product that was at least of the same value as his enhanced richness is merely stoking up a problem in the future.

It is fair to say that uncontrolled redistribution of wealth by the private sector is the most insidious aspect of modern economies.

Amongst the largest wealth redistributors as a result of the departure of the entrepreneur were the Private Equity fund managers. As their name implies they were involved in acquiring and managing unlisted companies. However unlike other fund managers they did not hold investments to earn dividends and make occasional capital gains. The private equity fund managers were there for a short period to restructure the financing side of the businesses that they purchased. This generally involved raising vast amounts of debt to replace the share capital of these companies and then to pretend that the remaining equity was worth much more than before. They were so immensely successful that a whole new industry grew up as a result of what were often known as the Leveraged Buy – Out businesses and many of the participants became fabulously wealthy. This is not the place to examine in detail what the Private Equity firms did and how they operated. I shall address this in a later chapter. The important point for the purposes of this chapter is that the wealth created by the underlying companies was their turnover. As a general rule these Private Equity companies did not increase the turnover and therefore the wealth produced by these companies by a single £. They were in any event buying existing companies. The money that they accumulated for themselves and the managers whom they frequently backed in their acquisitions (the managers often had control of the companies in what were called management buy outs) was therefore a simple redistribution of wealth. There was no wealth creation. Somebody somewhere sooner or later had to pay the price. By that time however it was too late. The Private Equity players had got away with the money.

How were they able to do so. They were able to maintain – wrongly – that the companies that they had bought were worth more than they were worth before they acquired them and that their additional value was the result of replacing some of the equity with debt. So long as that fiction was sustained they would enjoy their money without any alarm bells ringing. Only when the added risks that had been placed upon these companies in the form of additional debt resulted in failures of these companies was the fiction realized. By then it was too late. Too much had happened. There were too many others who could be blamed for the failure. To this day few Private Equity firms have been held to account for these vast redistributions of wealth.

Not only the Private Equity firms and their clients – the managers – profited but also the army of lawyers, valuers and accountants who assisted them. They too profited from these vast redistributions. The politicians were well pleased though because they thought – wrongly - that new wealth was being created and in any event unemployment was being alleviated.

The problem of unemployment came about largely as a result of the industrial revolution. There was always some unemployment in all but the smallest of economic units. However the introduction of machines that could do most of what man could do albeit quicker and more precisely made the problem appreciably worse.

The principle of rewarding the labour force with sums that an old entrepreneurs who risked their own capital would have been happy to receive, made the problem of redistribution of wealth. It was easy to make money – less easy to create wealth. It has been referred to as a great Ponzi scheme. The description is not inappropriate. More and more people came to be employed in redistributing wealth. The bonus system played its part. The principle was that if your bet came off you got a bonus, if it did not then the shareholders whose money you were betting with lost out. Heads you win tales they lose. It was a Goldilocks economy and like Goldilocks it was fictitious.

Not only did money start off being the servant but became the master of the economy but economists came to believe that the real economy could be controlled by turning on and off the supply of money. They still do.

In the 1930s the problem of unemployment grew to massive proportions as the great depression took hold of many Western countries. Economists like John Maynard Keynes considered that money could be deployed as the driver to bring people back to work.

His theory was that the ability of industrialists to produce goods was limited by the demand for such goods. Accordingly if more money was given to consumers they would spend it on more goods. Producers would hire the unemployed to satisfy the demand for the additional goods and in that way unemployment would be reduced.

Keynes was not able to put his theory to work because the problem was solved for a time by World War 2 which created employment in the military for 6 years, reduced the workforce as a result of the casualties of war and for 20 years or more created more employment as a result of the post war rebuilding and the introduction of social programmes.

Keynes's principles are very popular today. There are in fact no other ideas about how to increase output and reduce unemployment using market forces. The policy has many problems.

The first problem with giving more money to people to spend it is how to distribute it. There are unsurprisingly many volunteers each with self serving and ostensibly altruistic arguments. The principle argument by the volunteers is always the same. If the government gives the money to them unemployment will be reduced and the economy will grow as a result. The employed propose that they should get tax cuts. They will then spend the money, that will cause factories to hire the unemployed to produce the goods that they buy and everybody will be employed and more prosperous.

The unemployed and their advocates propose that the government should give the money to them. They will spend it and create job opportunities. Alternatively the government can indulge in building programmes that will require the hiring of the unemployed or at least some of them.

Irrespective of which of the volunteers for the handout of these "bonuses" in money wins the argument one thing is certain and that is that wealth will have been redistributed from those who previously had money to those who receive the new money. If this additional demand for goods results in new goods being produced that would not otherwise have been produced then new wealth will have been created. If that wealth is consumed then after that time we are back to where we started. It is only if the new wealth produces additional recurring wealth, in short it

43

is reproductive wealth such as a factory or ship or a farm that any unemployed who are deployed as a result of the new money created will continue to be employed.

Unfortunately it is just as likely that those who receive the new money will buy existing assets, possibly financial investments – savings – that will increase in nominal value – inflation – as a result. In short it might achieve nothing even in the short term, aside from a redistribution of wealth as explained above.

These vast redistributions of wealth that I have described and that are the hallmark of the modern industrialised economy should theoretically have been controlled by proper accounting. It is surely acceptable, one would argue to pay one's executives whatever the business can afford. It is also perfectly acceptable to pay bankers and lawyers amounts that enable the buyer of a company to make a profit by merging it with his existing business.

Unfortunately relying upon accounting has proved to be an inadequate control. There are good reasons for this that are dependent upon fallacies of valuation, that I shall address in a subsequent chapter. For the purposes of this chapter I can merely say that there is a process that may or may not involve borrowing and that allows overly optimistic valuations to camouflage wealth redistributions that defeats the most rigorous accounting principles. The following example will make this clear.

Company A develops a new product. It is financed initially by equity provided by its owners who carry on business from a small office. The product is successful and attracts many potential customers.

An investment bank is interested in expanding the reach of this company and calculates that its potential for future expansion is such that it is possible that in 10 years time it will generate 100mm of profits. As a result the company is valued at £1Billion. The investment bank sells shares in the company to its customers who buy all the shares at the stated value of £1Billion. The investors are all savers including some pension funds.

The company is floated on the stock market and maintains its market capitalization value at around £1Billion for 5 years. In that period several bankers at the investment bank receive substantial bonuses as a result of the bank's fees. The lawyers, accountants and valuers do likewise. Their fees are paid from the proceeds of the Initial Public Offering of £1Billion.

After 5 years it becomes clear that the future profits of the company are only likely to be £10million. The market capitalization drops to £100mm.

The companies that have acquired the shares at their market value have shown an asset on their balance sheets based upon the company's value of £1Billion. In reality they overstated their balance sheet asset value by 10 times. The accounting has failed to recognize the problem because the valuation at which the investment was shown in the company's balance sheet was the one at which the shares were traded on the stock market.

The process of redistribution generally starts with one party making a profit. The party who suffers the corresponding loss frequently has no contact with the party who profited. He may only discover his loss many years after the profit was made as the shares in the company in the above example are sold and resold.

Accounting cannot prevent overvaluations. The last line of defense is proper valuations. These cannot be left to the market but must, as I shall show in a separate chapter devoted to the subject of valuations, be calculated separately. Only in this way can the massive redistributions of wealth be prevented.

The failure of modern economists to understand the operation of an economy is a failure of politics. The first duty of the politician is not to create perpetual economic growth but to keep the peace. Politicians in democracies have grown to believe that the best way to keep the peace is to promise and hopefully deliver perpetual increases in prosperity. They believe that this can be achieved through market forces and they point to the economic failure of the Eastern Block countries prior to the fall of the Berlin Wall in 1989.

This is not the place to discuss the advantages and disadvantages of socialism and capitalism, or indeed to properly define a modern economy in these terms. However the market has proved inadequate as a means of maintaining a stable economy. Market forces could persuade a business to outsource its manufacturing. A business that seeks more profitability cannot be blamed for that. However the politicians should keep in mind the benefit of the nation. Exporting manufacturing that results in large number of unemployed persons is not a good thing for the nation. Politicians should control actions of that kind.

The benefit to the employer should be offset against the cost of keeping the unemployed on welfare, and a national decision should be taken before such an important move takes place.

Managing an economy is not easy. The capitalist system says "leave it to the market you cannot control it, it is too difficult". The result is social dislocation, vast redistribution of wealth and eventually revolution. The socialist system tries to control the economy. Perhaps it is too difficult to do so. The result is economic inactivity and stagnation.

Somehow it is the task of politicians to take the best parts of these two systems, to use the good and discard the bad. To date they have opted for the market system but have failed to identify and deal with the bad.

2. PRODUCTIVITY, GROWTH AND GROSS NATIONAL PRODUCT

As if it is a birthright most economists and politicians as well as most commentators assume that every economy in the world will grow and grow indefinitely. Their reason tends to be that in their experience economic activity has grown consistently and they therefore conclude that it will continue to do so for ever.

This is very similar to the argument that world sporting records – at least those concerned with speed and distance – will continue to be beaten. It ignores the logical principle that the rate of improvement gets smaller and smaller as records are beaten and that the regularity with which records are beaten will also fall.

In 2007 the Western world fell into serious economic difficulties. The symptom of the problem was massive borrowings much of which cannot be repaid. The solution proposed by all politicians and experts is "growth". They predict that we will "grow" out of the economic problems. Nobody is willing to contemplate what to do if there is no "growth". It is for this reason that an examination of the concepts of productivity, growth and gross national product is so important to a proper understanding of economics and social problems of today.

Gross domestic product (GDP) and its offshoot Gross National Product ("GNP") are the measurements governments use to calculate whether the country is growing richer. GNP measures the wealth produced by the residents of a country and therefore removes production within a country by foreign businesses as well as the production by British people abroad. For present

47

purposes we shall use GDP as the measurement of wealth produced in a country.

The measurement has not been around for very long. It was created in the 1930s after the economic collapse of the time that became known as the Great Depression. The GDP of a nation is the amount that is consumed by the nation in a year. It could equally well be called Gross National Consumption, but since one man's consumption equals another man's production the two should be equal. In a self contained and balanced economy that principle would be true.

If in a year a nation consumes more than in the previous year we say that we have "grown" richer. The UK has according to government statistics grown richer year by year between 1955 and 2010 by around 2.3% per annum on average. These statistics are based on real value figures. In other words they are adjusted for inflation. These are therefore supposed real increases in living standards.

There are many problems with "growth" of GDP. Politicians and economists talk about growth as if it makes us all richer. They also talk about it as if it affects us all in more or less the same way. It does not. Nor does it really represent increases in living standards.

The first problem with this measurement of consumption is that it is an average. It does not guarantee that every person in the UK has grown richer in a year by the percentage increase in GDP. If some part of the population has grown richer by more than the average then the rest must have grown richer by less than the average. Indeed some may have grown poorer. If 10% of the population increase their consumption by 50% in one year and the economy has grown by 3% then the remaining 90% of the population are worse off collectively by 2% (of GDP). In short the consumption of the rest of the population will have decreased. They are worse off. If the majority is worse off can we really say that we have "grown". Yet that is what the figures show.

GDP growth only makes us all richer if we share the increased wealth equitably. There is no logical reason why we should not do so particularly in a complex advanced industrialized economy. We are all interdependent and it is impossible to say that for example the increased wages of a footballer are entirely thanks to him. He was assisted in his endeavours by coaches, trainers, physiotherapists, doctors, clerks, managers, owners, advertisers, TV producers and a whole army of others in society. Arguably his school teachers and the groundsman of his school football ground had something to do with his success. The same can be said for most other activities.

The real problem is that the increase in what people earn is determined not by GDP but by the "market" which often means the perception of value that might be earned in the future, for example as a result of an advertising campaign. This prediction will almost certainly be wrong.

The second problem with GDP is that it does not reflect changes in the population. The UK has seen an increase in population of about 10% in the past 10 years. If the newcomers produce and consume at the same rate as the rest of the population then increases in GDP that represent consumption by these newcomers do not represent increases in individual average wealth. GDP should be measured in terms of an average per capita. In most cases this will represent a substantial reduction in the rate of "growth".

The third problem with GDP is capital usage. GDP measures consumption when an item is purchased and not when it is actually consumed. In the case of food and services the time that these items are purchased is normally the time when they are consumed. In the case of other items including for example clothing, fridges, TVs cars and computers these items are "consumed" over a longer period than a year. In some cases these items can be consumed over 10 years or more. In others like ships, planes and real estate the period of consumption is considerably longer. GDP treats all items as being consumed when they are bought. It does not follow proper accounting rules. Proper accounting rules require the buyer to treat the purchase as a capital asset and to reflect the deterioration in its value as consumption over its life. Proper accounting therefore reflects a mismatch between the position of the seller who correctly shows the goods produced and sold as income in the year in which the sale takes place. The buyer on the other hand shows the item as being consumed over its life.

This is not a serious problem so long as the principle is applied consistently. The difference is after all only one of timing. Problems arise when long life assets are not consumed by ordinary use but are destroyed by some accident or fire or some major catastrophe or simply because their owner wants something newer. Such an event will accelerate the time when the goods are replaced and will create more demand for production of such goods. Thus a catastrophe causes an increase in GDP, whereas in fact in terms of consumption, wealth and well being nothing has changed. Indeed those who have suffered the destruction will feel and indeed be worse off. Yet GDP will increase as these goods are prematurely replaced. Somebody has to pay for this. Often it is government or insurance money. The effect on GDP however is on paper at least positive. The destruction of large parts of Germany and Japan in the Second World War created massive demand for restructuring. That restructuring produced enormous GDP increases. However people did not feel richer. They were not. The "growth" merely returned them to the position in which they had been before the catastrophe. One way of increasing GDP regularly is to destroy our homes and have them rebuilt every year. That will not make us richer but GDP will show substantial growth.

Fourthly there is a material discrepancy in the inflation adjustments to GDP because of the inflation calculations. It is true that the GDP calculations are adjusted for inflation. Any growth therefore is accordingly meant to represent real growth.

50

The growth figures can only be real growth figures if the inflation figures include all production in the particular country. In reality the inflation figures are based on a "basket" of goods that are actually purchased by the average person. Thus for example luxury goods such as yachts are not included in the inflation figures but are included in GDP if yachts are produced. Likewise new expensive homes are included in GDP but not in inflation figures. Homes are in fact a particular problem that I shall address later. Services of a particular type are not included in the inflation basket but are included in GDP. Services too cause problems and discrepancies and I shall address these separately also. The general point about inflation calculations is that if the prices of items that are included in GDP but not in the inflation calculations increase by more than the general rate of inflation there will be apparent growth but in reality none at all. To take a yacht as an example suppose that the same number of yachts are produced in one year as in the previous year but that their price increases by 50% whereas the rate of inflation was only 5% there would appear to be growth in the economy - specifically in the production of yachts. In fact there is none. The growth is really just inflation. There is no doubt that inflation in luxury items has been substantially higher than for ordinary items. Indeed it was inevitable as vast sums were redistributed This could be a reason why there appears to be growth but in fact there is none.

Housing also creates problems with GDP calculations. If the price of new homes increases by 10% there would appear to be an increase in GDP of 10%. If this is higher than the rate of general inflation then there would appear to be growth whereas in fact there is none. Housing is taken into account in calculating inflation but it is not the cost of new homes that is taken into account. It is the mortgage payments that are taken into account in calculating inflation. This latter figure is affected firstly by interest rates which can be kept artificially low - as governments have done recently - and secondly by the fact that most mortgages are based upon historical house prices, some of them bought 20 years ago. Thus mortgage payments may be reducing and therefore appear to be deflationary whereas the houses that are constructed show massive inflation. This gives the appearance of growth whereas in fact there is none. There are other ways in which housing costs are taken into account in calculating GDP. Rent for example is taken into account and one year is compared with another. If more and more homes are being rented instead of being owned then GDP shows an increase whereas in reality no such increase takes place. Housing produces anomalies that are recognised and have caused mortgage payments to be taken out of GDP and included depending on the preferences of the government of the day.

Housing and mortgages give rise to an even more serious problem when comparing prices, productivity and interest rates. As interest rates are reduced the mortgage payments are reduced and the effect on inflation is negative. However reducing interest rates increases the value of properties. The result is that new houses appear to have a higher value for the purposes of calculating GDP.

What reason is there to suppose that inflation in luxury goods and services consistently exceeds inflation for ordinary goods and services. There is every reason. Inflation is the result of creating too much money that cannot be spent on new goods. The new money competes for existing goods and their price increases. There is little doubt that a considerable amount of the money supply increase in recent times has gone to the rich. They spend it on luxury goods and the price therefore rises. Large amounts have also gone into property. This causes an increase in the price of new property particularly highly priced property. The inflation index deals with the average house. If inflation in prices of those items that are not included in the inflation indices is higher than general inflation then there will be the appearance of growth but in fact no real growth. There is considerable evidence to support the theory that there has been no real – or at any rate no sustainable - growth in the British economy for at least 30 years. I shall deal with this evidence later.

Fifthly there is one problem with GDP that is not often mentioned and that I mentioned in the first chapter. It is the principle of reciprocity. GDP is calculated on the basis of the sale price of goods sold or acquired. All economic activity involves the production and exchange of goods and services. Money is merely an intermediate stage in the process of exchanging such goods and services. If the money used to buy goods is borrowed by the buyer then there is an implicit promise that the buyer will sooner or later produce more than he consumes. This means that he will either reduce his consumption with a consequent negative impact upon GDP at a later time or alternatively he will produce more than he did before. The GDP increases of the past 30 years in the UK have been practically matched with equal increases in debt. This means that one sector of the economy has been growing but the other has been merely promising to grow. If the second sector does not manage to grow it will have to reduce consumption in future in order to pay its debts. Such reduction will result in reduced production and reduced GDP. We are probably in that phase as I write.

If the borrower fails to reduce his consumption and fails to increase production of useful end products the result will be a bad debt. The current financial crisis has given rise to a massive amount of bad debts the total of which cannot be predicted because values of assets on which the loans are secured is still falling. These bad debts should be deducted from GDP on the grounds that they represented either a sale for an overvalued consideration or alternatively a gift. When the whole banking system is riddled with bad debts the impact on GDP could be considerable.

Economic analysis is often unnecessarily complicated by interposing money in the analytical process. Growth could exist even in times of barter. In order to examine this fifth problem better assume that there is a simple economy in which there are food producers and clothing manufacturers. The food producers provide all the food that is necessary for the whole community and the clothing manufacturers do likewise. Both sectors have only the bare minimum. The food producers discover a new way of producing much more food but the clothing manufacturers are unable to increase production. The food producers can deliver the greater volumes of food to themselves – after all they deserve it. However they will only deliver the clothing manufacturer's additional food if they can get something in return and the clothing manufacturers are unable to increase their production of clothing. If the food producers deliver more food to the clothing manufacturers it will be on the understanding that the latter will at some time in the future discover a process to produce more clothing. Alternatively they will have to wear less clothing themselves and deliver more clothing to the food producers. If the clothing manufacturers never produce more clothing they will have to wear less themselves and deliver more to the food producers. This is the problem of reciprocity.

It is only if production increases are widespread and reciprocated that a new discovery will make us all richer. Production increases by one side but not the other side to a transaction are of limited value.

The principle of reciprocity is best demonstrated when one considers the Chinese economy where economic growth has been spectacular over the past 20 years. Most observers are aware that China is still intrinsically a very poor country. Although there are many multi millionaires and billionaires in China the rural poor and many of the urban poor are very poor indeed. Many Western economists have challenged China to ensure that the wealth that they produce – clothing, cars, electronic equipment and now more and more sophisticated goods – should not be exported to the West. They do so on the basis that the massive foreign exchange surpluses that China has been accumulating is offset by massive deficits in the West. It has also resulted in unemployment in the West as previously profitable businesses in the West are now carried out in China much more cheaply.

There is a very good reason why China does not keep the clothing and other goods at home and that is lack of reciprocity. If they were to give the clothing and other consumer goods to the rural and urban poor what would they receive in return. The latter have nothing to give to the producers. The West has infrastructure. So the Chinese producers can be seen not only visiting Western countries in the same way that the Japanese did in the 1970s and 1980s, but they are to be seen buying property and companies in the West in return for the clothing and other consumer items that they export to the West.

There is also the issue of end products to be considered. Governments and politicians have assumed that any new product that is used in the production line increases GDP. This, as I explained in the previous chapter is a serious mistake. Only new products or innovations that result in increased production of the end product will increase GDP and then only, as explained above if there is reciprocity. Increases in production of office activity that does not increase production of the end product only result in redistribution of wealth and not in wealth creation.

New inventions also give rise to pricing issues that are relevant for the purposes of calculating growth and GDP. There are two types of invention. One invention that pays for itself, and another replaces something else. Where a new product replaces another the result is often a transfer of wealth from one producer to another. Thus for example if TV's replace going to the cinema as a form of entertainment wealth is transferred from cinemas to TV manufacturers. Initially the cinemas will struggle on and incur more debt. In the long term however as one new industry emerges another dies. GDP will reflect these effects but there will be a delay as the old industries try to resist their inevitable demise. The result is sooner or later no growth at all. One should therefore beware before trusting that technology, innovation or new businesses will resolve all our problems and create unlimited and perpetual growth. Not all innovations lead to growth. Many will lead to redistributions of wealth.

New businesses are either wealth incremental or zero sum gain businesses. Economists must be wary to distinguish between the two. Most businesses are zero sum gain businesses. It is highly exceptional in a modern economy to discover something that is entirely new and pays for itself. Most IT discoveries are only of benefit for office work, which at best is parasitic upon the end products that are consumed and does not affect the rate of production of such goods and at worst it a useless activity in terms of GDP growth.

New inventions also create a problem for GDP. There is no benchmark against which to test their real value. If I produce a new item of technology and sell it to my friend for £1 trillion then GDP will be seen to have grown by £1trn. If that technology is worthless that is a fantasy. If my friend cannot pay me back it is also a fantasy. GDP ignores this problem.

It is likewise with services. Services come in many shapes and sizes. A new service that is vastly overpriced results in immediate increases in GDP. If it is overpriced the result will be a bad debt. The banks are full of bad debts right now. Frequently these overpriced and possibly worthless services are capitalized and shown as assets of the purchaser of the end product. It will be some time before that purchaser discovers that his expectations have not been fulfilled. By then of course the "growth" in GDP will have long been recorded.

Whether goods or services are overpriced or worthless the result will be reflected sooner or later in a write off by the lender - probably a bank – and by the borrower. Such bad debts and write offs are not reflected in GDP calculations.

In order to see whether GDP increases are being share equitably and whether we are in fact better or worse off than we were before other measurements need to be deployed.

There is considerable evidence that things that we were able to afford many years ago cannot be afforded now. The reasons for this are either one of the faults in calculating GDP that I have outlined above or alternatively that there has been substantial redistributions of wealth under cover of apparent growth in GDP.

Fifty years ago we could afford pensions based on final salaries. This was not something that only the public sector provided. Most major firms provided such pension arrangements for their staff. Their employees were able to retire in comfort with a pension equal to around 2/3rds of their final salary. Over the past 20 years one company after another, and now the government have decided that the country cannot afford that. Why? The answer we are told is that we are living longer. That is something that needs to be considered but it should not just be accepted without calculating how much longer we are living and relating the answer to the growth in GDP.

It would be foolish to say that if we were living one day longer and the economy has grown richer by the equivalent of 20 years then we cannot afford to pay pensions for one additional day. Yet most commentators accept without questioning that if we are living longer, no matter by how little we cannot afford pensions no matter how much our economy has grown. The longer this explanation goes unchallenged the more it will become accepted. None seem to make the calculations or even consider that there is a relationship between these two items of data. They are content with the claim that we are living longer and therefore cannot afford more pensions. It makes us all feel good that we are living longer, a testament to the education and skills of our doctors, we are told. How can we blame the government for doing something we all regard as good.

The right approach of course is to calculate how much longer we are in fact living and then compare the increase in the amount of pensionable life (the period when we are consuming more than we produce – pensioners normally produce nothing). Only if the rate of increase in GDP is less than the rate of increase in pensionable life is there a problem.

It seems that in the past 30 years life expectancy has increased from 72 to 80, a period of 8 years. The retirement age was 60 so the average pensioner was reliant on a pension for 12 years. That period is now 20 years, an increase in pensionable life of 67%. Yet our GDP figures show that the economy has grown by 91% in that period. That ignores interest rates. Annuity rates depend upon interest rates. Using a 5% rate of interest an annuity for 12 years costs 11.28% per annum. That means that for every £100 in a pension fund a pension for 12 years equal to £11.28 per annum could be purchased. In order to maintain that same level of payment for 20 years the capital sum required would be £141. That is only a 41% increase in cost. So the conclusion as regards pensions is that we are being deceived, perhaps through ignorance rather than malice, I do not know. We have, apparently grown richer by 91%, we are living longer by 67%, and the cost of maintaining a pension for that additional period will be 41% more than before. It is clear that, assuming that the GDP figures are correct, the additional life is outstripped by the increase in GDP. We are therefore not only able to maintain the same pension provisions as before but could afford to increase it to take account of the additional growth in wealth. So where has the money gone. Only one explanation is possible. Others have got more than their fair share of the additional growth in GDP and they are refusing to put some of their increased share at the disposal of our parents. It is not an attractive argument. If the same argument was made about caring for children there would be an outcry. Those who took more than their fair share of GDP growth are the real cause why we cannot afford to pay pensions in the same way as we did before and not our increased longevity. It could of course be that the GDP calculations are wrong or partially wrong.

Another and possibly easier way of looking at this is that if we are growing older the population will be increasing. The population has increased by around 10% in the past 30 years. Yet GDP has increased by 91%. GDP per head is therefore positive and if we all share more fairly in such growth we can afford pensions.

It is irrelevant that the mixture of workers to non workers is different. It is irrelevant that the number of children in the mix is smaller because people are having children later. If GDP per head has increased we can afford to pay for the increased population without decreasing our living standards.

The real problem is interest rates. The government has decided to reduce interest rates and thereby redistribute wealth from investors and savers to borrowers. The borrowers tend to be the economically active. Savers are mainly pensioners. The government has therefore through the private sector indiscriminately redistributed wealth from pensioners to workers. This was redistribution by stealth. It was not subject to consideration by parliament. It was less honest than the state sponsored piracy of old. It was just done under cover. Now we are told that pensions are unaffordable.

The same is true about, education. We are told that we cannot afford free tertiary education whereas we could afford it in the 1960s. Indeed then we were able to afford a grant. The explanation is that more of us are going to University. Yet nobody does the maths. In fact the number going to university in the UK these days is distorted by the change in status in the 1990s when all previously Polytechnics became universities. The number of students at any one time is not easy to obtain. The Office of National Statistics does not produce readily accessible information to show comparative student numbers over a 30 or 40 year period. There is of course no doubt that student numbers have increased. The only reliable information is that total full time undergraduates in 2008/09 throughout the UK were 1,044,720. There were 152,770 overseas students, presumably all full time students. That leaves the UK domiciled student count in 2008/09 at 891,950. The GDP grew between 1970 and 2010 at an average rate of 2.22% per annum. If our student numbers had grown at that rate then we can, unless there has been redistribution of wealth away from education - remember it was number one priority not only to Tony Blair but to many governments before him - then our student numbers in 1970 - including of course all the Polytechnics - would have been not less than 370,600. This is just compound interest. If student numbers were 370,600 in 1970 and they grew at the same rate as the economy - 2.22% per annum - then student numbers in 2010 would be what they are today. I have been unable to find reliable data that shows the number of students including those at Polytechnics in 1970 but it is highly likely that there were more than 370,600. It follows that either the GDR numbers are wrong and we have not grown at the stated rate, or alternatively the part of the growth in the economy that should have gone to education has gone elsewhere. Where has it gone. Nobody asks. Perhaps the GDP figures are wrong or misleading.

Once again a simple calculation of GDP per head will lead to the conclusion that education is affordable. If GDP per head has increased then even though many people between ages of 19 and 24 are learning and economically unproductive compared to some earlier time it means that we can afford it, so long as GDP increases are shared equitably. If there are more teachers at University and these teachers before that were working in industry earning less then so long as they are not earning too much more than they had been before they can be afforded.

There can only be one reason why student education is unaffordable and that is that some are taking more than their fair share of the increases in GDP.

It is unnecessary to justify an argument that people who go to university will benefit the economy more when they graduate. That may not be true. However it does not matter. Proper analysis of GDP will reveal that we can afford to pay for higher education so long as GDP per capita increases and so long as everybody does not take more than their fair share of such growth.

It is undoubtedly the unfair sharing of economic growth that is at the root cause of all the problems that we face and in particular the inability to afford what we could afford many years ago.

It is likely for example that it is not the cost of tutors at universities that is expensive but the real estate, which was caused to rise by government reducing interest rates.

Health is another area where GDP seems to indicate negative growth. There was a time when prescriptions were free, all operations could be afforded. We had enough nursing homes provided for our old age. Dental care was free. Most of these benefits have gone or been gradually eroded. Why is it when we are getting richer. The answer, we are told, is that we are living longer. As I have shown above we are not living that much longer. There is a relationship between so called GDP growth and increased longevity. So long as our increases in life span are less than the increases in GDP then we should be able to afford everything that we could before. GDP has been increases - allegedly - at around 2.3% p.a.. That means that we can afford to increase our life span by 2.3% per annum of our current age (about 80). That is about 1.8 years per annum. Nobody expects that kind of life span increase.

One could easily draw up a list of those items that we could afford 30 or 40 years ago that we cannot afford now, although we are allegedly so much wealthier. Libraries, that have been around for hundreds of years are now under threat. Prescriptions for health are increasing. Public transport fares keep increasing regularly in real terms. Local taxes increase regularly at substantially above the rate of inflation.

Another problem with GDP is the services provided in the sale of existing assets. The sale of existing assets does not constitute part of GDP as no new wealth is created. Yet the charge by lawyers estate agents and others for these services are counted as part of GDP. The problem becomes more acute when one considers the sale of existing companies and securities. There the fees charged by professionals and bankers are vast. They do not create anything consumable of value. Yet their fees, charges and profits are considered to be part of GDP.

The same applies to profits from the sale of existing assets. In certain cases these give rise to profits of companies or paper profits. These profits are reflected as part of GDP. It follows that when for example a company invests in another company and the latter company is sold at a substantial profit that increase in nominal value is considered to be an increase in GDP. It is not. The same company remains in existence.

Theoretically and practically the figures entered in GDP calculations depend upon proper accounting. If the accounting is inaccurate for GDP purposes the results will be incorrect.

There are three ways of calculating GDP. All should produce the same results. The simplest way is the aggregation of incomes. This merely requires all the incomes and profits earned to be aggregated. Thus all salaries wages and fees, all dividends and interest income and royalties and such like as well as rents and undistributed profits of businesses are added.

Salaries, wages and fees reduce the undistributed profits of a business and so on the face of it the calculation is sound. However there is a serious problem with the calculation if the salaries wages and fees are capitalized by the business that pays them. How is this done.

The business pays, shall we say a vast sum of money for a new computer system in the belief that it will enable the business to make huge profits in the future. Those involved in installing the computer system are paid their fees. They make profits and pay very large salaries and bonuses. These payments by the computer system installer and its retained profits are seen as increases in GDP. The corresponding payment by the business that paid for the system however is not shown as a drain on profits but as a capital asset. The result of course is that GDP appears to have occurred but in fact the real rewards – if they are ever to emerge – remain unproved.

This problem makes GDP calculations in a situation where there is substantial borrowings and capitalization of expenditure extremely unreliable. It also leads to grossly unfair sharing of wealth as those who charge fees on increased theoretically higher values of property and companies claim their share of GDP growth to be based on these increased and artificially inflated values, which are not themselves reflected in GDP. Consequently their share of GDP growth is unfair. Others consequently have to get less.

Judging by the discussions and arguments from government and private companies hit by pensions the sums involved are substantial. They are certainly not trivial. The unfair sharing is therefore acute. Government appear unaware of these problems, and choose to focus instead on the victims of this redistribution of wealth and to explain – untruthfully - why they have to suffer.

Part of the problem of course is that governments and economists, for reasons that are not apparent, seem unwilling or unable to consider that there is not necessarily a relationship between what a person puts into an economy and what a person takes out of it. They assume that if a person receives salary or fees of £1 million it must follow that he has added value to the economy of at least £1 million. The rest is a gift to the rest of us.

In fact there is no evidence that the income that any of us take is equal to the value of what we put into the economy. With many office jobs for example it is arguable that no value is put into the economy. Yet the incomes can be substantial. It is assumed that only those who are economically inactive take more out of the economy than they put in. That is a mistake. Many highly paid people take considerably more out of the economy than they put into it. They are effectively redistributing wealth from the rest of us to themselves. Yet these are the people whom the government wants to keep in this country because they can help us to "grow our economy". It is the curse of economics that it is susceptible to such inaccuracies and nonsense can avoid challenge so easily.

One thing that is not taken into account in GDP is Do It Yourself work. When I build an extension to my home the bricks and timber that I buy are considered to be part of GDP. My labour however is ignored. This is a mistake. If I worked for my neighbor and charged him to build an extension and he worked for me to reciprocate our charges would be part of GDP but not if we do it ourselves.

Politicians and economists believe that money can effect the real economy or make us produce more goods and services. This is the economic equivalent not just of putting the cart before the horse but of making the cart pull the horse. There is no evidence that this theory can work.

The principle is that if we give people money to spend they will spend it on new products. The danger is that they will use it to buy existing products thereby increasing their price. No government has found a way of achieving what the theory claims to achieve.

Governments and economists have placed excessive faith in the power of money to create real economic activity.

Economic growth requires a number of conditions. Firstly it requires the capacity to produce more goods. This can come from – usually - employing unemployed workers, which is frequently the cause for concern but it also requires the capital and equipment for the purpose. It requires either surplus money in the hands of purchasers to buy such goods together with the inclination to do so, or the ability of purchasers to produce more goods themselves that the unemployed will produce when employed. In short a widespread demand and capacity for all sectors of the economy to produce more.

This combination of conditions is so exceptional that sustainable and real economic growth is difficult to achieve. The best that can be achieved is temporary growth funded entirely by borrowed money, which is the situation in which we now find ourselves. The problem is that we cannot repay our debts and there is a limit to the debt that we can sustain.

There is no right to ever increasing economic wealth. In an advanced economy optimal economic activity will be reached just as optimal performance is achieved by an athlete or a car. Politicians will not accept that there is potential for infinite increases in wealth. They will not address the possibility that GDP will not increase. If they did they would have to address the possibility that unemployment will not be reduced except by some drastic and radical action on their part.

Governments cannot influence real economic activity except to the extent that they incur expenditure on infrastructure directly. All they can do is redistribute wealth. They do so by keeping interest rates low for example thereby penalizing savers and benefiting borrowers. They indulge in printing of money, issuing bonds and spending the money and by quantitative easing – a process whereby the central bank buys bonds from the banks thereby freeing up capital for them to lend - and now credit easing. None of this will have any effect unless there is demand for goods and services and the ability to reciprocate by those who buy such goods and services.

It is very difficult in an economy that is mature and produces all that is required to increase production. There must be a plan B.

Unfortunately it is not there. Plan B should be one that assumes that there is or will be no more growth. Plan B would involved increasing the amount of leisure time and reducing the amount of work done per individual. It will involved sharing jobs because the principle of paying for idle people is unacceptable. Sooner or later all economies will come to that stage.

The theory promoted by Keynes and still followed by those who believe that there is a simple solution and it just involves either shuffling money around through the tax system, or manipulating interest rates or adopting some sort of monetary stimulus, was never properly tested. There is no evidence of it having the desired effect.

The refusal by politicians and economists to accept that there is no right to perpetual increases in GDP has led to the paralysis of both. They continue to hope that by manipulating the amount of money in the system they will "kick start" or "stimulate" the moribund patient. They indulge in "kicking the can down the road" hoping that their excessive burden of debt will be miraculously relieved by some technological innovation. There is no plan B. Indeed plan B to the economists and politicians is invariably some other way or idea about how to create growth artificially. It is only when they accept and acknowledge the perpetual economic growth like perpetual record breaking performances in the field of sport is impossible that they may eventually get back on the right track. For the time being they are miles away and will guide their economies to more and more disasters.

The Japanese economy slipped into economic recession around 1989 and has never recovered. The government has stimulated and increased the supply of money until the Japanese government is now the biggest borrower in the world. Yet none of it had any effect. The reason for that it is blithely said, is that they did "too little too late". They clearly did not do too little. As for too late what is too late? Perhaps it is too late for other too.

The major problem faced by governments and economists of an advanced industrial society is unemployment and how to solve it. Praying for growth is not a plan B. It is necessary to decide how to employ the unemployed if there is no more growth. Unless and until economists and politicians accept that there is no more growth and that most economic activity is in redistributing wealth they will be unable to come up with a proper and realistic plan to overcome unemployment, short of war.

One major error that economists make in considering GDP growth is that they focus only upon the producers. If the producer has enough capacity to expand then there should be growth. They do of course consider that demand should also exist but their focus on demand is limited to consideration of whether the consumer has sufficient funds to purchase the asset in question.

Economists do not consider that consumers have a limit to what they can use and enjoy. If consumers have enough water to drink and clean and perhaps fill a swimming pool they have reached the limit of their demand. They might have the financial ability to pay for more water but if the water company produces more water as a result of "efficiency" they are wasting their time. The consumer will not buy more water.

The same mistake is made nowadays with new technology. Printing is now so easy and transmission of information so extensive that more and more is being produced. The consumer only has limited time to read. If a consumer has only 2 hours a day for reading and as a result he buys 1 book per month there is no point at all producing 2 books per month. He cannot read them. When considering the production and sale of leisure items this factor is generally ignored. It is merely assumed that consumers will buy more and more books, will consume more and more information, will read more and more information.

When consumers were persuaded to spend time communicating with one another on their PCs nobody considered what these consumers would have been doing with their time otherwise. In fact the habits of those consumers had to be changed. Instead of going to pubs they spent time at home with their PCs. There are only 24 hours in a day and only so much time to be spent. That is another aspect of capacity that is ignored by economists.

3. VALUATIONS - THE FALSE PREMISE

The basis of most financial disasters is a wrong valuation. This is true whether the valuation is of a capital asset or of the services provided to a business or its cost of direct labour.

There are many different kinds of value. There is cost, which is self explanatory. Investment value is the value of an asset that depends upon the appropriate rate of return that can be earned from the use of that asset. Resale value is the price that a buyer will pay for something in the open market. There is so called going concern value and break up value. The former is the value of a business that is generating income. The latter is the value of an asset that is not deployed in any business, even though it may come to be after sale.

The investment value of an income producing asset, which depends upon the rate of return that a long term investor reasonably expects to earn on his investment depends upon the sustainable income that the investment will generate. Sustainable income suffers from a number of problems all of which are the result of the inability of anybody to forecast the future. The income might depend upon the likes or dislikes of customers, who might be fickle. The future rate of inflation also cannot be determined. Even where an asset is for example leased for a long term the customer might become insolvent. If the asset is leased at a fixed rate the rate of inflation might cause the expected return to be too high or too low.

Investment income is frequently inflation linked. Thus most companies that depend upon the retail market should have income that increases with the general level of prices sooner or later. There will be large differences from time to time because certain commodities – oil and gas to take one example – often increase in price at very different rates than the general rate of inflation. Nevertheless over the long term general price inflation will sooner or later affect all items that are bought and sold.

Rent – unless it is state controlled, which it often is even in advanced developed countries – also increases with inflation.

Taking property and corporate valuations as examples, because these are the major investments in any economy we see that there have over time been certain standards for valuing these investments.

Corporate valuations depend upon the goods or services that are sold by the corporations. If the goods or services are discretionary the profits of the corporations are likely to be less stable than if the goods or services are necessary utilities. Thus for example the income of a water or electricity company is fairly stable, and so is that of a food company. The income of a travel company however is less stable because they do not sell necessaries. How does this instability in income affect the rate of return that forms the basis for valuing the company.

For simplicity companies are valued at a multiple of current or latest earnings. A company with stable reliable income that is not likely to increase in good times or decrease in bad times will probably be valued at a multiple of 10. That means that the income of that company is 10% of the investment value. One can say that the yield is 10% of the investment value. That does not mean that as an investor in such a company one will receive 10% of the price one pays for the shares. The dividend will generally be only a proportion of the company's profits and so will be lower than the above yield – probably below 4%. That means that dividend cover is 2.5 time – its profits are 2.5 times its dividend.

The part of a company's income that is not paid to shareholders as a dividend is retained in the company and should increase its value because its assets – cash generally – will increase.

With a travel company because its income is potentially unstable the multiple is likely to be lower than that of a utility, unless of course the latest income figures reflect a low point.

Company valuations therefore rise as profits, or expectations of profits rise and vice versa. However the expected rate of return on company income will depend upon the expected rate of inflation and the rates of return on other investments.

Thus for example if inflation is 10% or more then the expected rates of return for a company whose income is expected to increase in line with inflation should not change. Its income is inflation proof. Its valuation as a multiple of earnings will remain the same as if inflation was 2%. This is because a company's nominal profit will be equal to its present income plus the rate of inflation. The company that earns income of 10% currently when inflation is nil will earn 20% if inflation increases to 10% per annum. Its real rate of return remains 10%.

In theory one should take the average income of an unstable company and use the same multiple as for a stable company or perhaps something lower to take account of unusual aberrations.

The principle of valuations is that in the long term an investor in one company should earn a return that is the same as an investor in another company.

Unfortunately a rather dangerous convention has grown up in recent times of forecasting profit increases, usually based on recent performance and an assumption that they must not only be sustainable but can go on indefinitely and valuing the sustainable income on this wholly fictitious future level of income. This is a serious mistake and has given rise to deleterious consequences both to investors and savers and eventually to governments.

Thus for example a business whose profits have increased at 10% per annum for the past 5 years is assumed to be able to continue the trick for the foreseeable future. As a result the value attributed to that company in terms of the multiple of earnings can be not 10 times but can be as much as 20 times or more. In the case of some of the technology companies valuations have been as high as 50 or even 100 times earnings.

These alarming multiples do two things. Firstly they say that the earnings of those companies are likely to increase at a very fast rate in the very near future. Secondly and more ominously the buyer takes all the risk that this might not happen and pays the seller for the privilege of taking that risk. This is a wholly absurd situation that defies logic and any sensible principle of valuation.

The vendor of a stock that has shown substantial increases in profits in the past says to the buyer "this company's profits are expected to increase substantially in the future, one cannot be certain that they will do so but you have to pay me the price that assumes that the profits will achieve that level. If they do you will get a modest return on your investment since you will have already paid me for the future anticipated increase in profits. If future profits do not achieve that level you will suffer the loss because you will have paid me for the privilege of getting the opportunity to buy this great investment. It is only if the profits made by the company turn out to be higher than currently expected that you will profit. I require a price from you that reflects this increase in anticipated profits although it is by no means guaranteed". I doubt that anybody in their right mind would accept such a proposal. Yet that is what happens with hot stocks every day.

The same is true about real estate. Real estate is valued on the basis of yields. This achieves the same result as using multiples and is the other side of the same coin. A yield of 10% is equivalent to a multiple of 10 times. A yield of 7% is equivalent to a multiple of 14.29 times. There are some subtle differences between company valuations and real estate. The most important is that company valuations are based upon after tax income but real estate valuations are based upon pre tax rental income.

Traditionally real estate valuations have been around 7% per annum. Thus a property with an income of 7,000 per annum would have a value of 100,000. That yield would be somewhat lower in the case of high street shops and somewhat higher in the case of a warehouse in a remote area. The reasons for the difference in these yields is sustainability. A high street shop could easily be re - let once the lease came to an end. A warehouse in a remote area might remain empty after that time. The investor will therefore require a higher yield on the warehouse because of that risk. Subject to those restrictions, which were entirely reasonable the rate of return was around 7%. The rents were of course inflation proofed and were set to increase in line with market rent increases at regular periods. In some countries the rent increased in line with the general rate of inflation.

Somehow the yield of around 7% came to vary by rather large amounts. The rents remained relatively stable in order to reflect the ability of tenants to pay. However capital values increased alarmingly as a result of the reductions in yield. This was said to be because of the demand by investors for property. It was a matter of supply and demand. Essentially the buyers are so keen to obtain an investment in property that they are willing to accept a lower yield than before. Why would they do this? The response is always the same "because they expect property values to increase". This is a rather strange explanation. Property values can only increase if one or two things happen. The rent could increase, or the yield could reduce. The prospect for rent increasing at a faster rate than general inflation over the long term is remote. It may do so for a short term but it is not likely to be a widespread increase in rent over a sustained period let alone in perpetuity.

The only potential for an increase in the capital value of a property is therefore a reduction in yield. The principle of valuing property at a lower yield, and therefore a higher capital value, is therefore that yields are expected to fall and fall for ever thereby giving rise to ever increasing capital profits to the investor who accepts a lower and lower rental yield in return for the privilege of making a capital gain. It is a game of musical chairs. An example will make this clear.

An investor who has paid 100,000 for a property yielding a rent of 7,000 per annum sells that same property to buyer A for 110,000 representing a yield of 6.36%. Buyer A accepts this lower yield (the rent remains the same – 7,000) because he expects to sell to Buyer B at a yield of 5.5%. He does so and sells for 127,000. Buyer B accepts this lower yield (the rent is still 7,000) because he expects to be able to sell to Buyer C for a yield of 4%, and does so. Buyer C pays 175,000. This could go on indefinitely. The yield becomes an irrelevance. Even if yields are down to 1% it is still possible to double the value of the property by selling at a yield of 0.5% and then again at a yield of 0.25%.

This is rightly described as a Ponzi scheme. Yield becomes irrelevant. Investment value becomes immaterial. Capital gain and resale value is everything. No longer is the property sold for its yield. It is sold for a resale. So long as there are others around who are willing to pay more and more for the property it will – ostensibly – increase in value again and again. However the intrinsic (the investment) value of the property remains the same. It still only produces a rent of 7,000 in this example. This kind of situation should act as a warning sign to all because the resale value has exceeded the investment value. Yield has become irrelevant. Property is traded in the same way as gold. Gold has no intrinsic value. It only has emotional value. It yields nothing. The argument in favour of ignoring yield when valuing property is that it should be treated in the same way as gold. Why not? What are the dangers of this approach?

The answer is that it is simply unsustainable. Sooner or later the merry go round, or the game of pass the parcel will cease. Investors can only make a return on the property not in the conventional way, from the rental yield, but by resale at every reducing yields. In order to make a monetary profit they have to sell. In order to sell the putative buyer must believe that he can find somebody sooner or later who is willing to pay more – sell at a lower yield than the one at which he bought - for what is after all the same property producing the same rent in money terms. Why should more and more investors not pay more and more for a property?

The answer is firstly affordability. There are a limited number of people with sufficient liquid resources to be able to pay more and more for a property and as more and more money is tied up in a property there is less and less to be spent on something else. Furthermore once a property has been passed from one person to another the first person is unlikely to buy again at the higher price. It is a game of chicken, who will be the last person holding the parcel. When the music stops the person holding the property will only be able to rely on the rent, which is still only 7,000.

All that has happened in the meantime is that vast sums have been redistributed from buyer to seller until an eventual loser has been discovered. The loser is probably highly leveraged and goes bankrupt so the bank ends up losing.

Why can this game not go on for ever? Simple. Buyers will have a choice whether to buy or rent and if rent is significantly cheaper they will rent. It is true that certain properties have an emotion or prestige value but most properties do not fall into that category. They have primarily a use value. If I can buy a property yielding 2% and I can invest my money at 5% I will clearly rent and invest my money at 5%, live rent free and pocket the additional 3%.

The liquidity problem can of course be overcome, as it has been in the recent past by the banks. They will provide more and more cash to enable buyers to pay more and more for the property. They will do so subject to a limit. That limit is reached when the amount of rent is less than the interest on the loan.

For a time governments can assist this dangerous game by reducing interest rates. However sooner or later a limit will be reached and the rent will be insufficient to pay the interest to the bank. At that time the market can be said to have peaked. The decline to true value will then start.

This game of pass the parcel need not be carried on through property. Any other asset will do. It could be a box of old toys. These can be passed from one to another at ever increasing prices making a profit for all who have participated in the process. When the nerve runs out someone will be left holding the box of old toys whose value will be the same as when the game started.

This process is not dissimilar to the pyramid selling of the 1970s, which was outlawed because of its intrinsic dangers. Pyramid selling involved the sale of something useless to buyers who sold the same useless item to others and so on. Those who managed to sell profited. Eventually one ran out of buyers. They were the losers, and there was nobody else to whom to sell.

That is precisely what has been happening to property prices.

It is extremely dangerous to allow resale value to exceed investment value. It should never be allowed for an extended period.

Corporate valuations do not suffer from the same problems as property valuations. The reason is that most investors in the stock market are looking for income. The yield is therefore a large part of the investment strategy. That has not stopped an army of investors – some call them day traders – who spend their time looking usually in vain, for quick capital profits.

Irrational valuations as was the case with internet companies and in the way I described earlier in this chapter, do however appear from time to time and the principle that a buyer should pay a seller for the future profits that are by no means certain is so foolish that nobody should indulge in it. It is a slippery road towards the one in which the real estate market finds itself.

Corporate valuations are affected by interest rates. As interest rates fall the comparatively higher return from stocks grows so that they look particularly attractive. The result is that stock prices will rise as interest rates fall.

The recent move by the central banks of the developed and over leveraged countries to print money and buy bonds has resulted in inflation in bond prices and a lowering of bond yields. That has kept stock prices up above the level that they deserve to be.

Inflation tends to have an adverse affect on stock valuations despite what I said earlier. Inflation usually results in a drop in bond prices as investors expect more return from bonds in order to compensate them for the rise in inflation. This drop in bond prices affects stock prices as well because the relative return for stocks is now too low. Stock prices therefore fall.

None of this sounds very scientific because the theory is that bond prices will only fall temporarily as inflation adjusts. However markets do not operate rationally. They assume that if inflation increases to 5% it will remain there for ever. That is a mistake but that mistake forms the basis for such incorrect valuations in unstable inflationary times. It is true that inflation causes people to panic and that panic is reflected in the pricing of stocks and bond prices.

Corporate valuations have also been affected by an insidious development that matured in the 1980s – the leverage buy-out business. I have discussed briefly the affects and dangers of this business and the way in which vast sums of wealth have been redistributed to a significant minority. I shall now describe how the principle operates.

A company with assets (property, machinery and other current assets) of 100mm and with income of 10mm per annum is entirely financed with share capital. Its balance sheet is simple. It has assets of 100mm and shareholder's funds of 100mm.

A leveraged buy-out fund, possibly backing its managers, makes an offer to buy it for 100mm. The offer is accepted and the deal is completed.

The buy-out fund immediately borrows 60mm from the bank at an interest rate of 5% - 3mm per annum and uses these funds to pay back to shareholders. The newly leveraged company's balance sheet and profitability is now altered.

It still has assets of 100mm but its share capital is now 40mm and it has borrowings of 60mm. It's profitability (I ignore tax for the purposes of this example) has reduced from 10mm to 7mm after paying the annual interest of 3mm.

The company's profile is now altered. It has shareholders funds of 40mm and profits after interest of 7mm. That represents a yield not of 10% as before but of 17.5%.

The company is immediately sold on the market at a multiple of 10. This means that the remaining shares are worth 10 times the adjusted income of 7mm. The newly valued shares are worth 70mm. The buy-out fund has made a profit of 30mm. But has it.

This is how leveraged buy-out or private equity funds have operated since the mid 1980s when the wonders of leverage were discovered and money became readily available. It is however a fiction and the fault is one of valuations.

The original company with no leverage and 10mm of profit was trading at a multiple of earnings of 10 time (or a yield of 10%). That company had no borrowings. Accordingly if the value of its assets were to fall or its income was to fall nothing disastrous would happen. It would continue in business and its share capital would have fallen in value.

Assume that the profitability of the old company had fallen because of a permanent fall off in trade by 50% to 5mm. The result would be that the value of its shares would fall to 50mm.

Now suppose that happened in the newly leveraged company. The profits would reduce from 7mm to 2mm and the value of its shares would have fallen from 70mm to 20mm, a reduction in value of 71%.

If the drop in profits was more than 7mm the new company would be insolvent and have to be wound up.

It is clear that the new company is at considerably higher risk than the old. It is clear that the share capital of 40mm that was left after the leveraging, and that was sold for 70mm was of substantially inferior quality in terms of risk than the 100mm before the borrowing and the reduction in the share capital. Yet somehow the valuers would value it at the same multiple of 10. This is a serious mistake.

The reality is that by leveraging the old company with 60mm of borrowings nothing was really achieved. Although the old company had share capital of 100mm that was not really equity in terms of risk. It was notionally made up of a tranche of debt of 60mm, the return for which was the same as that charged by the bank (5%) and a tranche of 40mm of equity the appropriate return on which was 17.5%. The weighted average rate of return of these two notional tranches of investment properly adjusted for risk, was 10%. It was this before the borrowing as it was after. I like to classify the risk of investments in the company not formally as debt and equity because that gives a false impression. It gives the impression that the debt is a low risk and equity is a high risk. I like to classify the investments in the company as being debt risk and equity risk no matter how the liability side of the business is financed. This would avoid valuing the new company following a leveraged buy-out as if new value had been created.

Who were the losers from this game. It was either the seller who sold at an undervalue or the eventual buyers of the newly leveraged shares that were valued at the same multiple of earnings as a company that had no leverage, when it should have been valued at a considerably lower multiple because of the increased risk in the "new" equity. Alternatively the bankers could be the losers because they are probably taking an equity risk but earning a debt return. Take your pick. The consequences are all too plain. The owners and promoters of these leveraged acquisitions are vastly wealthy. No new wealth or GDP growth has been achieved. It follows that somebody somewhere must sooner or later suffer the corresponding loss.

Valuations of existing goods suffer from a serious deficiency – assumed proportionality. They differ from newly produced goods in one very material way. Whereas consumables such as sugar, coffee, wheat and such items have a market price based on the sale of all the goods produced and marketed this is not the case for existing goods the most obvious of which are house prices and the stock market.

Stock prices and house prices are assumed to have risen or fallen proportionately to the price of those houses or stocks that are actually sold. Thus for example if there are 20 million homes in the UK and in a particular month only 2,000 are sold the market assumes that the remaining 19.998 million houses have increased in value in the same proportion as the ones that were sold. This is of course nonsense. Yet it is how we base our valuations of these existing assets.

Thus for example if of the 2,000 homes that are sold only 1,000 were for sale at an average price of 200,000 but there were 2,000 buyers the buying pressure would have forced the price up in order to persuade owners who were not willing to sell to do so. If this buying pressure resulted in the price of these 2,000 homes being increased to 210,000 the market assumes that the rest of the 20 million homes also increased by the same percentage.

Politicians and surprisingly economists have in the past been delighted by the phenomenon of increasing house prices. Owners were happy that their wealth had increased. They borrowed more money and spent it on discretionary items, such as clothing and vacations abroad. They voted for the government in power. What could be bad about it. It was of course fantasy. House prices increased only because of house price inflation. Money was created by banks and put into the housing market. Interest rates were reduced. More and more people borrowed on the assumption that house prices would not fall. In fact the real use value of the land was exactly the same as it has been for 1,000 years or more. Of course value had been transferred from the holiday market and clothing markets to the property markets. However there was a very large transferor of value – pension funds. Pension funds were depleted of value. There was a zero sum gain. Pension funds lost money that emerged in the property market.

The phrase that became current amongst ordinary home owners in the 1990s was "my home is my pension". They were right. Whereas previously these people had investments in a home and a pension, now they had only a home. Their approach however was very short sighted because they could hardly sell off part of their home to make up the deficit in their pensions. They would have to "downsize". This process, if carried on would result in lower priced houses increasing in value and more expensive houses falling. Of course with the lower priced houses there was nowhere to go.

The increase in value of homes was therefore illusory. It was a zero sum gain. There is no doubt that owners felt good about their position but they were wrong. The land that they owned was the same land and had the same use value – as a dwelling – that it always had. The loss of pensions was yet another example of the redistribution of wealth without any new wealth being created.

The true value of a stock market should be based upon the assumption that all stocks are sold and purchased. It is the same with real estate prices. Valuations that are based on the assumption that if a small proportion of these assets are sold and are subjected to market pressures of supply and demand that process will be reflected in the wider market is incorrect. Yet that is the basis for valuing existing assets.

4. UNEMPLOYMENT AND MECHANIZATION

Mechanization, whether on the factory floor or in offices has one objective and that is the creation of more profits for a business by reducing costs. The inevitable consequence of this is unemployment. Businesses are constantly trying to reduce employment costs whether on the shop floor or in offices.

With the industrial revolution there was a shift of employment from the shop floor to offices. The number of workers on the shop floor reduced and those employed in offices increased.

When mechanization was introduced on the shop floor the workers saw the writing on the wall as their numbers dwindled. Office workers are in general more resilient and imaginative than shop floor workers. They constantly find new ways of persuading the producers that their services are required. In many cases this is merely a perception. In others office workers try to win market share from one producer who is then forced to employ other office workers to retaliate. The result is more office workers with little benefit to the economy in terms of productivity except that more of the producer's income is shared with more office workers. His profits could indeed decline but he will be persuaded that without the benefit of the services of these office workers his profits would have declined further. That is how office workers justify themselves. Of course certain office work is the inevitable cost of doing business and governments have assisted in compelling producers to employ more and more office workers doing work that has no benefit on the eventual production of the finished product, except to add to its cost.

Government bodies now carry on a large number of activities in any modern economy – principally education and health and maintaining the basic infrastructure of roads. Often they are involved in providing rail services, telecommunications and utilities. No profits are made by governments but governments seek to reduce costs wherever possible in order to reduce taxation.

Most forms of mechanization involve a redistribution of wealth from one sector of an economy to another. Usually no additional wealth is produced. The value of mechanization in offices is particularly questionable. Sometimes there is new wealth produced as a result of mechanization. The industrial revolution was an exception to this rule because during that period the widespread use of machines meant that all sectors of the community produced more goods and services.

Those who lose their jobs may not be useless, they may not be the worst or least productive employees. They are always the unfortunate ones.

Mechanization has moved in recent times from the shop floor to offices. Receptionists have disappeared and are replaced by irritating answering machines that are despised universally by all who try to make contact with any business. Different levels of sales forces are displaced and replaced by teams working in sweat houses in India or China. Government employees are being dismissed and replaced as the government tries to automate all its functions through the internet. All these activities result in people losing their jobs and a redistribution of jobs and wealth, sometimes to other countries. The ultimate function or service remains the same. No additional new wealth is created. Indeed the wasting of the customer's time is considerable. When a business automates its telephone system and dismisses some telephone operators it saves money. It does not however take into account the additional time that is spent by its customers who are waiting on the phone listening to irritating and irrelevant messages that are designed to answer all possible questions. This wasting of time is a drain on the economy. Yet its impact is ignored.

It is noticeable that office workers these days spend more time at work than they did 30 years ago. With all the electronic means of communication one would have expected the opposite to occur. The reason for this unexpected development is simply that these workers are wasting more and more time dealing with parties at the other end of the phone than they did 30 years ago. Yet economists assume that such forms of mechanization must be useful and beneficial to an economy.

Of course what one business does to the employees of another business is done to its own employees by other businesses. The time wasted is vast and a material drain on the quality of life of people and the economy.

With globalization productive capacity has chased cheap labour and manufacturing has been transferred from the West to the East where goods can be made much more cheaply. This results in large redistribution of wealth as the business leaders, bankers and lawyers in the West get richer, and some in the East get significantly richer. Others in the West pay with their jobs. These moves may be good at the corporate level but they are bad for the country where jobs are lost to the East.

The savings that are assumed to occur as a result of moving manufacturing to the East are marginal. The fact that a pair of shoes can be made in the East for $2 instead of $20 in the West does not mean that the producer in the East will sell for $2. He will not. He will sell at the highest price he can that will get him the business. That is probably $19.   The result is that the savings in the West to the business is marginal. Wealth has been transferred from the West where the employee loses his job, to the East where a worker makes a modest living and the factory owner makes a vast profit.

Governments were wrong to ignore this development and to regard all forms of competition as progress. The consequences were and will continue to be quite serious and detrimental. Governments have a duty to protect their citizens. They cannot be said to be doing that by allowing something bad to happen to their economy. Doubtless they will say that in the long term this competition will make us all more efficient. This has been shown to be a mistake. Factory owners in the East should produce shoes for their own bare footed people, and they would have to do so – in the above example – at $2.50, thereby making a modest profit, and Western shoe manufacturers should resume their shoe making activities. It makes no sense to make billionaires out of factory owners in the East while their own people are bare footed, whilst at the same time costing Western employees their jobs.

As a general rule it is unwise and bad for the national economy – even if it is good for the particular businesses - for business to replace people with machines or to export activities that were previously carried on at home unless the following tests are satisfied;

1. Is there a shortage of labour. If there are unemployed people around then it is probably a bad idea to increase the number of unemployed. Only where there are no people who can do the job should a job be done by a machine or in some other country. The fact that it can be done cheaper elsewhere is not sufficient justification.

2. Has the customer's time been taken into account before deciding that the supplier's costs will be reduced. There is no point saving time of the supplier's staff when the consumers who are themselves staff of some other enterprise spend more time doing what before took less time. Customers are themselves staff of some enterprise or other and if one organization wastes the time of the staff of another it will sure be done to him later.

3. Is the job that is being made more efficient by introducing mechanization a wealth creating job or a wealth redistributing job. If it is a wealth redistributing job there is little point in redistributing it further. Nothing will be gained by the economy. Redistribution of wealth without wealth creation is merely a way of participating in the wealth created by others. There is no point in redistributing such wealth again and making the redistribution process more efficient. One cannot make an activity efficient if the end product on which the activity relies is not affected.

4. It is often said that the private sector will take up the workers dismissed by the government and that government prevents the private sector from expanding by taking much of the talent. The theory is that government should sack workers, reduce the deficit, reduce taxes and those who benefit from the reduced taxes will be hired by the private sector. The reduced deficit will enable the private sector to borrow more. This should be tested on the basis that if it does not happen the tax benefits will be reversed retrospectively. If the private sector needs employees that are government employees it merely has to make them an offer. The government should be regarded as having a pool of trained employees available to work in the private sector as and when required but employed by government to carry out government bureaucratic work when otherwise not required by the private sector.

5. Before manufacturing is exported overseas the exporting company should be compelled to pay the unemployed persons a percentage of the savings it makes as a result. The welfare of the erstwhile employees is the responsibility of the employer and if he profits by sending work overseas he should be compelled to support those who suffer as a result. The cost of

maintaining those employees should not fall upon those businesses that do not benefit from the transfer of work to cheaper countries.

6. Employers should be compelled to offer reduced working time to all employees and reduced wages when machines are introduced or there is less work available so that the burden is shared equally and there is a benefit in return – more leisure time for all.

7. Unemployed workers should share their work with their erstwhile work mates if there are too many of them.

There is a touching belief that unemployment will be reduced by more education and qualifications. This is a myth that I shall address in more detail later. It is based simply upon the evidence of the past that educated people have been more adept at grabbing for themselves a larger proportionate share of the profits of producers without necessarily providing any benefit to them in terms of production.

Educated people are more likely to be wealth redistributors and not surprisingly they benefit themselves at the expense of the real wealth creators. The assertion that education is likely to reduce unemployment is pure fantasy and is based on the fact that as there was greater demand for office work it was easier for educated people to get jobs. Now that there are more people working in offices than in factories and fields the position has been reversed. The matter is not only one of supply and demand but also of affordability. The productive sector cannot continue to support an unlimited number of office workers.

Government of course are now in some difficulty. Since the majority of workers are employed in offices it would be difficult for them to try to move them away from office work. It is hard for them to tell the office workers that their work is unnecessary, or at least too highly rewarded for the value that it provides.

Unemployment was once considered to be the curse of the unskilled workers. That is no longer exclusively necessarily the case. There are now many skilled jobs – including lawyers, accountants and doctors – that are hugely oversubscribed. The jobs are simply not there although the skills are. The rules of supply and demand cannot be defeated by education.

The constant attempts to improve efficiencies will only make that unemployment problem worse and the introduction of IT into offices has one aim and one alone and that is to reduce costs at the expense of increasing the unemployed.

One cannot leave a chapter on unemployment without addressing the issue of economic growth that we discussed in an earlier chapter. The inevitable conclusion of the chapter on economic growth is that economic growth will not come to the aid of the unemployed. Indeed as monetary wealth becomes concentrated in the hands of a large minority the plight of and the number of unemployed will only increase.

Theoretically the unemployed constitute a pool of excess capacity. If the unemployed could be employed producing goods and services that are required by the rest, and the rest have the reciprocal capacity to produce more goods and services to repay these erstwhile unemployed the problem of both unemployment and growth will be solved. Unfortunately the unemployed need to be employed by somebody who has the financial resources to make the goods and services that they are able to produce. There must be a market for such goods and services. The concatenation of circumstances is difficult to imagine. It is likely that only government can overcome this problem and there is no reason why the government should not be the employer of last resort, thereby providing a trained labour force if it is required by the private sector.

The concentration of massive amounts of wealth in the hands of a few results only in more and more saving. There is only so much that a rich man can spend. If wealth is distributed more widely it is more likely that those who benefit will spend the money by employing the unemployed. There is a lot of work that needs doing. One only has to look around one's own community to see it. There is work for everybody to do, so long as the wages that are available are not shared disproportionately.

When the beneficiaries of the vast redistributions of wealth that occurred over the past 30 years are concentrated in a small number of individuals the chances that they will spend all their money on new goods and services becomes more and more unlikely. The result is that unemployment will become worse and worse.

It is the duty of any government that wants to be taken seriously in combating unemployment that wealth is not concentrated in too few hands. It is far better to spread wealth thinly than to allow a small number to have more than they can realistically spend.

The unemployed give rise to a particular problem when it comes to the payment of social security or unemployment or other benefits to them. The employed tend to be resent those who receive something for nothing.

Such resentment tends to be well hidden so long as the standard of living of the employed keeps increasing. However when a drop in living standards is required, because consumption has run ahead of production, which is the situation in which we now find ourselves, the resentment grows when the employed are expected to suffer the consequences. They inevitably consider that it is the "scroungers" or the "work shy" who should bear the burden of reduced consumption and not themselves. Terms like "indigent idle" have been around to describe the unemployed for generations. People who work claim that they "work very hard for their money". Politicians constantly reinforce that belief. It is merely a form of flattery. Many employed persons do not work hard at all. Most who work in offices do so because the work is easy. Certainly it is nothing like as hard as working down a coal mine.

It is understandable that those who are employed resent having to contribute to the cost of living of those who do no work at all. Governments have an obligation to ensure not only that the wealth produced by a nation is shared equitably but also the burden of producing that wealth.

Governments have thought rightly that by making provision for the economically inactive to receive a minimum standard of living they are more likely to keep the peace. That however ignores the other side of the coin. Government has to make sure that the burden of producing the wealth of the nation is also shared equitably.

It is the duty of government to ensure that there is work for all. If the market is doing its job in this respect so be it. However if it is not then government must intervene. There is always work to be done, whether in cleaning or tidying public spaces, or indeed, for those who have office skills, in keeping the bureaucracy up to date. Governments should be the employer of last resort. All unemployed should be employed by the government. That way a pool of employees will be trained and ready for work in the private sector as required. Government training tends to be very good, particularly when it comes to law and administration. The burden of keeping the unemployed employed doing government work, even inessential work will have to be carried by the rest of us. Taxation will rise as a result but it will be a small price to pay for having a ready pool of trained employees for the private sector as and when required.

There is a curious feature of employment that seems to operate contrary to market forces. If a law firm has 20 jobs but 2,000 qualified applicants each of whom can do the work more or less as well as the next, the law of market forces says that the result should be that the wages of those who are employed should go down until the cheapest ones are employed. That does not seem to happen. This is a phenomenon that has not been properly explained or addressed by economists or indeed the employers who seem to be missing a trick. The explanation offered of course is that the employer wants the "best" and one has to pay for the best. There is of course no way of knowing whether those who have been selected are indeed the best. Indeed with mechanization of the interview process it is likely that the choice is made of the best students and not the best employees.

However it would be very easy in the example given to ask those applying for the few jobs available what wage would ensure that they walked away. Nobody does that. Clearly there is no attempt to ensure that the employer pays the minimum possible as required by the laws of market forces.

The reality seems to be the result of two factors. The first is that if the new employees are willing to work for less then their bosses too will have to take a pay cut sooner or later. The second factor is that those who carry out the employment and set the terms are themselves employees and not the employer who ultimately bears the cost.

It is of course true that each individual is unique. It is however also true that all law firms for example claim to have hired "the best". The laws of economics should not be suspended in this way. If there are too many lawyers, accountants, doctors or bankers or indeed people applying for any job market forces should ensure that the price of employment is driven down if there are insufficient. This can only be done by a different process than the one in place whereby the employer or somebody who works for the employer, sets the wage and people apply for it. This is not how market forces are meant to work in a free market.

Jobs should be advertised on the basis of a bidding process. Whether a company is employing a CEO or a driver an auction should be put in place with a price set by the job seeker. It is only in that way that market forces will ensure that the right compensation package is awarded. Individual applicants will be able to evaluate themselves. One who has a weaker CV may be willing to do the work for less as a result and that may be good enough for the employer.

The market for jobs seems to be dominated by an insane chase for the "brightest" graduates with the best academic results at higher and higher salaries that are not necessary but whose effect is only to ensure that the bosses' salaries remain high. This is only possible because the real owners of the business are too remote from the hiring process. It is a totalitarian approach to employment and the setting of wages, whether at the top or bottom end of the scale.

5. UNEMPLOYMENT, TAXATION AND WELFARE

Politicians are for ever on the look out for simple solutions, mantras that the masses find attractive, and unhappily a focal point to unite people either favourably or critically. The unemployed fit this need in an advanced society where the majority are employed and that provides welfare payments for its unemployed.

The problem of unemployment has baffled economists for generations. It has not been solved. The number of unemployed has waned from time to time but it keeps recurring.

Politicians find it convenient to classify all the unemployed in one or two simple categories. Those on the right like to think that aside from a very small number who are unable to work there is a small number of people trying to find work but the majority on welfare simply do not want to work because life is better on welfare. If only these lazy scroungers could be forced into work we would have economic growth, very little unemployment, lower taxes and we would all be better off.

Those on the left agree that there is a small number unable to work but that the majority of the rest are actively seeking work and the number of scroungers is really very small indeed.

The majority of those in work apparently favour the opinion of the right wing of the political spectrum on this matter. They go even further and consider that the majority on welfare are cheating or defrauding the system.

Government policy when times are bad has therefore tended to be focused upon dissuading those on welfare to continue to be lazy.

The real problem that any government faces when tacking the undoubtedly high welfare bill is that unemployment pay is not very high at all. Indeed it is impossible to make ends meet with unemployment or the basic welfare cheque. The government therefore has to contribute more. It provides housing allowances for those who cannot pay for accommodation. This can be quite substantial and has to rival what those in work pay for their accommodation. The larger welfare cheques however go to those who have a large family. It is difficult to penalize children who are by law not allowed to work.

In reality the unemployed and indeed the employed fill a number of different categories. There are probably more than I can enumerate here but the following are a few of them. I start with the categories of the employed.

1. There are employees who work for a very small wage, probably below what their job is worth. They require welfare payments to live decently. They probably do not particularly like their jobs, and certainly resent the fact that they do not earn a living wage. It is however the best that they can do and they would rather work than live off welfare.

2. Some employees earn an appropriate wage for the job. The do not like their job but have to work. They would not work if they did not have to.

3. Others in category 2 might love their work and would work even if they did not need the money.

4. An increasingly large number of employees are vastly overpaid. They love their jobs and would work for considerably less but vast sums of money are offered to them.

5. Some in category 4 do not particularly like what they do but the money is too good for them to leave and do what they want. They look forward to a time when they have

enough money to do what they would really like to do – perhaps nothing at all.

Of these categories the first and second are the most likely to resent welfare payments to scroungers. All categories are likely to consider that they work very hard, deserve all that they get and that the scroungers do not deserve what they are paid.

The unemployed also fit into different categories, rather than the simplistic one that politicians find it convenient to use. The following are a few of the main ones.

1. There are the genuine scroungers. These are able bodied persons who find it preferable, no matter what their circumstances, to live on welfare. They could find work but choose not to.

2. Others would love to work for any remuneration, because it is better for their peace of mind. They prefer to have something to do. They look and look for work but all the jobs, even in category 1 of the employed workers, are taken.

3. Some unemployed persons are willing to work but only if the wages are worth their while. They would rather be unemployed then work for a pittance. The inconvenience of working is simply not worth the wages on offer in those jobs that are available.

4. Another category is the unemployed worker who will only work in a position that he or she considers is consistent with the status to which he or she considers appropriate having regard to his or her training, qualifications and ability. There are jobs available but they are not the "right" jobs.

Clearly those who merely refuse jobs can afford to do so because of the availability of welfare payments.

It is easy to see which people in the categories of employed workers might resent most those in the unemployed categories.

The problem that politicians face is that they all try to address the problem with a "one size fits all" solution. Since there are so many different categories this is often inappropriate and it is not possible to analyse the different categories without interrogating the unemployed – a difficult and time consuming task.

Of course there is no doubt that if there were no welfare payments for unemployed persons there would be no unemployed. People would be forced to work in one way or another. It is likely that there might be more crime and more begging too, but all would have to live by their own endeavours. That however, is not how a civilized society likes to live. Welfare is the price for unemployment. It is also the price for not having too many beggars and too much crime.

Looking at the categories of employed and unemployed there is a principle that can be identified. Wages are the reward for the efforts of work. Work is considered to involve an output, a cost, a disadvantage. Wages are the reward for the inconvenience or discomfort endured by the workers.

Of course there are those who earn less than the value of the effort they put into their work, and those who earn considerably more. That is how Western advanced industrialized economies work.

If the effort or discomfort involved in working is exactly equal to the benefit from the wages then clearly the unemployed would be getting something for nothing.

Where the effort or discomfort involved in working is considerably less than the benefit from the wages – this is the case with those who are overpaid – the argument against the unemployed receiving something for nothing becomes weaker.

Governments all assume that workers all get a wage that is equal to the effort or discomfort involved in working. That is a mistake.

To many work is a pleasure and they would do it for nothing if they could afford it. There is a large number of workers who fall into this category. Of course those on welfare do not have this luxury.

It is this disparity between the employed and unemployed that enables the employed to be so easily critical of the unemployed.

The employed persons' perception of themselves as being paid exactly what their effort is worth and the underlying assumption that they receive little benefit, pleasure or reward from the work itself is the foundation of a good argument by the unemployed.

The assertion by the employed leads to the inevitable conclusion that those who are paid more endure more suffering and discomfort by doing their work than those who earn less. Of course the reality is exactly the opposite. It is those who earn more that have the more stimulating and enjoyable work.

So we are faced with a situation in which those who are highly paid win twice. Firstly they win because they get pleasure and satisfaction from the work itself, and secondly they get paid more. Of course their argument is that they get paid more because of the greater value of what they do. This however is a different question that I have addressed elsewhere in this book.

It does not really matter however whether the employed are overpaid or underpaid. In principle there is effort and discomfort in working and so long as there are others able and willing to work who cannot find jobs because there are simply not enough jobs to go around a question must surely arise as to why those willing and qualified workers who are unemployed should not share in that discomfort and effort. There is certainly no moral reason why they should be paid for doing nothing.

Politicians like to deal with economic questions and the issue of unemployment on the basis that the matter is simple. They like to think that it can be solved with some kind of injection of money into the economy or by the simple manipulation of interest rates. They like to think that our right to perpetual economic growth will somehow sweep up all the unemployed and remove the problem.

When Margaret Thatcher became prime minister of the UK in 1979 she introduced policies that were clearly going to have a detrimental effect on the unemployment figures. She claimed that her policies would result in a "temporary" and "very small" increase in unemployment, that would soon be reversed as people suddenly became more productive as a result of lower taxation.

The unemployed figures increased from 1.5mm to around 3.5mm. Today they are still around 2.5mm. They never came down to where they were and the increase was certainly not small. The promised economic growth did not materialize enough to absorb the unemployed.

Politicians like to deal with the problem on the basis of the world as they hope it will be if they are given enough time. This is a mistake. Only now is reality. They should deal with the situation as it is now.

The situation today is that there is an army of qualified and able bodied unemployed who are equally able to do the work that is done by those who are fortunate enough to have jobs.

The focus of governments upon what the unemployed receive and what workers are paid is wrong. The focus should be on the effort of work, upon its inconvenience and discomfort.

If there are employees who are "working very hard" for their money they should be offered the benefit of working less hard and taking time off for more leisure – with corresponding reductions in pay of course if they can afford it.

In short the effort of working should be shared. There is no excuse for able bodied and qualified people to be unemployed. It is also a great waste.

The employed who deride the unemployed do have a point. However if asked whether they would be willing to share their jobs they would certainly object. Such objections are inconsistent with their claims that they are working hard for their money and do not want to give it to scroungers.

When factories in Germany were not getting the work that they expected some bosses offered the staff two alternatives. They would either reduce staffing numbers by 30% or reduce wages – and hours worked – by 30%. The workers accepted the second alternative.

There is no reason why the unemployed should not be given the same opportunity to share in the discomforts and effort as well as the benefits of receiving wages with the employed. There is no reason other than luck why some qualified people are in work and others, equally qualified are not.

There is a lot to be said for a policy that requires shorter working hours and earlier retirement.

How does a government pursue such a policy. Those who like their jobs, enjoy their work and in general find that the benefits from their wages far exceed the discomfort of working will resist any attempt to cut their working hours. They will argue that the unemployed are less qualified or less able.

Those whose wages are below the bread line will not be able to reduce their working hours and wages.

On the other hand there will be a large number of employees who would welcome the opportunity to work shorter hours and to share their jobs with others who are unemployed including a large number who are not on welfare.

It is the task of government to address this issue and it has to do so by considering the various categories of unemployed and of employed.

Starting with its own army of employees it can issue instructions reducing the number of hours worked per week and recruit many of the unemployed to share the jobs that the government performs. Only where replacements cannot reasonably be found will employees not be required to work part time.

Governments have the ability to employ large numbers of people with different qualifications. They can employ cleaners, porters, receptionists and armies of office workers. They have jobs for skilled craftsmen and technicians. They require helpers at schools and hospitals. The possibilities are endless.

The private sector will be harder to change. Employees should be given the right to nominate the number of hours or days that they wish to work. Some will retire earlier, women and some men may wish to work part time because it suits them. Others may want to travel and can afford to reduce the number of hours that they work. If they are given that right employment contracts will fill a whole spectrum. Some may want 12 months leave of absence. Anything should be permitted so long as jobs are made available.

There will be many who refuse, even though they can afford to reduce their working hours. These will generally be those who get more out of their work than the effort they put into it. Their taxes should be raised to make it less worth their while.

The cost to business, aside from the inconvenience of having to employ more people than before will not be substantial and the government should assist with any additional costs. The welfare bill will practically disappear.

It is the availability of jobs or lack of them that causes unemployment. All efforts by government to assist the unemployed have to date been in helping the unemployed to jump the queue. They are taught how to get ahead of their competitors, either by gaining qualifications or writing a good CV. That does not reduce the number of unemployed it merely determines who gets the few jobs available. It is a practically worthless exercise.

6. BANKS, HOW THEY OPERATE AND HOW THEY CREATE MONEY AND CONTROL HOW IT IS SPENT

I do not intend to go into too much detail about how banks create money. There are sufficient web sites that will explain the procedure is detail and with clarity. Here however is a brief summary.

Money in the form of paper was originally backed by gold and the goldsmiths were the original source of paper money. I would deposit gold at a goldsmith and he would hand me an IOU for the amount. I would later buy something for gold and instead of cashing in the IOU and handing the gold to the seller from whom I had purchased the goods I would hand him the IOU.

Goldsmiths soon found that it was only necessary to have a certain amount of gold and that they could issue IOUs to a person that exceeded the amount of gold that person had deposited. In return that person would himself give an IOU to the goldsmith promising to hand over the rest of the gold (the difference between the gold he handed to the goldsmith and the IOU the goldsmith had given to him).

That is how banks now carry on business. The only difference is that nowadays instead of having physical gold they have an amount owed by the central bank that takes the part of gold.

Whenever a bank makes a loan it creates money. I go to the bank to borrow £100mm. The bank does two things. It credits my deposit account, which is the bank's liability to me with £100mm, and it debits its loan account, which is the amount that it had lent me. That is its asset.

Its balance sheet is now greater by an additional 100mm of assets and 100mm of liabilities. Some banks today have balance sheets that are the size of the net worth of many small countries.

When I draw down the deposit of 100mm I merely use the money to pay my creditors. I borrow for example to buy a property or a company. The money goes to the seller who deposits the money with his or possibly the same bank. That banking sector as a whole has not changed the total amount of assets and liabilities.

The bank in this example does something else. It decides where and how I am to spend the money. I am not allowed to use the money as I please. I have to use it for the stated purpose. They are therefore intrinsically involved in deciding whether the value of what I decide to buy is a good valuation. If they are wrong, as they were with AOL for example (wrong by $140Bn), I will not be able to repay them and they have lost their asset.

The liability however is still on their books as a liability. The bank or the banking sector still owes those who sold the property or the company to me at what the bank decided was the right valuation.

It is of course not the banks but bankers who make those kind of mistakes. Nevertheless by targeting particular assets and enabling borrowers to pay vast sums of money for them this will cause inflation in the price of those assets. It is targeted inflation but inflation none the less. It happened to property values and it happens regularly on the stock market in the price of companies.

By creating money that did not exist previously banks have the ability to redistribute wealth without creating any wealth in the way I have described earlier. The amount of money created to the extent that it represents more than full value is the equivalent of printing money and giving it to the recipient for nothing. When I take the 100mm in the above example and give it to my lawyers who have overcharged because their charge rate has been increasing at inflation busting rates for many years, they have redistributed wealth to the lawyers and away from the rest of us. When I pay more than the property or company is worth the banks have redistributed wealth to the extent of that overvaluation to the vendor. It is the same with what I pay in fees to my accountants and my staff. It all represents dilution in the value of the money that was previously available to the rest of us.

If such money is spent buying staple goods and services there will be general inflation. If it is limited to buying property for example there will be inflation in property values, leading the banks to make bigger and bigger bad bets for an indefinite period and creating more and more money in return for nothing.

This is redistribution of wealth in huge amounts. Because of the kind of people who receive it the inflation will appear in particular sectors such as for example property values and stock prices. It is inflation nonetheless and redistribution of wealth for which somebody will have to pay sooner or later.

What is wrong with banks making loans secured against a valuation? Nothing whatsoever so long as the valuation is right. In the short term we can be reasonably certain that valuations are right. However the longer term nature of many liabilities particularly where real estate is involved increases the likelihood that the valuation is incorrect and as a result large sums of money can be redistributed without any wealth being created.

Some assets, such as consumables have only a limited life use value and few if any banks have lost money by lending on security of such assets. It is only when dealing with assets whose value depends upon a longer, sometimes an indefinite period that the value of the underlying security can fluctuate so seriously as to result in a redistribution of wealth without any wealth creation and possible detriment to the bank itself.

Here are a few examples. Many banks hold long term bonds. Bonds are IOUs where the borrower agrees to pay the bank back the money he borrowed with interest at a fixed rate over a long term. If the rate of interest on these bonds changes the value of the bonds also changes.

When there is no general inflation the rate of interest on long term bonds can be relatively low (around 4%). When inflation was high, for example 10% bond yields were around 15%. When inflation came down to, say 2% bond yields fell dramatically resulting in the value of the bonds increasing materially. The value of a bond varies in inverse ratio to the level of interest rates in the market. As interest rates fall the value of a bond rises and vice versa. Thus the buyer of a 20 year bond with a face value of 100 yielding 15% will be able to sell it for 224 if interest rates were to fall to 5%. That is a massive profit. Value has gone into the hands of the investor. There has been a redistribution of wealth to him. No wealth has been created. All that has happened is that for whatever reason inflation has fallen. Of course it is the future rate of inflation that is important but markets do not operate that way. In general if there is no inflation today financial markets will assume that inflation for the foreseeable future will be modest. If inflation is high today they will assume that inflation in 10 years time will remain high. It is of course nonsense but that is what happens.

So who would be the loss maker at whose expense this profit of 124 in this example was made. The answer in this case is simple. The loser is the borrower - the issuer of the bond. He still has to pay a rate of interest of 15% when he should be paying only 5%. It was a gamble that borrower and lender took. The gamble proved profitable to one and equally unprofitable to the other. Vast amounts of money were redistributed but no wealth was created. That is how banking works.

Another very recent example of the extraordinary nature of long term investments comes from the real estate market and the introduction of the Euro. Prior to the introduction of the Euro in 2000 the Italian Lira was a high interest and high inflation currency. Interest rates were around 10%. Property values were based upon the assumption that this is the appropriate rate of return on bonds and therefore property rents should be around 10% of property values.

When the Euro was introduced long term interest rates were around 5% and the rents payable before in Lira were payable in Euro. Property values however were then revalued so that the rent yielded about 6%. Property values soared. Property owners profited. It is by no means clear who were the ultimate losers but losers there undoubtedly were.   Massive sums of money or purchasing power were redistributed without any new wealth being created. Banks in this case profited because the value of their security on their property loans increased.

When a bank values a company they are valuing its future cash flow for a long period. It is normally assumed that a company's profit trend will continue forever. Nothing is forever. Competition ensures that things will change. Sometimes changes occur very rapidly. When a bank gets its valuation wrong the consequences are enormous and the purchasing power that is redistributed is enormous. This all happens without any new wealth being created.

Banks do not only lend money to businesses. They also lend to consumers. We all know what lending and borrowing is but here is a definition in economic terms.

Borrowing is the arrangement that exists whereby the borrower is permitted to consume more than he produces in return for the promise to consume less than he produces at some time in the future.

Whenever a bank lends money to a borrower it does so on the understanding and the belief that the borrower who wants instant gratification and thereby will consume more than he has produced will at some stage in the future reverse the process and consume less than he produces. It is a risk that the bank takes. It is a gamble.

The bank assesses the prospects that the borrower will be able to reverse the process. The surplus wealth that the borrower produces will at some stage be consumed by the depositor who has lent the money to the bank – and has therefore produced more than he consumed. When the borrower and depositor reverse their consumption and production habits the money disappears and things return to normal. The bank's balance sheet returns to the level at which it was before the loan. That is how lending is meant to operate. It is how a balanced economy is meant to work.

In order to appreciate the magnitude of what has happened over the past 30 years consider what happens first when a bank makes a loan. As explained above it creates money by doing so. The amount of the loan appears in the books of the bank as an asset. The money however that is given to the borrower is used by him to pay wages, fees (lots of fees at ever increasing inflation busting rates) and to the extent that the borrower is acquiring a capital assets such as land or other goods such as cement or metal rods as proceeds for the sale of such items. To the extent that the borrower is paying for manufactured goods all such proceeds ends up in salaries and wages or profits of one or more people. Only land is really an exchange of one capital asset (land) for another (money). Leaving the land aside for the time being then the money that forms the loan ends up in the hands of individuals as payment for their goods or services. Thus although the bank records the loan as an asset that in theory does not affect the economy the money that it represents ends up as income of a number of people.

The fact that the loan is an asset of the bank means that it expects to get its money back. The people who get the money are supposed to produce an asset as a result of their work. This in the past would have been a factory or ship or aircraft but nowadays is more likely to be some computer game or piece of software that in many instances does not have any realisable value (e.g. Software that is specifically made for a particular business). In any event if the goods or services provided by those individuals does not produce enough revenue in the future to enable the bank to get its money back the bank will suffer a loss. Those who have received the money from the bank do not have to pay the bank back. The bank made a bet that by paying these vast sums of money to these individuals it will be repaid. If it does not however the bank is in trouble because the ultimate beneficiaries have taken their money. More importantly those at the other end of the flow of money have shown the income that they have received as pure income, unfettered by any conditions. The bank loan - the opposite end of the flow of money, treats the payment not as a corresponding loss but at a contingent asset, subject to probable repayment at some time in the future. The payer takes the risk, the receiver takes the income.

This disparity in timing itself creates an imbalance in the system because one cannot know the value of the asset that the borrower is creating, he will only know when it produces income. He hopes that it will be enough to repay him for having paid all those fees, wages, sale proceeds and profits to various parties.

Thus we have a situation whereby the first step in the production process is that numerous people receive income and profits that they are free to spend. In return the payer (ultimately the bank) expects to earn income and profits in years to come to repay him for the substantial up front payments that he made.

There is a clear trend here whereby present and short term payments are being made in return for possible income in the future. The bank and the borrower are making current payments and expect a return on their investment in the future. That bet could be spectacularly wrong as in the case of some Internet companies. There is nothing new in this except that the volumes have expanded out of all proportion until bank lending is now so huge that in many cases the balance sheets of large banks exceed that of a small nation. And the value of these balances sheets are dependent on the banks getting their bets right.

The banks have not properly considered the effects of new technology upon their whole loan and investment portfolio. They do not ask the right questions. They do not ask whether the new technology pays for itself and whether it is business efficiency improving or quality of life enhancing. They do not calculate whether the profits that they project for the new technology, doubtless based upon market research by highly qualified consultants, will adversely affect other businesses. They do not calculate whether new technology causes additional unemployment and therefore a redistribution of wealth, and whether the unemployed can indeed be employed elsewhere or not.

One only has to switch on a business programme to witness the euphoria based upon the electronic toys that are the basis for most new business ventures these days. Experienced analysts look with amazement at these toys and make assumptions about the viability of the businesses that sell them. They do so without regard to the basic economic principles that I have outlined here.

It is hardly surprising that the banks have so many bad loans and get their calculations so wrong.

If banks focused on whether their valuations depend properly upon redistribution of wealth or are genuinely business production improving they would not make so many mistakes. Instead they content themselves with such simplistic questions as whether it is a good idea that will pick up. That is puerile and facile. They should always consider whether a new product is genuinely incremental or a zero sum gain business that will sooner or later replace another business and they should then exit the business that is being replaced. They make no such judgment.

The approach of the banks to new businesses will result not necessarily in wrong valuations for the new businesses but in losses elsewhere. A bank could easily shoot itself in the foot by backing for example an Internet company all of whose income is being taken from a pub company in which the bank has a substantial investment. In short the bank could be right about the future for the technology company but could lose money by backing it because it is heavily invested in a pub company that will lose out £ for £ as the technology company makes money. This is just a simplistic example   but it happens and banks must be on guard against such possibilities. They are not even thinking about these possibilities.

The above is a description of classical or utility banking, namely banking that is connected to borrowing and frequently to capital expenditure.

There is another kind of banking - investment banking - that has come to be known as "casino banking" of late because it involves the taking of huge and often complicated bets on investments and other kinds of securities and financial instruments.

The investment banks - this is the American term - were created in the 1930s as a result of the great depression. One of the features of the great depression in the US was that there was huge inflation in the stock market, but not elsewhere. Ordinary people were piling into the stock market and many made fortunes, sometimes paper and transient fortunes but in any event their net worth increased beyond their wildest dreams. There was euphoria about the stock market. It was generally thought that you could not lose. Shoe shine boys were giving advice about stocks, which ones were likely to increase in value and which ones were not. It was a mad frenzy. You had to be in it to make a fortune and many took the bait and piled in.

The result in the short term was of course more self fulfilling price increases resulting from the buying pressure that existed. In short the result was inevitably what happens when there is more money chasing the same existing goods – inflation. Unfortunately every bubble bursts sooner or later. This one did too. However not before many people thinking that they could make more and more money borrowed as much as they possibly could to invest in the market. The banks were happy to lend, just as they have been the past 30 years on real estate values irrespective of how the buying pressure increases the nominal value of the assets that the borrowed money is used to acquire. They took security, on the shares that the borrower was purchasing but also on the borrower's other assets which in most cases borrowers were willing to give because "you can't lose". They did. The bubble finally burst and share prices crashed. People lost their homes and some committed suicide. Many paper fortunes were wiped out.

The supply of money had increased with loans, secured against assets that had increased in nominal value because of the additional money that the banks created. There were those who believed, and still apparently do, that inflation of long term assets is good but inflation in consumable assets is bad. That is a mistake that we seem bound to repeat over and over. Inflation is bad, whether it affects the price of bread or land. It is disruptive, indiscriminatory and redistributes wealth unpredictably.

The reaction of the authorities was to compel the banks to divide their activities between ordinary banking - taking deposits and making loans - and investment banking, the higher risk activities that involved investing in share, underwriting share issues (forecasting the price at which a new issue of shares will be bought), pricing all kinds of instruments. This type of banking activity was meant to be for the real professionals, for those who could afford to lose money. The rewards were potentially enormous but so were the risks. The result is that many banks split. J P Morgan split into Morgan Guarantee (the utility bank) and Morgan Stanley (the investment bank). These new investment banks were not permitted to take deposits and generally did not lend money in the conventional sense. They did underwrite bond issues. A bond is an IOU whereby the borrower is a well known and large company whose credit is often better than that of most banks. It does not need to borrow from the bank. It can borrow at the same rate as that at which the bank can itself borrow or perhaps cheaper. The investment banks would underwrite the issue of the bonds. Effectively they would buy all the bonds (equivalent to lending the money to the borrower / bond issuer) and sell them on the market. These bonds were tradable securities. Individual investors would buy them. Ordinary utility banks did not issue bonds.

The UK had a different system. It had merchant banks and ordinary utility banks. The merchant banks had a different background from the investment banks in the US. They arose because they were able to trade internationally. If I wanted to buy coffee from Kenya the vendor in Kenya would want to know that he could get paid. My liability to him would be guaranteed by a bank in Kenya. That bank would have an associate in London. The shipping documents would be sent to the associate in London. When the ship arrived in London I would go to the associate in London and collect the shipping documents. These were documents of title. The associate in London would only release them against my payment. As soon as the associate in London had my money he would tell the bank in Kenya that he had the money and the bank in Kenya would pay the vendor. I would take the shipping documents to the port and collect the coffee from the ship on showing the mate the documents. The London associate would then pay the bank in Kenya and all subject to a commission would be satisfied. The activity of the two banks was known as merchant banking. The two banks were originally merchant bankers.

These merchant banks expanded their activities to include what the investment banks in the US did. They raised equity from wealthy clients. They managed investment for their clients. They underwrote share and bond issues. However they also made ordinary loans to their clients. They were not high street banks but they did have clients and took deposits from them.

There was no need to split the activities of the two types of banking in the UK because an effective split already existed. In any event the UK public never took up the mad investment frenzy of their US cousins.

Amongst one of the major activities carried out by the investment and merchant banks was foreign exchange activities. The merchant banks were of course ideally suited to this activity and London as a result remains the leading city in the world where foreign exchange activity takes place today.

Foreign exchange transaction were originally intended to facilitate the sale of goods between countries where one currency was used and another country that used a different currency.

In 1980 the Thatcher government decided to allow banks to do whatever they wanted. The distinction between merchant and high street banks disappeared. There were other activities involving the stock market which was run by jobbers and brokers and were replete with restrictive practices but which as a system worked perfectly well. She abolished these restrictive practices as well. Henceforth the banks could do anything including buying and selling shares and bonds, underwriting, trading in foreign exchange and anything else. The market, we were told would control any excesses.

In the US the separation of the banks was enshrined in law under what became known as the Glass Steagall legislation (named after a Senator and MHR). The legislation was repealed by President Clinton in the 1990s.

Many are today convinced that the abolition of Glass Steagall and the disappearance of the merchant banks in the UK were contributing factors that led to the collapse of the banking system in 2007. The jury is still out on that and decisions about going back to the separation of activities are still being considered.

However one thing is certain. The banks partook in a frenzy of betting on any instrument that they could create, and there were many. You could take a bet on anything. You could bet that the market could rise or fall, that a sector could rise or fall, that the property market could rise or fall, that one or more foreign currencies could rise or fall. Options were issued enabling these gamblers to limit their risks in return for a premium and to win if they got it right. Most of these activities were zero sum gains to the economy. The number of possible transactions was unlimited. Their number grew and grew. Geographic restrictions were removed so that I could take a bet on the value of the Peking stock market or the Bombay bond market.

A new instrument - the daddy of derivatives - was created, namely the interest rate swap. This exchanged floating rates of interest for fixed rates. There were inflation linked investments. You could buy an instrument linked to inflation in one or more countries.

There was an explosion in the number of collective investment funds. You could invest in an "index". You could "short" and "index". You could buy futures and options to limit or increase your risk as you wished.

It was one big gambling casino. And most importantly there was no limit to the number of times you could place your bets. With the introduction of the PC programmes were invented to do the work of an individual.

Whereas in the past the number of financial transactions was limited by the number of physical transactions that the money was supposed to serve this disappeared. In theory I can now sell forward (agree to sell at a particular price at a future date) more shares or bonds than actually exist because I do not have to sell physical shares. It is just a bet. Nothing changes hands. A calculation is made at the time I am meant to deliver the instrument as to the price of that instrument and either I or the counterparty win. The other loses. It is a complete zero sum gain.

Not a single additional widget is constructed. Not a single additional tomato is grown. Not a bushel of wheat results from the vast profits that are made and lost.

The players are of course the banks and funds and other institutions all dealing with our own money. They use either depositors money or shareholders' money. In practically all cases the shareholders and depositors are not aware of the risks being taken with their money. It is none of their business, until it is lost of course.

But in amongst all this there is one winner. It is the individual who transacts the deals. Each bet involves two parties. One will win, and the other will lose. The winner gets a bonus. The loser merely blames the market and at the very worst loses his job. The next day the loser might win and the winner of the previous day might lose. Again a bonus is paid to the winner and nothing is taken from the loser.

It is not difficult to realise that every time a trade is made or a bet is taken money drains out of the system in a flood of obscene bonuses. The benefit to the economy is nil. As I said above not a single additional bushel of grain is grown.

It is argued simplistically that by giving large sums of money to these individuals as bonuses that is good for the economy because they spend it. Strange that when it is suggested that money be given to people on welfare so that they can spend it this argument is rejected as nonsense. It is of course self serving nonsense. All that is happening is that wealth is being redistributed without any wealth creation.

These sums are massive. They can be measured in hundreds of billions. These sums alone could bring the system to its knees. When somebody gains where no wealth is created a loser has to be identified. That lose we now know is the taxpayer who had to bail the banks out.

I described earlier how money was supposed to work. It was meant to be the servant of the real economy. It was meant to assist the exchange of goods and services. Borrowing and lending was meant to be temporary and to bridge the gap between the time when one set of goods and services was exchanged for another. Bank lending came to overpower the real economy. Through the process of lending and over valuation of assets it became possible to redistribute vast sums of money into undeserving hands. Those who came to hold the power to demand delivery of goods and services – the rich - were not those who created real wealth, but those who were able to redistribute wealth to themselves. These people dealt mainly with existing assets. They bought and sold them, they repackaged them, they pushed prices up by persuading banks to lend more and more.

The process of wealth redistribution through the private sector always starts with the beneficiary gaining. Identifying the person or persons who have to bear the corresponding loss occurs later, often many years later, by which time the causal connection is lost.

7. THE EVOLUTION IN THE FUNCTIONS OF MONEY

Money has been around for many centuries. Its form has changed from gold and other precious metals into paper backed by gold and later into paper without any implicit backing by gold. Nowadays it consists largely of bank balances and it is transferred increasingly electronically.

Money has always had three essential functions.

1. It is a medium of exchange.

2. It is a store of value.

3. It is a measure of value.

At the end of the chapter I will address another modern function of money that was never intended when money was created. It is this modern function of money that has overtaken in importance the three classic functions that money was meant to achieve.

MEDIUM OF EXCHANGE

Prior to the introduction of money people exchanged goods and services directly. This was cumbersome and inconvenient and had clear limitations. The introduction of money enabled all kinds of goods and services to be exchanged through the medium of money. Goods are sold for money and money is then used to buy something else, not necessarily from the same person or at the same time and not in the same amounts. Money made possible exchanges in smaller fractions. In a pure barter economy it may have been necessary to exchange 1 cow for 3 lambs, money enabled the owner of the cow to exchange it for a leg of lamb and 10 chickens.

Most economists regard the introduction of money as a replacement for the barter system. That is a mistake. Money merely makes barter more workable. It does not replace barter. Every economy involves the exchange of goods or services for other goods or services both within one country and between countries. The fact that money is used as an intermediate step in the process does not alter this fundamental fact. Failure to appreciate this fact leads to confused thinking and wrong conclusions. In particular it leads to the illusion that anybody who accumulates money has done so as a result of creating wealth. It ignores the possibility that money can be accumulated simply by redistribution and the impoverishment directly or indirectly of others, not necessarily in the same country.

The supplier of goods or services does not require money for its own value. It has none. He wants it in order to buy goods or services in the future. If no such goods or services are available the consequences will be felt in ways that cannot be predicted. Initially the supplier will consider that he has given a gift of his goods or services because he has received nothing in return.

This is a problem that is featuring regularly with regard to China which now produces much of the goods that we in the West consume. It is the problem of mutuality. It appears that nobody, including the Chinese have considered what the Chinese want in return for their goods and services. To date the answer has been "government bonds". That is a facile response. Bonds and other paper investments are yet another interim stage before the holder claims goods and services from the debtor country. Ultimately the producer wants something tangible to buy in return. The money he receives is an interim phase in the process. Where credit is granted - this is what happens when a country with trade surpluses cannot buy anything in return - the creditor - whether a country or a producer within a country, says in effect that he expects something of value to be produced in the future by those who have "bought" the goods that he produced. In reality of course the creditor will use his purchasing power to buy limited goods and services that others would have purchased instead. The result is inevitably inflation in the prices of those goods and services that the producer acquires including investments in the stock market and real estate.

Has anybody noticed how much of our real estate and companies are now owned by foreigners. That is one thing that can be supplied in return for production. We can sell our infrastructure in return for the T shirts that the Chinese supply to us. The problem is we can only do this once.

Money has no intrinsic value. It represents merely the right of the holder to claim goods and services of an economy at some time in the future. In all discussions about economics it would be helpful to ignore money and the holding of it or to regard the holding of money as purely having this feature. Much economic discussion leads to error because the experts confuse the real economy with money. They treat money as if it has some intrinsic value, as if it has some special features. It does not. It is merely a right to claim goods and services that will be produced in an economy.

A stable economy is one that is able to produce goods and services in return for goods and services that it receives from another country. Thus in the case of China it is essential that the US and UK in particular produce enough goods and services to provide to the Chinese. Such goods or services should not be capital goods such as real estate or companies. They should be goods or services that are manufactured or produced regularly. A lot of attention is paid by governments to its domestic deficit (the excess of spending domestically over income). Not enough is paid to the current account deficit. That, we are told is controlled by the market that values the currency of the country. That is a mistake. It is important to ensure stability between any two countries. Certainly there will be deficits and surpluses from time to time, but these must be reversible from current

120

production and not from capital. Why? Because capital can only be used once.

A STORE OF VALUE

In a pure and primitive economy barter economy I would have to exchange goods for goods of equivalent amount with the same person. I would for example have to exchange 20 sheep for one cow. I would have difficulty though exchanging a cow for 10,000 eggs since I would have no need for 10,000 eggs all at once and they would go off before I could eat them. Logically therefore I should take delivery of the eggs daily or weekly for a number of years. Money achieves precisely that and makes it easier to carry out the exchange. I sell the cow for money and use the money to buy eggs whenever I need eggs. I could also buy the eggs from different suppliers. I could one day choose to buy tomatoes, or perhaps a couple of hens. Money can be used to carry out the exchange later.

As a store of value money makes possible borrowing and lending. Borrowing and lending represent the deferral or acceleration of consumption. Thus borrowing involves the borrower consuming more than he has produced. The borrower promises to consume less than he produces at a later date and to give the surplus production to the lender later. Lending involves consuming less than the lender produces in return for a reversal of the process later when the borrower repays the debt.

A MEASURE OF VALUE

This is an important feature of money and the most problematic. Clearly goods have to be priced in terms of money so as to be exchanged for money. It would not be possible to exchange goods for money unless we knew what how much in money terms particular goods were worth. If prior to the introduction of money I could exchange a cow for 20 sheep and following the introduction of money a cow was priced at £20 and the sheep

121

were priced at £2 each something would be wrong. The sheep would have to be priced at £1 so as to maintain the relationship of value that existed before the introduction of money. This problem of relative worth occurs also when a new currency (such as the €, or the Australian Dollar) is introduced.

This means of measuring value gives rise to all kinds of issues such as inflation, exchange rates and the ability to measure wealth creation such as gross domestic product. It is perhaps this feature of money more than any other that is appreciated and used more than the others by lay persons. Everybody knows the price or value of their goods and services, and what is more or less expensive. Things become more complicated when capital goods are purchased and interest rates are applied to borrowings. Then the expertise of the lay person diminishes markedly. However as a general rule we all know how to measure the value of what we buy and sell in terms of money.

MONEY IN RECENT TIMES

Money was intended and for generations fulfilled this function properly, to be subservient and subordinate to the real goods and services of an economy. It was never intended to either have a life of its own or to be treated as a means of driving or affecting the production of goods or services in an economy.

By being associated with and subordinate to the goods and services in an economy the use of and the value of money was controlled and stable. The goods and services of an economy are by their nature limited. There are after all only 24 hours in a day, a finite amount of land on which crops can be grown and a limited number of people who are able to produce those goods and services. A natural limit to the number of deals that could be done existed.

Over the past 30 years money has acquired a unique feature that it was never intended to fulfil. It has become a surreptitious means of transferring vast amounts of wealth from person to person without any wealth creation. It has always been possible to redistribute wealth even in a purely barter economy. Thus for example a person could find a shepherd willing to sell 5 sheep for a cow and a dairy farmer willing to sell his cow for 4 sheep. The person could introduce the parties and keep the additional one sheep for himself. Wealth could in this way be transferred from the shepherd to that intermediary. The economic cake is exactly the same size as before - one cow and 5 sheep. All that has happened is a transfer of wealth without any wealth creation. The economic cake is the same size. One additional portion has been taken simply because the appetite of the dairy farmer is less than expected. However such opportunities were rate because both the shepherd and the dairy farmer knew the substance of the trade. With money the interaction between the eventual buyer and seller is so complex and unclear that opportunities for making vast profits without adding anything of value are multiplied. Companies are sold at vastly inflated prices. Bankers and professionals charge hugely inflated fees for their services. The deals are complicated by borrowing and the costs are capitalised and treated as having a realisable value, whereas at the end of the day the company being sold is essentially the same. The same opportunity exists with real estate.

This fourth use of money is dangerous and requires controls that to date have not been exercised, or at least not effectively by the regulatory bodies. Money has become a Trojan Horse within a modern economy for the wholesale and widespread redistribution of wealth without wealth creation. This redistribution of wealth creates massive imbalances and potential economic disruption as well as social disorder within an economy and between nations because it requires large sectors of an economy to become worse off as a direct consequence of others being undeservedly better off as a result of these redistributions.

There is another insidious by product of this feature of the use of money. As long as it remains so easy to profit from large scale redistribution of wealth the incentive to create wealth by slowly building or constructing some new business or product will remain unattractive. The incentive to create wealth disappears or diminishes substantially.

It is this reason and this reason alone that has resulted in so few new businesses being created, and so little hard work being encouraged. Why would anybody want to go through the risks of producing real wealth. Why would anybody want to take the risks associated with inventing something new, building up the necessary infrastructure and then selling the product at a profit, when it is so easy merely to redistribute wealth in a comfortable office.

Money is merely a right to claim the delivery of goods and services produced in an economy in the future. It has however now achieved a life of its own. It is now passed around and transferred in the form of fees or the results of substantial bets from one to another. There is a minimal pretence of association with goods or services but it is only nominal. Bets are taken not only on the stock market and the currency markets where literally trillions are traded or at risk at any one time. The form of betting is ubiquitous. When a new company is floated on the stock market ridiculous prices are paid. The difference between what the seller deserves and what the buyer is willing to pay depend upon future expectations of growth, a vague and subjective concept that varies from buyer to buyer. Companies like Google, AOL, Microsoft, Facebook and such like are worth vast sums of money at least on paper. To the extent that these valuations are excessive they represent a redistribution of wealth without wealth creation.

The real estate market also has participated in this insidious activity. Wealth has been redistributed in most cases without any transaction even taking place. Yesterday I had a home that was worth 100,000, today it is worth 1,000,000. I have become richer without producing a bean. It follows that somebody else must have got poorer.

Let me be absolutely clear about this because politicians are not willing to make these allegations in case they lose votes. Whenever there is no new wealth creation - as where a company or piece of existing real estate is sold - and somebody grows richer as a result of some transaction the inevitable consequence is that somebody else must grow correspondingly poorer. The corresponding impoverishment could take place many years later by which time the person who received the benefit will have lost all connection with the adverse consequence that he caused.

The process is complicated and frequently unclear. If I sell a house that is worth 500,000 for 1,000,000 there has been a redistribution of wealth of 500,000 from the buyer to myself. If I do not sell my home and it merely increases in value the identity of the loser cannot be immediately identified. He is anonymous. Yet a loser or losers there most certainly will be because no new wealth has been created.

Every time a footballer receives an increase in salary for doing the same job as he did before the increase - playing for 90 minutes - somebody has to or will have to pay the price. The fact that it does not come directly from our pockets does not mean we do not pay. We do. Nobody, particularly governments, should stand by idly as vast increases in salaries are dished out to the army of sports stars and celebrities. It is a most dangerous move and unless it is stopped the consequences will be very serious. Unless there is clear and tangible real wealth creation in return for their efforts the rest of us somewhere and at some time will have to pay for it.

The bill will not necessarily come through instantly. It can be delayed through the process of borrowing and lending. It will however be felt and we will have to pay for it sooner or later. Thus increases in salaries or fees are not something we can merely admire or envy. They constitute a real and potential danger of instability to the economy. The consequences could be felt in a different country where people might starve as a result. That the consequences will occur is not in doubt.

Governments have a duty to make sure that wherever there are inflation busting salary awards they are at least matched by an increase in real wealth creation. If they are not then others will have to get poorer sooner or later. It will be no surprise that those who are asked to become poorer - even though they do not know the direct causal connection between their impoverishment and the enrichment of others - object, in some cases very strongly indeed.

Who are the people who are benefiting from these redistributions. The beneficiaries are clear. We know them all. We read about them in the press. They are all those who have had inflation busting salary or income increases without creating anything new. In an advanced industrialised society the beneficiaries are the celebrities, TV personalities, professionals, office workers, bankers, fund managers, advertisers, lobbyists and such like. You read about them in the papers regularly as their excesses are uncovered.

In general it is not difficult to see how wealth has been redistributed. All that is required is a comparison of wealth over a period. If some are appreciably richer and others are poorer the transference of wealth is obvious. Relative wealth - where the gap between rich and poor widens - is not a good measurement of this wealth transference, because much of the gap can be created by real wealth creation. If real wealth is created and the creator gets richer by more than the wealth he created then he has transferred wealth to the extent of the excess and others will have to become poorer as a result. If the creator of wealth becomes richer by something less than the amount of additional wealth that he created then the gap between rich and poor may increase but the poor are marginally better off. Such

126

improvements in living standards of all are what some economists call the trickle down effect. Wealth trickles down. It does not of course trickle down when no new wealth is created but some persons become wealthier. That is the danger created by money.

Trickle down is often an excuse for the accumulation of vast sums of money. Money will trickle down if the holder has the need or desire – however extravagant that might appear to others – to spend it on new goods. Often however where vast sums are accumulated the number of options for spending money is limited. The holder has so much money he does not know what to do with it. He will trickle down some of his money but the rest he will be compelled to spend on existing goods that create inflation. That will probably be the stock market or property. He might leave the money in the bank or invest it in bonds. It will not all trickle down. The theory of trickle down only applies to a very limited extent and then only if the money is spread widely and thinly.

The majority of us in an advanced industrialised society are involved in the redistribution of wealth. To the extent that we pay ourselves vast inflation busting increases in salary we are stealing money from the rest who are not identified and may in some cases not even be born. Many will be in different countries.

Yes even the passive act of sitting on an investment or a property that increases in value far above the general rate of inflation is causing wealth to be redistributed into the hands of the owner. Since no new wealth has been created others will have to pay for it.

No government or economists seem to be aware of this concept or the dangers it creates. They seem to think that inflation in property values or the stock market are a good thing. They are not. They are potentially destabilising and create potentially massive imbalances in an economy and the social order that forms part of a civilised society.

The past 30 years has seen only the beneficiaries of the redistribution of wealth. We all seem to have benefited. Most of us are after all property owners. Now it is time to pay. The wealth that has been so surreptitiously redistributed should be redistributed back where it came from. Much of the redistribution has shown up in the form of bank borrowing. That is normal and part of the obfuscation process that camouflages the process of redistribution of wealth without informed public scrutiny. If money is to be first given to the beneficiaries of redistribution and we do not want those who have to pay the price for it to associate themselves with this generosity we borrow the money. That defers the problem. It is only when the borrowing has to be repaid that problems arise. Who should pay for the borrowing. Not those who have benefited of course. They have long since made off with their money. In the case of the banking crisis it is the rest of us of course who have had to pay for the redistribution. It is the rest of us who are at the other end of the transfer to the footballers, the celebrities, the TV personalities, the investment bankers, the fund managers, the professionals and the army of freeloaders who have paid themselves inflation busting pay awards and seek to continue to do so.

The consequences of these inflation busting wealth transfers to the substantial minority depend upon the circumstances and how the economy reacts. There are essentially two possibilities. Either the rest of us have to take pay decreases, or lose our jobs or pay higher taxes to pay for these inflation busting pay awards. If we do so (as are the citizens of Greece and Ireland) the redistribution is complete.   That would be a mistake. It would only encourage those who benefited to repeat the exercise. We see the arguments and threats being made by the bankers to leave the country if these redistributions do not continue. It is extremely difficult even for the very rich to take a reduction in income and living standards. However it is easier than for the poor to do likewise.

The other alternative is a general rise in the rate of inflation and equally large inflation busting pay awards to compensate for the redistribution of wealth that has taken place. In short general inflation in incomes to equal that of those who have benefited from the redistributions that have taken place to date. This is a very blunt instrument because not all will have benefited to the same extent.

Governments have been negligent and continue to be by not acknowledging the dangers of redistribution without wealth creation. Nobody talks about it. They talk about massive and imprudent lending. They talk about unemployment. They talk about education and budget deficits and banks that are too big to fail. They do not however address the underlying cause except in an oblique way. They attack bankers' bonuses on the grounds that it "sends the wrong signal". They attack bankers' bonuses on the grounds that some of the banks are state owned and they "owe it to the rest of us" to restrain their greed. How sweet. Whether banks are state owned or not is irrelevant. They are an instrument that through the process of borrowing camouflage and confuse the connection between the beneficiary of a redistribution of wealth and those who have to pay for it. Bankers who receive inflation busting pay awards and create no wealth are merely redistributing wealth to themselves. They are however not alone. There is an army of professionals doing the same thing outside the glare of publicity.

Any government that ignores the distinction between real wealth creation and redistribution does so at its peril and is failing in its duty. The distinction is vitally important. Any government that permits wealth to be redistributed in vast sums without the source of the redistribution being immediately identified is laying a trap for itself and will have to pay the price in due course. Any government that fails to appreciate that in a modern industrialised economy more and more people are consuming wealth and not producing it and fails to ask "what do all these people do" is failing its duty.

129

Of course most of us would like to think that we create wealth. We are the exceptions. It is the rest who merely redistribute. Many would like to think that only governments redistribute wealth. They are wrong. Most of us in a developed Western economy are in the business of redistributing wealth. That causes a danger that needs to be addressed and controlled. In subsequent chapters I will show how wealth is redistributed in various activities and professions. At this stage it is merely important to appreciate that money and the way in which it is controlled presently enables this process to take place in vast sums.

The fact that we were running out of things to do because of mechanisation was appreciated in the 1970s, when there was a lot of discussions about how people would be kept busy. Most at the time considered that we would have more leisure time. There is no evidence of people working less hours now. Indeed an attempt recently by the French government to reduce the length of the working week in order to share employment more equitably met with a near revolution. Why do we work more hours. The answer is very simple. We work more hours because we are not restricted by the production of anything tangible in the number of hours we work. If we were there would be an automatic limit to the number of hours we work because the production process has its own limitations. Take for example a house. It has to be built brick by brick. Yet the architectural designs have not been automated to a large extent. The result should be a reduction in the number of hours worked by architects and reduced fees. Nothing of the sort happened. The architects still charge the same amount and instead of producing one plan they produce 20. The same would be the case with regard to the production of cars. There is a natural limit to the amount of cars that can be produced. There is however no limitation on the number of hours that an individual can spend recirculating wealth. It can go round and round more and more rapidly, creating nothing but redistributing wealth again and again. That is why there are no leisure hours for those of us who work in offices. We can find unlimited ways of expropriating others of their money. If such transfers of wealth were restricted to activities that were connected only to the real economy there would be a natural limit to the wealth that could be transferred. It is this disconnection between money and the real economy that it was created to serve that has led to the opportunity for the massive redistributions of wealth that occur daily.

There is only one realistic way of controlling the excesses that can be brought about through inflation busting pay awards. Income tax should be increased gradually so that it is simply not worth while at the top end. Thus for example anybody on a salary of more than 200,000 should have to pay 90% income tax. That will put a stop to such absurd pay awards. That would of course put a stop the unrestricted activities involved in wealth redistribution. It would simply not be worth the while of those involved. We shall deal with taxation in a later chapter. However for the time being it is important to appreciate one aspect of high taxation on incomes. The threat of raising taxes is met with the reaction of the interested parties that they would leave the country and go elsewhere, where their wealth creating skills would be appreciated. The consequence is that no additional taxes would be collected. That argument misses the point of high taxes. No more taxes would be collected it is true. High taxation does not raise more taxes. It means that wealth redistribution is minimised. No longer will employees take massive salary increases for doing the same job - a wealth redistributive process. They will work fewer hours and there may be more jobs available for the young as those with sufficient resources decide to pack it in. As far as going abroad is concerned of course that should be welcomed. They would create job opportunities as they leave. The wealth that they were in the habit of redistributing to themselves would remain in the hands of others and be distributed more equitably. Corporation tax collected will also be increased as the profits from which these vast salaries were paid are retained in companies so that more profits remain in the business.

What about the real wealth creators. The answer is simple. There should be no tax on capital gains. Anybody who creates wealth and grows a real business - financial services will be excluded as they are from many reliefs in an advanced tax system - will receive his profits tax free. This benefit will accrue only to the real entrepreneur, the one who actually risks his own money. Those who use other people's money and take risks with other people's money will not benefit from this advantage.

8. WEALTH CREATION OR REDISTRIBUTION

How does one distinguish between wealth creation and redistribution of wealth. This is the important and difficult task that faces governments and economic managers of modern economies if they are to do their job properly. To date this distinction has been ignored. Nobody is willing to address the problem. Indeed governments and economists assume that if a person becomes wealthy he is a wealth creator. Nothing can be further from the truth.

In an earlier chapter I advised that economic issues should be examined by ignoring money. Real economic activity involves the production and distribution of real goods and services. Measuring such activity however cannot realistically be done without using money – the universal economic measurement. It would be better if possible if one was to measure the amount of livestock consumed, or the amount of grain produced, but that would make statistics very cumbersome. Some goods would have to be measured in terms of tons, others in gallons or litres, some in bushels and such like. There would not be one single measurement as there is for example in the calculation of a country's GDP. Measuring real production would however be more realistic.

The acquisition of goods and services is real economic activity. The possession of money is merely an interim stage between the exchange of goods and services for other goods and services. Money has no intrinsic value. The possession of money merely means that the person who holds it has sold goods and services of a greater value than the ones he has bought. He hopes and indeed expects to make up the difference in the future. He is in the middle of the exchange process to the extent of this difference. Of course he might die and that surplus will be spent by his heirs so the process of exchange can straddle generations. Nevertheless the possession of money remains an intermediate process in exchanging real goods and services. It is a holding stage in the process of exchange. It gives the owner a potential claim over future goods and services. Economics is not about exchanging goods and services for money but exchanging goods and services for other goods and services, essentially economics involves barter with money as an intermediate step. Those who ignore this principle will misunderstand what happens in an economy and when things go wrong they will be unable to solve the problem.

Redistribution of wealth these days occurs invariably in the form of money. In ancient times when redistributions of wealth occurred as a result of violent action on land or sea such redistributions were of actual goods, and of land. Nowadays such redistributions are not possible. It is theoretically possible for redistribution of wealth to occur even in a pure barter economy but the opportunities in such a system are severely restricted. Thus for example I might know of a farmer who is willing to sell 4 hens for one lamb and another who is willing to sell one lamb for 3 hens. I can opportunistically interpose myself between the two, buy the lamb for 3 hens from the latter and sell the lamb for 4 hens to the former thereby profiting by one hen. No more hens are produced but I am richer by one hen at the expense of the first farmer who was not well informed enough about the relative market price of lambs and hens. These opportunities however would have been rare and the potential for profit in this way would have been limited because the relative values of the various products were well known and understood by all participants in the market place. The introduction of money made redistribution of wealth through opportunistic examples such as the one just described more widespread because a few pence could be added to the price of hens with little alarm being caused. However the sums involved would still have been very small because of the relatively simple deals that were done. Nowadays as I shall show later the sums involved are vast because we have moved away from exchanging livestock to exchanging ownership of joint stock companies and real estate.

Redistribution of wealth occurs when money - the right to claim delivery of goods and services in the future - is transferred from one person to another without a corresponding amount of real wealth being delivered in return.

The basic rule for distinguishing between wealth creation and redistribution as regards goods is simple. Real wealth is created when new goods are created. The farmer who breeds lamb or chickens creates wealth whenever a lamb is born or a chicken lays an egg. A house builder creates wealth whenever he builds a new house. The weaver who spun the cloth has created wealth. The carpenter who made a chair has created wealth. That is simple old fashioned wealth creation. Those involved in these processes are few and are easily identified. With mechanisation and globalisation the processes involved in the production of most goods is much more complicated today and those involved are more difficult to identify and classify. More importantly the relative worth of those who co-operate in the process of production is impossible to determine properly. Even something as simple as milk production could involve persons who never meet one another collaborating in bringing milk to the door of the consumer. These will involve those in the pasteurization process, transportation, the retailers and the army of officials and regulators involved in the many phases, and of course the bankers and other office workers who assist in marketing the product.

Services are intangible and therefore in many cases harder to categorise as wealth creating or redistributing. Services are wealth creating if they either make the quality of life of the recipient better or are an intrinsic part of the production of new goods. The services that are provided directly to individuals such as medical services are wealth creating because they make the patient feel better and enjoy his life more. Education services are generally wealth creating because they either enable us to enjoy our lives or enable us to produce goods or services that are wealth creating. Legal services to an individual for example in litigation to enable the individual to enforce his rights can be wealth creative if they are brought about to enforce one's rights with regard to a wealth creating activity. They are redistributive if they involve the enforcement of rights in respect of an agreement or arrangement that is redistributive.

There are many services that do not involve the direct creation. Thus for example retailing is part of the wealth creating process because it is part of the chain that delivers new goods to customers. Transport services are wealth creating if they involve delivery of new goods to their ultimate destination or transport individuals to the place where they wish to be entertained or work. To the extent that transportation services deliver people to work where they carry out redistributive activities such services are redistributive and not wealth creating.

Those who work in offices can be either wealth creators or wealth redistributors. Sometimes they can be both. Lawyers and accountants involved in the production of cars either as part of the negotiation process for contracts for components or in building factories or in evaluating the progress of the business are an intrinsic part of the wealth creation process. Bankers who have financed the factory where planes are made are an intrinsic part of the process of creating wealth. Those involved in setting future prices for grain or copper are part of the wealth creating process because they assist the farmers in growing and selling their produce. Those involved in taking positions or gambling on the future value of a financial instrument are not involved in creating wealth. They are involved in redistribution of wealth.

A lawyer or accountant who assists the banker in carrying out gambling activities or in performing a merger and then a demerger of a company that as a result produces not a single additional widget is not a wealth creator but a wealth redistributor whilst carrying out that activity.

It is not the job that a person does but the activity on which the person works in his job that determines whether he is a wealth creator or wealth redistributor. All will depend upon the circumstances and each situation needs to be considered separately.

It is not an easy task to distinguish the wealth redistributing activities from the wealth creating ones and it is impossible to make a rule for every situation. The main problem occurs when services are provided. In general redistribution occurs when the service is not associated with the creation of something new or is not a service provided directly to the consumer. This is not the same as providing a service that is useful. All services are perceived to be useful by their recipient. The important point is whether they assist in the creation of something that did not exist before.

Most services that are redistributive rather than wealth creating tend to be involved in the change of ownership of something that already exists. This could be a financial instrument or a tangible asset such as real estate or perhaps an antique. The difficulty in identifying wealth redistribution makes it even more important to control the process and any government that ignores it does so at its peril for reasons that I shall explain later.

As a society becomes more advanced fewer and fewer persons are needed to produce the goods and services that we all require. More and more persons therefore become involved in redistribution of the wealth that is created by fewer and fewer persons. Some redistribution may be necessary for the maintenance of social stability such as the redistribution by government of money to the poor. Other redistribution can be deleterious to society because it may result in those who produce least wealth possessing most money and therefore the right to enjoy the wealth produced by others. Uncontrolled redistribution of wealth is a pernicious feature of modern economics and has become possible by the creation of money through the banking system and the development of fiat money.

Money camouflages the unrestrained redistribution of wealth. Loans make it almost impossible to tell who has benefited as a result of somebody else's suffering. Indeed the experiment of fiat money and the explosion of borrowing that occurred in the latter part of the 20th century has still not reached a conclusion. We simply do not know what the consequences will be.

Where wealth is redistributed so that one person or group of persons is enriched the inevitable consequence is that somebody else must sooner or later be impoverished as a result. The person or persons who bear the burden of impoverishment need not suffer the effects immediately. They generally do not deserve to suffer the penalty. The redistribution that occurs through the private sector is indiscriminate. One cannot tell where the burden will fall. Those who profit do so without any alarm being raised. Those who suffer the consequences or pay the price are identified often many years later and may be completely innocent bystanders, possibly in a different country from that in which those who profited live.

There may be no contact or relationship between the person or persons who gain and those who suffer the corresponding loss. There is a fog that disconnects the gainers from the losers which is caused largely through the use of money. Borrowing causes this disconnection to be increased through the passage of time. After all how could I possibly have caused the starvation of somebody 10 years after I profited from some wealth redistribution. Yet that is what happens with widespread and uncontrolled redistribution of wealth. The profit from a redistribution could be in the US and the corresponding loss could be in Ethiopia many years later. However there can be no doubt that if there is no wealth created as a result of an economic activity then one man's gain must mean another man's consequential loss. The bearing of the consequential loss understandably causes serious unrest. Usually it falls upon the poor and least powerful. It is far easier for somebody to increase their living standards than to ask others to reduce theirs.

If the identity of the person who bears the cost of redistribution is established at the same time as the person who profits does so no such redistribution is likely to occur. It occurs by stealth. It is legalized theft.

Governments should therefore be very careful before they applaud huge increases in living standards. If such increases arise either partially or mainly from redistribution of wealth there will be serious consequences later.

Wealth creation results in immediate gratification of the creator and his associates. Enrichment without wealth creation is a time bomb and will result in adverse consequences later.

Unrestricted redistribution of wealth is potentially explosive because it frequently leads to inflation, unemployment and at worst revolution. It is for these reasons that it is essential that governments identify and control activities that amount to wealth redistribution rather than wealth creation. Unfortunately governments tend to believe that all economic activity particularly if it is carried out by the private sector is wealth creating. Most people believe that only governments redistribute wealth. That is a fundamental mistake. They also assume that the amount of money a person earns is at least equivalent to the amount of wealth that that person delivered to the economy. That too is a fundamental mistake. The amount of wealth that governments now redistribute is a trifle compared with the redistribution carried out by the private sector. The former is tightly controlled and scrutinized by press and parliament. The latter is presently out of control.

Attempts are being made to control the amount of borrowing – a fundamental part of the equipment that is necessary to accomplish successful wealth redistribution – but those who are carrying out the process seem unaware of the real danger that they are involved in trying to prevent.

Some politicians claim that a large proportion – possibly more than half – of government spending is redistributive. They regard all "entitlement" programmes as redistributive. That is a mistake. Many government programmes are similar to insurance or pension savings. The person pays during his working life and expects or is entitled to reciprocity when he retires. This is what insurance companies do. Is that wealth creative or redistributive. Insurance and saving are nothing more than a deferral of the time when a person consumes what he produced. The provision of insurance or pensions services themselves is wealth creative or redistributive depending on whether the money paid to the insurer or saver came from a wealth creating or redistributive activity. The action of government in paying these aptly named entitlements is no more redistributive that the action of insurers or of pension fund managers in paying the saver or insured party the money to which he is entitled.

Whenever a business that produces goods incurs a loss and particularly when it becomes insolvent wealth has been redistributed to the extent of the difference between the real value of the goods and the expected value of the goods that formed the basis for the initial business plan and the associated payments. The loss is not suffered fairly between all the parties involved in the process of producing the goods. It will probably be shared between the owners of the business and the bank and possibly some suppliers or other creditors. The professionals and employees as well as the component manufacturers will have been paid irrespective of whether the business is successful. Wealth will have been redistributed from the bank and equity investors to these persons in proportions that it is impossible to calculate. These redistributions of wealth could cross many national borders, so that the lawyer in London who collected his fees will have received wealth redistribution the corresponding cost of which is suffered by an equity investor in Tunisia and a bank in Austria or China. The bank in China might react by charging a wholly innocent customer a higher margin for a loan than he otherwise would have to pay. The equity invested in the project could have come from a teachers pension fund in Canada so that Canadian teachers will suffer as a result. That is one way in which wealth redistribution crosses borders and affects innocent people.

It is not easy to identify the cause of the failure, and who is to blame when a business fails. There could be many causes and some of the parties who were enriched may have had no part to play in the failure. Each party who benefited from the payments by the producer will claim that they provided proper value and the real fault lies elsewhere. That does not assist those who suffer the consequences.

When Eurotunnel - the tunnel between England and France - was built the estimates of total cost and potential revenue turned out to be vastly wrong. The amount of wealth redistributed ran into several billions. The fault was probably an overestimate of the number of potential passengers. New wealth was created. Nevertheless vast sums were redistributed to the extent of the difference between the cost and the real value of the project. Shareholders and bankers lost money, others such as the providers of the components, the professionals and the builders gained. The latter took few risks. In other cases it is not so easy to identify the cause. I mention Eurotunnel merely to illustrate the size of the problems nowadays and the amounts redistributed. It was the same with the development of Canary Wharf where vast sums were redistributed between the time of the original development and the eventual apparent success of the venture.

The value of and size of the Eurotunnel project is nowadays dwarfed by today's electronic companies. Many new companies were created as a result of the electronic revolution. The electronic companies did not possess many barriers to entry. A new car company has a very high entry barrier because the creator needs to provide a lot of capital to build a factory. There is a long time between commencement of building of the factory and the sale of the first car. An Internet company does not need many barriers to entry. Many of the PC and Internet millionaires and billionaires created their business initially using nothing more than a computer in their homes.

The Internet and electronic revolution of the 1990s will be considered later. For the time being I merely point out that the size of these companies and their valuations is so vast that if the valuations are wrong or there are failures the consequences to those who suffer the loss that corresponds to the enrichment made through the redistribution of wealth will be disastrous. There was a dot com bubble in the 1990s but this appears to have been forgotten. Doubtless there were winners and losers as a result of that event.

The process of redistribution of wealth through overvaluation of assets was widespread in the past 30 years or more through the real estate market. For most people purchasing their home is the largest business deal that they ever do. Overvaluation of a new home where real wealth is created and of used home both constitute a redistribution of wealth. The sums involved in the real estate market were insignificant compared with the values of Internet companies but the number of real estate transactions was enormous. Nearly everybody who owned a home was involved either actively or passively in profiting from increases in real estate, a subject that we will treat in greater detail later.

Vast sums of wealth were redistributed by selling new homes at inflated prices. However most activity was in the existing homes market.

The selling of an existing home creates no wealth whatsoever. The stock of homes remains the same. Whether the home is sold directly or through an agent the profit made constitutes a redistribution of wealth to the seller from the buyer.

The process is complicated because of the borrowing with which the purchase of most homes, whether new or old is associated. The borrowing creates a fog between the beneficiaries and those who pay the price for the wealth redistribution. I shall address the borrowing process later. It is significant that many if not most of the sales of existing homes would not have occurred if values had been stable. The evidence of this is that now that property prices have stabilised and are indeed falling in many parts of the country the number of sales of new homes is very small indeed. The ever increasing values over the previous 30 years seduced many to believe that property values could only increase. So they bought bigger and more expensive houses. Later these same people planned to sell up, cash in and buy smaller houses in which to spend their retirement. It is important to appreciate that existing homes that are sold create a redistribution of wealth whenever they are sold at a profit that exceeds the general rate of inflation. Those that are sold through an agent result in redistribution without any wealth being created to the agent even if no profit is involved. The same redistribution occurs when lawyers and valuers are paid. To the extent that taxes are paid for a sale of an existing home wealth redistribution occurs from buyer to the government.

Even those who did not participate in the sale or purchase of a home but who owned a home were affected by these increasing values. They borrowed against the apparently increased value of their homes and spent that money on other luxuries that they would not have been able to afford in their wildest dreams. The redistribution in wealth that occurred in the case of property can be seen when one considers the barriers to property ownership for the young. Our children cannot afford to buy the homes that we had when we were their age. We have transferred wealth from our children to ourselves. Those who profited either because their property increased in value by more than others

143

and sold out made actual redistributions. Others became nominally wealthier and promised to realize that additional wealth when they retired and traded down. This process is still to unwind and we do not yet know what the consequences will be.

The process of enrichment followed by a later impoverishment is as I said before masked by borrowing.

In years long since gone if I wanted to buy or build a home I would first have to save up the money to do so. I would have to consume less than I produced for several years, unless I was fortunate enough to produce something of great value very quickly. When I had accumulated enough money to buy or build my home I would do so.

It was of course possible that the price of my future home increased while I was saving to such an extent that my savings made it impossible for me to ever catch up and make the acquisition. If so I would keep my savings and the house would not be sold to or be built by me. Home ownership would be postponed perhaps indefinitely as the prospect faded over the horizon further and further from my reach. On the other hand I would still have the money that could be used for some other purpose.

In fact house prices did not increase until they became a "must have" asset and getting on the "property ladder" became something to which everybody aspired.

The ability to borrow money to buy a home made it possible to first gratify my desire to buy a home earlier than I otherwise would. I would be able to consume more than I produced on the understanding that in future I would produce more than I consumed. However the borrowing process meant that if the value of the home increased I would profit instead of the previous owner, and if the home was new I would profit from increases in value instead of never being able to afford to buy a home. The dynamics of home ownership changed. The bank lent

144

me the money and I was able to profit from increases in value of the home.

Of course property – or at least the land - lasts for ever and so it is possible to inherit a home. The stock of house building therefore in principle has a limit. Once everybody has their own home growth in house building will only occur as a result of people buying a second home.

The introduction of borrowing into the process of buying a home means however that one other rather powerful party is involved in the potential for transferring wealth. Banks will sell their loans in whole or in part to other banks. Often these other banks will be located in different countries where the original lender was located and where the real estate was located. Thus if such loans go into default the pain will be felt in some country other than the one where the property is situated.

Default might not occur for many years after the loan was made. In the meantime the bank will have treated the loan as an asset - a "performing asset" to use banking parlance. It will have taken its profit annually from the loan - its profit is the margin above its own borrowing cost that it charges to the borrower. It will have paid its advisers and lawyers. It will have paid its staff, many with substantial bonuses. All these parties will have been enriched even though the loan was potentially bad. By the time a default occurs those who have profited will have received their money. The result is that the bank might lose money but the professionals and staff will have benefited as a result of a deal that in the end turned out to be bad. The home owner will also have lost money. Wealth has been redistributed.

This may sound trivial because of the amount of any individual loan but when all real estate transactions of the past 30 years are added together the sums involved are seen to be massive, enough to bring a country like Ireland to its knees. Now replace real estate with an Internet company such as Google or Facebook and you will see that the potential amounts of wealth redistributed are enormous - certainly enough to cripple the world economy.

Despite the view of governments as redistributors of wealth they do in fact create wealth. They build and maintain roads, schools and hospitals as well as offices. They provide the police and the military. These make us more secure and better able to enjoy our lives. They provide medical and educational services. All of this is wealth producing. The only redistribution occurs in respect of social security. That is a very small amount and not to be confused with the entitlements that I addressed above.

The fees charged by the wealth managers and the rewards that they pay to themselves increase in line with increases in the value of the stock market. Many of them do very little for their money. Yet what they receive for their services is substantial. The buying and selling of existing shares is, as explained above, not wealth creation but redistribution because the value of the share before and after are unaffected by the transaction. This activity has always existed so it is important to examine what has changed in recent times.

The change in the past 30 years has been in volume and in the number of people involved. The City of London has changed considerably over the past 30 years. In 1983 the City occupied approximately one square mile. It then expanded upwards and outwards into Broadgate which multiplied the amount of office space substantially, and later into a new city in what was known as Docklands. This was an even greater enterprise than Broadgate.

The number of people working in what is known as the City has grown massively. So have their salaries. Some of these people, a very small amount, are involved in real wealth creation. Those who provide financing for capital projects or for the financing of trade provide a wealth creating function. The vast majority produce nothing and have been described as "socially useless" and their activities as "casino banking". Broadly speaking the rest take bets. Those who finance real wealth also take bets but their function is necessary to the process of wealth creation. The function of what the banks call "taking positions" creates no wealth at all. It is the equivalent of shuffling ownership of existing assets around. In some cases no assets change hands, bets are the whole substance of what they do.

The sums involved are alarming. They run into trillions. In reality the bets are taken between banks or financial institutions so there is a zero sum gain. So long as enough bets are taken the banks should break even. Unfortunately there is a massive fraud perpetrated against the rest of us. It involves the so called bonus system. Every time a bet is made there will be a winner and loser. The winner gets 20% of the winnings, the loser pays nothing. When the position is reversed the same happens. Thus every time a bet is made 20% of any profit leaves the system. The more bets are taken the more leaves the system and goes into the hands of the employees who risk nothing except perhaps their jobs, which are exchanged frequently.

The system and the amount of loss by way of redistribution of wealth depends upon what is known as volatility. There will be no profits or losses unless prices change frequently. The prices change with the bets that are taken.

It is all done with our money and most of us do not know what is going on. Indeed we are not allowed so much as a vote when our money is invested through a fund which all pension and many other non pension savings are. The leakage of wealth by way of redistribution runs into billions just in the City of London. The bonuses paid for these socially useless redistributions of wealth are around $10 Billion a year.

The fund managers also play a part in this process of redistribution of wealth. They get paid very large rewards for managing and often just doing nothing with people's money. They might invest it in property or other shares that the beneficial owner could buy directly. In many cases the fund invests in Treasury securities that anybody can buy. Instead the fund manager charges a large fee for doing practically nothing. Certainly nothing he does enhances the value of the investments bought with the money of the individual, who in most cases has no idea what is being done with his money.

Large sums are redistributed in this way. Fees mount. Lawyers and accountants participate in this process of redistributing money from the savers. All are paid before the final accounting for an investment takes place. Most are paid whether the ultimate investor makes a profit or a loss. In many cases where the ultimate investor makes a profit the fund managers get 20% of profits. When the investor suffers a loss they pay nothing back, they merely "suffer" by getting 20% of nothing.

Computer services produce many services. Apparently computer fraud is now running into trillions per annum. That requires an army of computer experts who provide anti theft or anti-virus devices. All these services cannot be properly evaluated because we do not know if they achieve their objective. It is a form of insurance but we do not know how effective it is.

The number of financial instruments that has been created so as to enable as many of us to take bets or for bets to be taken on our behalf without in most cases our knowledge and certainly without our understanding is vast. There are futures and options on currencies and shares, on interest rates and on bonds. It is possible to sell what you do not own before buying what you have sold later. Commodities are bought and sold and options to buy or sell are regularly purchased and sold by speculators. Insurance products are sold without the insurers knowing what their risks are.

I do not think that there is any doubt that the City is now largely a centre for redistribution of wealth. It used to be a centre where capital for investment in wealth producing projects could be raised. Very little of that happens now. There are mergers followed by demergers of companies with some financial

148

engineering between each transaction and not a single additional item of wealth being created by the underlying company as a result. It not only carries out this function but has increased both the size of deals that it does and the number of people doing it. There are different types of instruments packaged together in funds, in funds of funds and in funds that are traded on exchanges. There are stock exchanges in every major capital city of the world. Yes we can safely say that the city is at the centre of the wealth redistribution process. They are amongst the worst offenders. It is just not appreciated either by those in the city or elsewhere that for every $ that a person in the city redistributes without wealth creation sooner or later somebody else somewhere in the world will suffer the corresponding loss. It is a zero sum gain. The person who bears the price for the wealth of the bankers may starve to death in Africa or Columbia. Nobody makes the connection because between the gain of the bankers and lawyers and other professionals and the suffering in Africa or Columbia there could be many years of events and any connection is camouflaged by borrowing that bridges the gap often in years between the receipt of benefit and the suffering of the corresponding loss.

There is little point listening to people in the City of London claiming that they are so good at what they do (gambling) that they win more than they lose and that the country therefore needs them. Even if this is true, which is doubtful, if I am right and they are merely redistributing wealth that does not exist somewhere else in the world people will starve, be impoverished or revolt and die as a result. That is not a process to which any civilised society should lend its name. The reality is that gamblers in London bet against gamblers in New York and there is no evidence that London's gamblers are better than those in New York. If there was those in New York would quickly be shut down. Why is such gambling not only carried on but increasing. The answer is that the commission (the 20% that is paid to the staff) is a sufficient incentive. Heads they win tails the client loses. It's a safe bet for the employees. All that is required is that the source from which this enrichment occurs is hidden. It is hidden by combining genuine banking activity with gambling. At the heart of this activity is redistribution of wealth in uncontrolled amounts. The investment bankers in the city could well be the cause for the riots in Cairo or the starvation in Africa. They certainly are the cause behind the cuts in government programmes in the UK and US.

One of the more serious dangers associated with uncontrolled redistribution of wealth is that it discourages wealth creation. Why should people work hard to produce something that requires a manufacturing process when it is so easy just to redistribute purchasing power away from others.

Aside from that however what are the direct consequences of redistribution of wealth. The main one is that those who have received the additional purchasing power will be able to mould the way in which society operates to suit their wishes. If wealth was distributed equally or more equally there will be enough people producing food and clothing, and probably housing, albeit of a modest kind. Much of the land will be given over to the production of food and rearing of livestock.

If wealth is concentrated in a few hands they will use their purchasing power to secure that the labour force is not used for producing necessaries but for producing luxuries. There will be a shift in the balance of an economy away from necessaries towards luxuries. Thus for example the builders will be persuaded to build a palace or many palaces instead of building simple homes for those who have less wealth. The result will be more homeless. They rich might want a yacht to be built. They will lure shipbuilders away from making and repairing fishing vessels. Luxury cheeses and wines will be produced so that the poor will not have their cheap wine any more. Land that would otherwise be available for the poor to have their modest housing will be use to build more and more extravagant houses.

It is possible that valuable farmland will be used to turn into hunting grounds for the rich. People active in farming could be turned away in order to serve as cleaners in the palaces. The result would be food shortages for the poor. Those who profit will describe it as progress or evolution. It could however turn into revolution and it is the job of government to make sure that this does not happen. They can only do that by maintaining a sensible and modest balance between the rich and poor.

Debt and increasing amounts of debt are a warning signal that there has been substantial amounts of redistribution of wealth but that the price has yet to be paid. The possession of money, and debt implicitly means that there is a corresponding amount of surplus in the hands of others, is an intermediate step in the process of exchanging goods and services. The provider sells his goods or services in return for money and expects to be able to use that money at some time in the future to buy something that he could not previously buy. Those who owe the money are the ones who will in principle have to provide the goods to the provider. In reality they do not. Indeed in most cases those who have the capacity in time to produce reciprocal goods are not able to do so and those who may have the ability do not have the capacity. The result is that the money owned by the provider is spent in competing for the limited goods and services already available. The result is what we call inflation.

Where there is debt it has been proposed that profits of a bank arising from such debt should be recognised gradually over the life of a loan. Accounting rules provide that fees earned by banks for example should be recorded as income over the life of the loan. That is not prudent. The results of a loan cannot be known until the last £ is paid back. No profits should be recognised until the loan is fully repaid. That is the only sensible way to reduce these vast redistributions.

151

The substance of the redistribution through the financial sector is that the people involved are grossly overpaid. Overpayment or overvaluation is the foundation of redistribution of wealth.

This phenomenon has been around ever since the basics of life were available to all, which occurred several decades ago in most developed Western countries. What has changed? The answer is the sums involved and borrowing sometimes over very long periods. The sums involved are vastly bigger than anything we have known before. The borrowing makes it more difficult to connect enrichment with the corresponding impoverishment.

How can governments overcome this epidemic of unrestricted wealth redistribution. It is partly the curse of an advanced economy. As an economy advances and we all have the necessaries of life fewer and fewer people are required to participate in the wealth producing and distribution process. One possible result should be an increase in leisure time. Unfortunately this has not occurred. Since it is now so easy to participate in the redistributive part of an economy, and since redistribution can go on indefinitely as wealth is redistributed again and again and faster and faster with computer systems there is no evidence of increased leisure time becoming a feature of an advanced economy. Those of us who do not participate in the redistribution process will become its victims, therefore we dare not stop and step off the redistributive merry go round. If it turns faster then we have to move at the new speed. Pensioners will continue to lose out as their investment income decreases so as to maintain the living standards of those who profit from the redistribution process.

Massive redistribution has occurred from pension funds to borrowers by the simple process of government manipulation of interest rates. Pensions that were expected to produce 7,500 for every 100,000 now produce less than 2,500. The pensioners merely shake their heads and are told that this is because they are living longer so they should be grateful. That is not the real reason for their impoverishment. It is unrestricted wealth redistribution. The pension funds were a huge source of wealth and once that has been tapped where will the redistributors go next to find their next fix.

There is only one solution and that is high taxation for the very high income earners. This will not raise more taxes in the long term. It will however put a stop to the pernicious redistributive processes and moderate them. It is essential that the process of vast enrichment at the expense of others is kept to a minimum and this can only be done by making it not worth while accumulating more wealth.

That process should be accompanied by freeing all real wealth creators from the burden of taxation. Capital gains should be tax free if such gains are made by producing real goods. This at least will ensure that those who produce real wealth will be rewarded. Those who merely find clever ways of redistributing wealth to themselves do not deserve rewards. The consequence is that the suffering of those who have to pay the price for this binge in redistribution of wealth will be protected. They are after all in most cases helpless and innocent victims.

Another way of at least putting a cap on redistribution is a 100% death tax. That at least will limit the advantages of redistribution to a life time. It is a drastic step but it may be necessary.

Anybody who doubts that there has been a significant change in the economy from one in which the vast majority are creating or distributing wealth to one in which wealth or rather the right to claim the fruits of real wealth is being merely redistributed should consider why all the technology that has been introduced into offices has not reduced the number of hours worked. The whole purpose behind the introduction of technology into offices has been efficiency, or shorter working hours. Nothing of the kind has occurred.

If the people in offices were occupied in producing real wealth and distributing it then efficiency in offices would have led to a

153

substantial increase in leisure time and reduction in the hours worked. The opposite has happened. The only sensible explanation is that they are occupied not in creating wealth where the amount of work is limited by the amount of goods produced but in redistributing the rights to acquire such goods and services. This latter process is endless because money can be re-circulated over and over and no matter how much efficiency is introduced into the process the total amount of wealth does not increase. The process merely determines how much of the real goods and services are consumed by whom. It does not make the economic cake bigger by a single cubic centimeter.

It is for this reason that I am amused when governments and indeed businesses try to improve efficiency. It is pointless making an inherently unproductive activity more efficient. I can see why a business whose existence depends entirely upon redistribution of wealth to itself at the expense of others may want to reduce its staffing levels but if the staff who are dismissed are then employed in some other similar activity that merely recirculates more wealth. They will have achieved nothing for the economy. Certainly the size of the economic cake will remain the same.

I do not wish to give the impression that all forms of redistribution of wealth are wrong. They are not. Redistribution of wealth, whether by the state or through the private sector is sometimes the only way that people can survive. Begging is wealth redistributive. So is charity. Taking advantage of a market to buy something cheaper and then sell it to somebody who is willing to pay more but is unaware of where he can buy what he wants is legitimate. However, unrestricted and surreptitious redistribution is pernicious. People should be paid for selling existing goods but it is essential that neither the goods themselves nor the fees charged by those who facilitate the sale are overpaid. To the extent that they are that is redistributive and there is a price to be paid by untold and unidentified persons at some unspecified time. Such transfers of wealth should not be permitted or at least not encouraged. Taxation can place a limit on this kind of pernicious practice.

Redistribution of wealth also occurs through the process of globalization and exporting of manufacturing, for example to China. An example will make this clear.

Suppose that trainers in the UK were being manufactured at a cost of £20. The corresponding cost in China is £2. So the UK retailer cancels the contract for trainers with the UK producer and orders his trainers in China.

The Chinese manufacturer will not of course sell for £2. He only has to sell at a price that is marginally beneficial to the UK retailer. He sells at £19. The factory owner in China makes a massive profit - £17 and becomes fabulously wealthy. The UK manufacturer goes out of business.

Wealth has been transferred from UK manufacturer to Chinese factory owner and workers, the former taking most of the profits.

If the Chinese manufacturer had not competed with the UK manufacturer but merely produced trainers that he sold to Chinese people for £3 the total wealth of the UK would have remained the same instead of falling, and Chinese wealth too would have grown. Total world wealth would have grown and many Chinese running around barefoot would be wearing trainers.

It is a simple example but it demonstrates the harm of wealth redistribution and how redistribution can masquerade as business efficiency. It is also an example of the harm of globalization.

9. INFLATION AND THE REDUCTION IN THE VALUE OF MONEY

"There was no inflation in times of barter". I remember this quotation by Mrs Thatcher as if it was yesterday. Whilst her statement was true it hid more than it revealed about the evils of inflation. Indeed right throughout the 70's and 80's when the UK and much of the world economy was riddled with high inflation I do not recall anybody explaining why inflation was so bad. Quite the contrary, I remember people saying how good it had been for many of us. I hope to remedy this deficiency and expose the myth that inflation in certain sectors of an economy, such as for example the real estate market or the stock market, is good whilst only general inflation is bad.

Experts in this field generally assume that there are some fundamental truths that do not require explanations. They hide behind technical statements like "monetary stimulus" or "fiscal tightening" or now "quantitative easing" as if there is some magic in these terms of themselves. They have as their task the manipulation of interest rates and most discussions by the experts is about which way the authorities are going to move rates - a function that should be left to the market in a free market economy, at least in theory.

If the authorities were to properly explain the procedure that their remedies are meant to achieve I believe they will realise - or if not ordinary people will do so - that it makes no sense at all, or at best has only a chance of working. No such attempt is made. Rather it is assumed that inflation can be countered by raising interest rates and that lowering interest rates makes us economically active and imaginative and consequently productive.

Mrs Thatcher never explained why inflation was such a bad thing. We all know how bad inflation is, or do we. We do know for example that in Germany before World War 2 there was hyper inflation and money became worthless. We know of the example of the lady who took her weekly wages home in a laundry basket, and left the laundry basket outside the bakery where she stopped to buy some bread. When she returned the basket had been stolen but the money was left on the pavement.

So what?

Hyper inflation destroys the trust in money. It becomes useless - some say worthless although it never had any intrinsic worth, it merely represents the right of the owner to certain goods and services for sale in an economy up to the value of that money. The problem of course is that if the value of the money (or rather the price of the goods in terms of that money - is changing constantly it is impossible to rely on the value that the seller receives. There is no doubt that in situations of hyper inflation people will resort to barter, thereby removing one of the main functions performed by money.

Unfortunately many people will be in the middle of a trading cycle (exchanging one item for another) in the sense that I outlined in an earlier chapter. I may have sold my house in return for enough money to buy bread and meat for the next 30 years. If during the 30 year period inflation takes place such that I can only buy bread and meat for another 3 years I will not be pleased. I will have suffered a redistribution of purchasing power from myself to the buyer of my house who will probably have profited because the house will have maintained its real value relative to the cost of bread.

The danger of inflation however that has never been articulated either by Thatcher or others is simply that it enables vast sums of purchasing power to be redistributed without any wealth creation. Borrower profits at the expense of lender, buyer at the expense of seller, investor at the expense of other investors or employees or other fee earners. There is massive destabilisation in the economy. The incentive to create wealth knowing the value of what you will create is threatened. Long term investments become risky because the entrepreneur cannot know what his labour cost is going to be, nor does he know what price the end product will fetch. Inflation of course does not hit all goods and services in the same way. Some items increase in price at a greater rate then others.

There is however no doubt at all that inflation is profitable to many. Why then is it so universally despised. Why do all experts and governments agree that inflation is a bad thing.

More importantly why do politicians and economic experts seem to agree that inflation in house prices and real estate in general and in the stock market is a good thing for an economy.

I do not know. Nobody has even addressed this question to my knowledge, except vaguely by saying that it destroys faith in money and depletes savings. Even now in the midst of the most serious economic crisis since the great depression there are not many experts who will say that inflation in the stock market or house prices is bad. They hope and pray that house prices will start increasing again as a sign of health in an economy. This means nothing more than they hope for inflation in property values. This, they assert brazenly, will "get us spending again". Spending apparently is what they believe keeps an economy going. They do not advocate producing more, merely spending. It is of course true that for every item bought there must be an item sold but buyer and seller do not necessarily live in the same country and where there are large imbalances in trade between countries - I shall address this in another chapter - this can be destabilising for both, as the Japanese found out to their cost in 1989.

The emphasis however is on giving people more spending money. If you give them spending money producers will produce more goods. That at least is the theory. One sees it expressed from time to time when labour unions advocate higher wages. They claim that higher wages are good for the economy because their members will spend more. That will lead to more production and more growth. If it was that simple why work at all. Only one sector of the economy would need to work. One sector would produce. The other would just be given money to buy those goods. It cannot be that simple. It isn't.

Economists and other experts pray that the stock market will keep inflating. Since this too constitutes a redistribution of wealth on a massive scale it is dangerous and in my opinion has contributed to the economic crisis in which we now find ourselves.

During the mid 70s in Britain inflation nudged 30% per annum. Salaries and wages kept in touch with these rates and increased by at least the amount necessary to enable people's wages to keep up with rising prices. That at least was fair.

There was one significant difference however. Borrowing costs (interest rates) never matched these high rates of inflation. Interest rates at the time never went much above 17%. We are in that cycle again today albeit at a different level. Inflation (RPI) in 2010 was around 5% in the UK whereas interest rates were about 0.5%.

Borrowers who were paying a rate of interest in the 1970s that was lower than the rate of increase in the price of the goods that they bought with the borrowed money made substantial gains. Since no wealth was created others have to pay the price. We do not know who these others were for certain. Maybe the victims are still being identified today. However we know that pension funds were large investors in interest bearing instruments. Their liabilities were to pay pensions to people based upon the final salary of the employees. As wages were increasing at a rate that exceeded the rate of increase in the wages and therefore the potential pension of the future pensioners pension funds got into difficulties. They had to be bailed out by their sponsors - the employers who set them up. This caused a drain on the value of the shares of the employers and therefore a loss to those who invested, including in some cases the same pension funds. Those were the clear losers. Pension funds today are still suffering. Indeed it is arguable that the pensions industry as we knew it - based upon final salaries - is on its knees. There are fewer and fewer such funds left, and there are no new ones starting. Savers on fixed incomes suffered hugely from this vast redistribution of wealth.

Inflation was not the universal demon it was made out to be. Many profited. Many others suffered as a consequence. Wealth, in money terms of course, was simply redistributed and people grew rich from doing nothing. The price was paid by others who were blameless. Massive instability was created.

That, more than the destruction in faith in money and its functions is the major harm wrought by inflation. If politicians and experts were to explain this more rigorously and were to define the harm of inflation more carefully they would not ignore such pernicious events as inflation happening in a small sector of the economy. If inflation is wrong because it creates redistributions of wealth in uncontrolled and unlimited ways then inflation in property prices must be equally bad. Indeed arguably inflation in such a large item of purchase may be worse than inflation in the price of a loaf of bread.

Milton Friedman - the Nobel Prize winning economist - claimed that it does not matter what you include in the basket of goods for the purposes of calculating the rate of inflation. Aside from new technology where prices tend to fall after their initial discovery, all goods, said Friedman, changed their value at the same rate over time. I wonder if he would have agreed if real estate were the asset in question. I suspect that he would.

Real estate does have one or two features that other assets do not possess. The first is - as Mark Twain once famously said - that they are not making any more of it. In short the option of increasing the supply merely because the price has increased is not available in the real estate market. Certainly it is possible to increase the number of homes being built but it is not the price of the bricks that tends to increase over time. It is the price of the underlying land. The second peculiar feature of land (and frequently that includes the bricks built on it) is that it does not depreciate. This makes it a peculiar asset in an economy. Usually property does not have to be rebuilt. The stock of houses is in general growing. Certainly blocks of apartments and houses are pulled down from time to time but in general when a builder builds a new home that will be a net increase in the number of homes available in an economy. Do these feature make inflation in property values any more or less insidious than inflation in other assets. I do not think so. If the danger of inflation is that it enables purchasing power to be redistributed without any new wealth creation then it matters not that the asset that enables this transfer of wealth to take place has the peculiar features set out here.

One other feature of inflation in property prices is that although very few houses change hands in a particular year and most houses remain in the same ownership all houses are assumed to have increased in value. The result is that banks lend money to those who do not move house on the basis that their house has increased in value. It is implicit in the calculation of a bank that all the houses against which they lent money, and they are willing to lend to all householders, can be sold at the same time. This is of course nonsense. If all houses were put on the market at the same time their price would collapse. This is a peculiar feature of house values and differs from the price for example of oil or sugar. The latter is a real value because it is the price at which all the oil or sugar produced can be sold. Indeed it is all sold. Houses are not sold. Their value is therefore artificial.

Certainly the particular differences between real property and chattels means that it needs to be treated differently and considered more carefully, something that I will address in

161

another chapter. However the fact that it has the ability to redistribute wealth without creating any new wealth is something that it shares with other chattels and as such inflation in property prices are just as harmful to an economy as inflation in other goods.

What should one do about inflation. How does a government cure it. All governments agree that it is damaging and that it must be stopped. Unfortunately they do not seem to agree that it should be stopped if it affects only a small albeit significant sector of the economy such as for example real estate and the stock market.

Milton Friedman proposed that the interest on borrowings should all be at the rate of inflation plus a margin. That, he argued would dissuade those who borrowed because the rate of interest on their borrowings was less than the rate of inflation in the assets acquired with the borrowed money.

Subject to one qualification - namely that the tax effects should be taken into account - I think he was right and that his proposed solution would work to take inflation or at least the effects of it out of a large part of the system. It would certainly make it not worth while borrowing because the rate of inflation in the asset one acquires with the borrowed funds is higher than the rate of interest on those borrowed funds.

Tax has to be taken into account because it would be improper to tax the lender on the part of the interest that represents the rate of inflation. Likewise it would be wrong to give the borrower tax relief on the part of the interest that he pays that represents the rate of inflation. The borrower who owns the asset should not be taxed on the "profit" when he sells the asset that represents no more than the inflation in the price of that asset. Subject to this qualification Milton Friedman's proposal was correct. For reasons not known to me no government has adopted his proposal on this matter.

Nowadays governments have through their monetary policy committees adopted the principle that the rate of interest on borrowings should be equal to the rate of inflation plus a margin. It would have been easier to adopt Friedman's policy and have done with the regular meetings of the national monetary policy committees whose wisdom seem to preoccupy all the experts in the financial markets. We are of course told that these wise men and women are able to anticipate inflation. The evidence does not support this contention. Indeed they seem generally surprised when inflation appears and are constantly chasing inflation and trying to balance the requirement for stable values with the wishes of the business community for lower and lower borrowing costs.

The dangers of inflation cannot be overstated.

An economy can only really grow if real wealth is created. That means that goods or services must be created that did not exist. It requires people to work. Inflation transfers wealth without any work being done. The economy does not gain anything. All that happens is that some of us grow richer while other grow poorer. The net gain is zero.

Even though appropriate interest rates can stop people gaining through buying something and borrowing where for example the rate of interest is less than the rate of inflation it is still important to appreciate the general harm that inflation creates. It persuades people that it is easier to gain through the manipulation in the rate of inflation than to work and create wealth. This is damaging to the economy and to the psychology of the society. Why should we create any wealth when we can gain more from merely borrowing and purchasing assets, or vice versa. A government has a duty to eliminate inflation. It does not matter if the inflation is only in the real estate market and the stock market or is more generalised. Inflation is insidious and is a cancer on an economy and every effort should be used to make it ineffective as a means of redistributing wealth.

10. REAL ESTATE AND ITS SPECIAL PLACE IN A MODERN ECONOMY

"Buy land, they aren't making any more of it" - Mark Twain.

Real estate has a special role to play in a modern economy. As homes are built and more people are housed an economy gets more prosperous. The potential for building homes is probably for practical purposes infinite as people could come to own two homes, or possibly three. It is therefore a potential source for infinite growth in an economy, even if there are no new discoveries or inventions.

Unlike most other items produced in a modern economy houses are not "consumed". They do not deteriorate, at least, not particularly. Indeed although blocks of apartments are from time to time demolished the stock of houses in an economy should, if they are built properly, increase perpetually as the population grows. Property should, with proper maintenance last indefinitely. Certainly the land remains intact.

This particular feature of property means that it should be given special consideration in any analysis of an economy.

As an economy moves from one where people are not properly housed to one where all are adequately housed there will inevitably be considerable activity in the building trade. This phase constitutes classic wealth creation. Tangible real wealth is created by all who participate in building and selling the houses.

Sooner or later a state of equilibrium will be reached in which only increases in the population create more demand for house building. At that stage the demand for new homes will reduce. Nevertheless any new housing will normally be a permanent addition to the wealth of the economy. It is not necessary to demolish homes every so often. This is both a benefit and a problem. Once equilibrium is reached there will be unemployment in the building trade because only increments in the population will require builders. That can be overcome by the building of second homes or even third homes adding to the prosperity of the population and its quality of life. Of course such homes need not be for the indigenous population. They could be holiday homes for visitors that thereby create foreign exchange for the local population that can be spent abroad. Housing for practical purposes in perpetuity is one way in which an economy can continue to grow indefinitely.

Real estate has another feature that distinguishes it from other commodities that has nothing to do with the fact that it is a durable rather than a consumable item. Real estate has a certain value and its value rises on the basis of a very small number of transactions in the market.

With most consumable commodities the market price is the price at which the consumable goods can ALL be sold in the market place. Thus for example assuming there are 1 million tons of wheat in the market at any one time. The market price for wheat will be the price at which all such wheat can be and indeed is sold. Certainly there will be buyers and sellers but all - aside from some that may be stored - can and will be sold at that market price, and although there are and will be fluctuations in that price the changes will not be substantial.

With real estate, in particular houses, this is an absurd assumption. Only the stock of new homes has to be and is sold. The market price of property should therefore be and generally is determined on the basis of these new homes. However the price at which new and the small number of existing homes that are sold determines the value of all other homes that are not sold as well. Most of us value our homes on the basis that they are similar to another transaction that has taken place. So if my neighbour sold his home for £1mm I assume that my home is also worth £1mm. If we were all to try to sell our homes at the same time two problems arise. Firstly there would be no buyers, and secondly and as a result the price would collapse. Indeed if there were no buyers they would be technically worthless.

Of course we could all merely exchange our homes, with older people moving into smaller homes and younger people with growing families moving into larger homes. However that is what occurs normally and accounts for the small number of sales of existing homes. The vast majority have no wish or need to move house and if all had to sell house prices would collapse as stated above.

Although a sale of all housing stock will have disastrous adverse affects on values, this has not prevented people assuming that their homes are worth and could realise what in practise is an impossibility. More importantly however banks also make this absurd assumption. This is surprising because banks are expected to make more rational and hard headed decisions. Banks are apparently willing to lend to all home owners a percentage, often a rather high percentage, of the value of their home, even though on any rational examination of the circumstances if all homes were put on the market simultaneously their price would collapse.

The value of houses generally is set by the small number of houses actually sold and this includes new and existing homes. However existing homes frequently do not need to be sold at all. It frequently happens that if a seller of an existing home cannot get the price that he considers appropriate, he will merely withdraw his home from the market. As I write estate agents inform me that there are few homes on the market. This reduction in supply helps keep prices artificially high. This is not something that can happen with wheat or cocoa. All that is produced has to be sold and this determines market prices. This ability to manipulate prices upwards by restricting the supply of existing homes for sale is another special feature of the real estate market.

Property values are also affected by planning. This affects mostly new buildings. Only land made available by the planners is available. Thus planners can affect the value of land by withholding planning consent. It is accordingly in many ways not a free market but controlled for policy and other political reasons.

Property is also not homogeneous. Each property can be described as unique, and although there are similarities there are always unique features. Certainly each location is unique. This is not a material difference as valuations tend to show certain consistency. However as between areas there are considerable differences in the relative values of similar buildings. Certain areas are not only more desirable than others such as for example properties with views over water, but opinions change from time to time and areas can be redeveloped and become as a result more desirable. Thus it is possible for owners to suddenly find that their property is worth more than it was a few years before.

Property values particularly in desirable areas in capital cities also tend to be supported by inflows of funds from various sources outside the country. Countries with large trade deficits such as the UK and US spend large sums of their own currency buying consumable goods from other countries. These other countries end up holding the currency of the trade deficit country. Not unnaturally they tend to spend it buying real estate in that country. There is after all nothing else that the deficit countries might have that they want. London is a prime example where property prices, particularly at the prestigious end keep increasing despite any downturn in the economy.

That may explain the more expensive end of the property market. Prices however have increased at all levels.   Why has that happened and in all countries

The reason is that the amount of money created by the banks has gone mainly into the hands of the better off, and it has done so in huge amounts. Professionals have received rewards for their services at inflation busting rates. Executives of large companies have had pay awards that vastly exceed the norm. Celebrities have also received excessive pay awards. It is not just the bankers who have profited. These sums have been so vast that they could not possibly be spent on food and other goods purchased by the average housewife. The result is that they were spent on real estate, both at home and abroad. The British and Germans in particular have been big buyers of overseas property. The Germans on the other hand, unlike the British tended not to be home owners in their own countries.

Inflation in property values does have adverse consequences. One man's gain is another man's loss. Who has lost.

Is there anybody out there who does not realise that those of us who have homes that we bought when we were young would not be able to afford those same homes at today's prices if we were in the same jobs today as we were when we bought them. What does that mean. It means that money or purchasing power has been transferred from the younger to the older generation. This transfer of wealth however is fickle. It can change back tomorrow if values fall.

The increases in the value of homes is nothing more than simple inflation with all the hazards that economists say they know is such a bad thing. Real estate values are merely a way of transferring purchasing power without wealth creation. The simple truth is that the purchasing power of a home owner is increased when property prices increase faster than general inflation and the purchasing power of those who do not own homes reduces. That is classic wealth redistribution and it has serious potential adverse consequences. Governments have tended to be very pleased by increases in property values because that persuades people to spend. They should not be so sanguine.

Property values are also affected by interest rates, inflation and taxation. Interest rates in particular have from time to time been maintained at artificially low levels so as to keep property prices high. Why? Because falling property prices put banks at risk. Keeping property prices high is not a free pass. Somebody has to pay for it. The parties who pay are the savers, many of whom cannot afford to have the return on their savings reduced in order to help borrowers who may not need the money. Interest rates are a blunt and indiscriminate instrument. They affect both those who can and those who cannot afford it adversely and they benefit those who need it as well as those who do not. I have already explained how property values are determined and the problems with valuations. That explanation applied to commercial property as well as residential property.

The value of a property depends upon the relationship that the rent of that property bears to the value. As the rent increases the value of the property increases proportionately so that the ratio of rent to value remains the same unless there are special circumstances, such as that an area is renovated.

Residential property prices have seen a very strange phenomenon in recent times and that is that the ratio of rent to values has been falling in many areas. The reason for this, it is said, is that the particular area is close to the centre of town or a prosperous area or located close to the sea or some such other criteria that fails to address the question because those aspects were the same for renters as for home buyers.

The reality is that house prices have been – wrongly in my view – affected by a new phenomenon – affordability. Affordability is calculated in terms of borrowing costs. Thus if interest rates are kept artificially low the buyer who is borrowing to pay for his home can afford to pay more. Consequently the capital price of the home increases. This is a serious mistake. Nevertheless it is the way in which banks have come to accept that a loan can be repaid and valuers who value properties on the basis of comparison with others have followed one another down this unwise path.

Affordability determines the ability to repay the loan. It does not make the home a better or worse investment. That can only be determined on the basis of the yield – the ration that the rent bears to the value of the property. If the capital value of the property increases faster than the rent then the yield falls. The person who buys a home is saving himself rent. It is unwise and unsafe to compare the rate of interest on a loan with the yield on a property. In effect the buyer is encouraged to say that if the rate of interest on the loan is 4% then the appropriate yield on the property is also 4%.

That is a big mistake and has accounted for a massive increase in property inflation. The appropriate rate of return on a loan – as we saw in connection with the valuation of leveraged buy-out companies – should depend upon the loan to value ratio and the risk of the underlying asset.

This is the way in which property acquisitions should be financed. The procedure is not dissimilar to that of the private equity firms in a leveraged acquisition. Assume that the property is worth 100,000 and that the corresponding rent would be 7,000 p.a.. The buyer borrows 70,000 from the bank at a floating rate of interest of 4%. His interest rate bill is therefore 2,800 per annum. The property is financed with debt and equity. On his debt the buyer is paying 4%. His equity is costing him (that is what he would have received if he rented the property out so it is an opportunity cost to him) 4,200 per annum. In percentage terms that is 14%.

That is how a private equity firm would value its acquisition if this was a company and a 14% return is reasonable because the chances that the property will fall in value by 10% or 20% is considerably higher than that it will fall in value by more than 30%, which is why the debt yield is so low (4%).

171

The current approach however is to ignore yield entirely from the valuation. Thus so long as the rate of interest on a loan can be afforded on the basis of the salary of the buyer the loan will be made. Thus the property in question might be sold for 200,000. This would represent a yield (ratio of rent of 7,000 to price) of 3.5%. Neither the bank nor the valuer takes any account of this yield although it represents a sensible measurement of the risk of the investment. If the borrower is able to fund a mortgage of 140,000 (70% of purchase price) at 4% interest the bank will lend him the money. A mortgage of 140,000 at 4% over 25 years will cost 8,962 per annum. That is considerably more than the rent on the property. Nevertheless the loan is made and the property is purchased.

How does such a transaction look in the world of corporate finance. Not very good. The income of 7,000 on 100% of the investment is reduced to 1,400 after the interest on the 140,000 loan at 4%. The equity return is therefore 2.33%. The investor is surrendering 60,000 of equity and is saving himself 2.33%, substantially lower than the return on the debt. The valuation must be wrong.

These valuations are the backbone of residential property lending. It is no surprise that the banks are in such a mess. More alarming is that individuals continue to buy property at these prices, on this basis and without any regard for the yield. Instead properties are bought on the basis of the publicity that shows how beautiful and desirable a particular property is.

The turnover in the number of homes achieved huge encouragement over the last 20 years from the TV companies. One could hardly switch on a TV programme without peering into somebody else's living room. People were hugely interested in listening to comments from estate agents about how to have a modern looking home which will sell well if all the walls were painted in a particular colour. Everybody felt that they were experts. Walls were knocked down and extensions were built regularly to achieve the desired modern look. This encouraged a lot of economic activity in the housing market as people expended their homes outwards and upwards. In most cases this expenditure was funded with borrowed money that depended upon the valuation of the home as well as the income of the home owner of course.

Even those who did not move house or install extensions borrowed to raise more money on their existing homes because their values had increased. The banks felt free to make such loans because they were secure that the underlying value of the property would not fall but would keep increasing.

What did people who borrowed more money "to release equity" on the security of their homes do with the money. In many cases they invested in other properties, often abroad but also in their own country. They bought homes for investment purposes or they bought second homes that they rented out only periodically as holiday lets. This pushed valuations up further.

In conclusion property has unique features. It has an inflation of its own with the ability to created huge imbalances in an economy as wealth is transferred from one sector to another without any or with small wealth creation (for extensions). The amounts involved are massive and the consequences equally so, far more than for example an increase of 5p in the price of bread.

None of the facts stated above are new. Only the conclusion is, namely that inflation in property values is detrimental to an economy because it enables vast sums to be transferred from one sector to another with serious adverse consequences.

There are of course positive features to real estate as I explained at the beginning of this chapter. It can be used as one of the best forms of continued wealth creation in an advanced economy where people will get to have two or more homes. However it has been far easier to redistribute wealth through property valuations where one has to do very little if at all to profit than through the effort of house building which is time consuming and arduous.

The dangers of real estate are all associated with borrowing. We shall consider borrowing and lending in another chapter. It is important to appreciate that borrowing involves an undertaking to consume less than one produces in the future. To the extent that consumption is reduced it inevitably must mean that production is also reduced, unless of course miraculously the borrowers are all able to increase production of whatever it is that they produce. Unfortunately most people in an advanced economy produce information and bureaucracy, hardly a valuable consumable item. If their borrowings are to be met with reduced consumption then it inevitably means that large borrowings will be followed by reduced productivity and reduced wealth in the future. That is the danger of borrowing associated with real estate. Governments that ignore massive borrowings to acquire real estate do so at their peril. The larger the borrowings the greater will be the reduction in productivity and consumption as debt is paid down in the future.

11.   BORROWING – THE MODERN PHENOMENON

Margaret Thatcher once said that she was keeping interest rates high in order to encourage saving and reduce borrowing. Nobody laughed. That was the nature of the lady. She said very mundane things as if they were words of great wisdom and required exceptional understanding of difficult concepts. The sages amongst her had never heard such ordinary things said with such enthusiasm and were therefore doubtless confused. Ordinary people loved it because somebody in authority was speaking a language that they understood. It proved that all that confusing talk that they did not understand was just so much unnecessary complication.

Of course saving and borrowing are two sides of the same coin. There would be no borrowing unless there was saving. As explained in an earlier chapter saving is the result of consuming less than one produces. Borrowing is the converse. Somebody after all has to consume the surplus that is produced by the saver.

As I have explained in the chapter on Money, banks can create money. They do so by making loans. In the recent past the amount of money in the form of balance sheets of banks has increased substantially. There has been little control over the amount of money around.

Borrowing involves the promise that the borrower will sooner or later reverse the process. In many cases that will be a difficult task for the borrower because it is difficult to reduce living standards. The assumption that a borrower will be able to increase production is normally just that, an assumption.

Borrowers have an advantage over lenders or savers. An insolvent individual borrower has his slate written off at death. Savings outlive the saver and are passed to his heirs. It is therefore essential that individual borrower pays back his loans long before he dies. Of course if the insolvent borrower owes the money to the creditor directly the wiping clean of the slate of the borrower on death immediately balances the account. The creditor loses his money and passes nothing on to his heirs. Unfortunately in this far more complicated world that is not what happens. Banks are interposed between the lenders and the insolvent borrowers. If the borrower is insolvent it is the bank that loses. The creditor is protected because it is owed money by the bank. So long as the bank can maintain its solvency – and it can be assisted by central banks to do so where necessary – the creditors will continue to be protected whilst the insolvent debtor has his slate wiped clean on death.

It is essential therefore that banks collect their debts before their customers die.

Borrowing inflates a bank's balance sheet because it causes – as I explained in an earlier chapter – the assets and liabilities to be increased. The repayment by the borrower of his loan does not of itself reduce the bank's balance sheet. It merely replaces the loan with cash. The way in which the bank's balance sheet was meant to be brought back into equilibrium goes back to the principle that all economic transactions are ones of barter. The debtor was meant, directly or indirectly to sell to the creditor or depositor goods and services that would extinguish the debt. The banks loan and deposit book were therefore means to be revolving accounting entries as first the creditor sells to the debtor and later the situation is reversed. The bank then repeats the process with the same or another debtor and creditor. Unfortunately far from reversing the process the creditors grew richer and richer and the deposits grew larger and larger. Debtors borrowed more to repay earlier loans and eventually they were unable to repay and large loans had to be written off. The assets over which the banks had taken security proved to have been overvalued, largely as a result of the inflation caused by the banks themselves printing money that chased property and stock values upwards without any intrinsic increase in the real value of these assets.

Borrowing has in the past 30 years been used to fuel economic growth. More and more goods – cars, clothes, homes – and services – mostly travel and more travel – have been supplied to consumers in exchange for a promise to pay in the future. Before the explosion of borrowing, consumers first saved – consumed less than they produced – and then spent. The explosion of borrowing accelerated production and consumption of goods and services because those who had saved and spent competed for the goods and services on the market with those who wanted to consume before paying. Consumption and therefore production increased substantially.

Over those 30 years in the UK the aggregate economic growth is practically identical to the aggregate increase in borrowing. It is fair to say that all the economic growth during that period was fuelled by debt.

This was always going to be a one off increase in production and consumption, or growth in GNP. Once maximum borrowing had been reached problems were bound to arise. Even if such maximum borrowings were not repaid aggregate consumption was bound to reduce because the increase in spending funded by borrowings was going to cease. Furthermore borrowers had to pay the funding cost of their borrowings which in the case of credit cards is not insubstantial.

For the reasons explained above individual borrowings had to be repaid at some time and therefore the more the borrowings there was the more rapid was the drop in consumption likely to be. In any event borrowing had to be repaid within the lifetime of the borrower and so there was a natural limit to this experiment of ever increasing bank balance sheets. Once the limit of borrowing is reached consumption by borrowers has to decline.

The result is economic decline to the sustainable level at which it was before the lending boom commenced.

Reducing consumption means reducing ones living standards and that is not easy. Stress and depression are a likely by product.

It is surprising that the increase in the supply of money – increased borrowing - did not result in alarm bells ringing. Of course additional borrowing was only possible because of the vast sums of cash that were paid to over-valued employees and for over-valued assets.

To a much greater extent than in the case of real estate has been borrowing for corporate acquisitions. The massive expansion since the 1980s of the leveraged buy-out business has led to previously unknown amounts of borrowing to acquire companies. These companies are then restructured so as to replace equity with debt and then sold on the basis that they are now more profitable. They are not. They remain the same companies producing the same numbers of goods and services as before. All that may have happened is that wealth may have been redistributed from equity investors to debt providers and to the private equity fund managers, who have become fabulously wealthy in the meantime.

Of course it is hoped that large borrowings can be repaid by increasing production rather than by reducing consumption. Reducing debt by means of economic "growth" has its difficulties. One of the most significant problems is that those who incur the debt are frequently those who cannot create economic growth. Those who invent new items or ideas are understandably reluctant to allow their innovations to be used to repay the debts of those who have borrowed too much. Indeed those who create new inventions and their advisers will wish to extract maximum value from such inventions. There is an army of investment managers, advertisers and consultants who will argue that the new invention will produce untold wealth in the future. The result is that the new inventions are sold for appreciably more than they are currently worth. They are sold in return for payments that represent future increases in profits or "growth" that may not occur. The result is more debt as those who create growth are overpaid. The corresponding debt of course ends up with those who cannot create any growth in the future.

Since the cash surpluses of those who receive them are no so huge that they cannot be spent they end up in the banking system as deposits directly or indirectly. The banks therefore lend this money to those who cannot afford to repay it. For years the banks have been satisfied that the wall of money that they have lent has had the undoubted effect of creating inflation in for example property prices. They have therefore felt secure that so long as they continue to lend more and more money the property inflation will ensure that they can recover their loans. True but only if the merry go round continues. Sooner or later it has to end because the ability of borrowers to repay their borrowings is limited to their income from other sources and these other activities do not have the "benefit" of the same inflation as property. When the borrowing stops property prices will start to fall. The result is losses that the banks will be unable to stop. They cannot tell where their losses will stop because they do not know how far property prices will fall.

In theory they will fall until borrowers are able to repay their borrowings. In short they will fall until they show the same trend as inflation of other goods and services.

In reality of course prices tend to overshoot and it is likely that they will fall below trend.

There has in the past been a genuine Ponzi scheme for personal borrowing as well. Credit card companies have offered credit card holders interest free holidays to take over the borrowings of new clients from their existing credit card companies. The result is that the old credit card company thinks it has been paid and the new one has a new customer. The process is repeated so that all borrowers seem to be repaying their loans. In fact they are not. Their borrowings are increasing materially. This is an insidious aspect of borrowing. Sooner or later as the borrower grows older the loans will have to be repaid. The borrowers cannot repay. The loans are written off and the borrower reduces his consumption because he cannot borrow again.

That is the nature of the disaster of borrowing for consumption.

Borrowing should be limited to either temporary situations that can easily be reversed such as for example the delivery of goods from abroad that will be sold in the local market, or for investment in an income producing asset that will repay the borrowing. Any borrowing that is not for such purposes should be marked "danger". This is not how we have behaved. We will now have to pay the consequences until a return to sanity.

For some reason the focus on over-borrowing has been mainly on government debt. Economists point out the ratio of government borrowing to GDP. This is understandable because the government is the largest borrower in practically any country. It is also the largest spender. However in many Western countries today personal and corporate debt exceeds government debt by a factor of more than 3 or 4 to 1. Government debt in the UK is around £1 trillion. Total debt, ignoring bank borrowing because banks are conduits, is around £5.5 trillion. In the US government debt is around $16 trillion whereas total debt is around $60 trillion. In Australia government debt is low but personal debt is huge. It is not difficult for governments to reduce their borrowings at the expense of piling debt on their citizens.

It is the proportion of government debt to government income that is important and likewise it is the proportion of total debt to personal income that is important, and not the proportion of government debt to total income, which is what is often used as the relevant benchmark.

Why can debt not keep increasing indefinitely? There are two reasons. Firstly there is the phenomenon mentioned above; the fact that insolvent debt is written off on death but deposits go on for ever. The individual – but not the corporate borrower – has to repay his borrowings. The second phenomenon is the cost of funding borrowing – interest. As soon as interest cost on an increasing loan exceeds the ability of the borrower to pay such interest from his surplus cash, he is in difficulty and his difficulties will only increase.

Thus for example if I have income of 100,000 which after living costs reduces to 30,000 then if I have been adding debt until it amounts to 500,000 and interest is 6% then the surplus of 30,000 is only sufficient to pay interest on that debt. If I cannot pay that debt then the interest will be added to the debt and the amount of debt will get larger and my ability to pay the interest on it – to say nothing of repaying the principal – reduces.

There is therefore a relationship between the total debt, surplus income available to fund debt and the interest on that debt. It is for that reason that governments have artificially lowered interest rates. This makes it possible for the total debt to increase before it becomes impossible to service that debt. It is also why governments pray for growth. In the above example the 100,000 represents my share of GDP. If there is economic growth that sum will increase and my ability to borrow more and to fund that debt increases.

If government debt is less than ¼ of total debt but the government spends 40% of GDP – the situation we face today – then we are ignoring the seriousness of the problem by focusing on government debt because the ratio of personal and corporate debt to personal and corporate income is worse than that of the government. It is for this reason that it is comical to hear politicians criticizing the government for having too much debt when the private sector's position is far worse.

181

If debt is a problem then all debt is a problem, not just government debt.

Debt that fuels increases in GDP – which is what has happened in the developed Western industrialized world over the past 30 or 40 years – has a limit that can be seen by looking at the position of consumers.

As a consumer borrows he can spend his income plus the amount of money he borrows. That position can go on for some time as he borrows more and more. Once a borrow has reached maximum capacity to fund his borrowings – and remember he has to repay his borrowings in his lifetime – he has to return to spending only his income. He will at best and for a short time have to pay interest on his borrowings. He can therefore for some time spend only his income less the interest on his borrowings. This can, in the case of credit cards for example be substantial. When he comes to pay off his debts he can only spend his income less the interest on his debts less the principal of his debts that he has to pay off before death.

The result is substantially reduced consumption.

Of course the amount of debt can be replaced by lending to another generation so that the total amount of debt that the banks have at any time remains the same.

However the bulge in spending that occurred when personal borrowings were ballooning and that presented itself in the form of increased consumption and GDP increases will never re-occur. It is a one off. It peaks. All that has actually happened is that during the period of increased borrowing the consumer has brought forward his consumption. Previously a consumer would save first – produce more than he consumes – and then spend. With the explosion in borrowing the consumer was able to bring forward his consumption and to spend first with borrowed money – consumer more than he spends. We celebrated this event as if it was the genius of our educated people that resulted in this increased prosperity. In fact it was nothing of the sort. It

182

was merely reversing the way in which we consumed. Those who saved first and consumed once they had saved spent as before. The new generation accelerated spending by spending first using borrowed money.

Now the time has come when that consumer has to repay his borrowings. He has to consume less than he produces. The government not surprisingly does not like this because it results in reduced GDP and reduced prosperity.

That is the phase in which the modern developed industrialized world now finds itself. The piper is demanding payment and we do not want to pay him.

12. EXCHANGE RATES AND FOREIGN TRADE

Exchange rates have in the past been based upon the amount of goods and services exported by one country to the other.

Thus if the UK exports cars to the US the UK exporter will require payment in £s. The US importer has to find these £s in order to pay for the cars. He goes to his bank and surrenders $s in return for £s. His bank will only have £s if some US exporter has sold goods to the UK. This would require the UK importer to go to his bank with £s and exchange them for $s.

The UK bank had £ and needed $ and the US bank had $ and needed £. They merely exchanged their £s for $ and were thereby able to satisfy their customer's needs.

There is perfect symmetry in this process. Somehow an imbalances in the goods and services exported and imported grew over a prolonged period. Countries created enormous balance of payments surpluses, which were of course offset by the deficits of other countries.

What was the rate of exchange at which the $ were exchanged into £. Originally the exchange rate was set by the governments. Exchange rates were fixed. Thus for example the exchange rate between $ and £ was at one time $4 = £1.

The massive imbalances between any two countries was for some time overcome by means of what are called "devaluations" in the currency.

If the UK exporters in the above example had exported £100mm of goods to the US and the US exported $1billion of goods to the UK at a time when the rate of exchange was $4 = £1 then the UK economy received goods worth £250mm but only sold goods to the US of £100mm. The UK had a trade deficit of £150mm and the US had a trade surplus of $600mm.

These surpluses and deficits are the international equivalent of borrowing and lending. The UK economy in the above example consumed £150mm more than it produced and the US economy produced $600mm more than it consumed.

Just as in the case of borrowing and lending the UK economy collectively will have to reverse the process at some time in the future. It will have to produce more than it consumes. Hopefully the US would reverse the process and consume more than it produced at some time in the future.

Politicians and economists generally claim that the solution to a balance of payments deficit such as the one in the above example is easily and painlessly solved by devaluation. Rather simplistically they say that devaluing the currency of the deficit country makes goods in the deficit country (the UK in this example) cheaper to the surplus country. The shoppers in the surplus country who previously bought their own goods (cars perhaps) would choose to buy goods from the deficit country instead and this will quickly reverse the imbalance. How does this work and is it that simple?

Suppose that £ was devalued (as did indeed happen) from £1 = $4 to £1 = $2. It is true that the price in £ of the cars that were exported to the US will fall in price by ½ when converted to $ as a result of such a devaluation. The US consumer will see the price of the UK car in $ fall by ½. That would indeed make them more attractive to US buyers who previously may have bought US cars. Unfortunately it is not as easy as that. The UK car manufacturers would have to produce twice as many cars at the old £ price in order to get the same amount of US goods in return. So they would effectively have to double their production and then make some more just so as to be able to buy the same number of goods as the US was exporting to the UK.

What about the accumulated deficit. Well that too will now cost more in terms of goods produced to reverse than before. The effect of this devaluation is that it is possible that a large amount of real goods that previously would have been consumed by UK consumers will now go to the US.

Of course the net effect is the same as for borrowing, either consumption has to be reduced or production has to be increased to make up for the excesses of the past.

But was it really necessary to reduce the value of the £ in order to achieve this reversal of the imbalance that was created. Is there any reason why goods that were cheaper than the same goods in the US and were selling well should have their price in $US reduced. What if the deficit only arose because the price of cars and cars alone was too high in the UK. Is there any reason why the UK car manufacturers alone could not have reduced their prices thereby making their cars more attractive to the US market.

The reduction in terms of $US of all goods and services sold to the US is rather drastic. It is indiscriminate and unnecessary. It inevitably results in wealth being redistributed from one sector to another without justification.

And what happens to all the goods imported into the UK. They are twice as expensive as before in £ terms. The UK consumers who buy US made goods may not want to pay double the price. They may therefore choose to buy locally manufactured goods instead because they will be cheaper. Thus goods that may have been exported may now be sold in the local market thereby negating the benefit of reducing the deficit.

All economic propositions are "if" propositions. One cannot be certain what will happen. Devaluation of a currency is not a panacea. Only hard work and producing real goods is and this can be done without interfering with the money side of the economy.

Politicians and economists think that it is not necessary to work hard to overcome economic imbalances. These can be resolved by means of manipulating the supply of and price of money. This is a big mistake.

Politicians have a strong desire to believe that it is easy to change economic facts without causing any pain to their voters. There is however no excuse for not questioning whether such pain free solutions are possible. The simple truth is that whether domestically or internationally when one consumes more than one produces sooner or later the process has to be reversed. There is no easy way of avoiding this. Central bankers can huff and puff and print money and manipulate interest rates. All that they achieve by this is the redistribution of wealth with unknown results.

Of course in recent times exchange values have been affected through general inflation. Inflation devalues the currency – or it should do so if markets behaved rationally. It means that the price of goods denominated in local currency will increase. In the foreign currency the price of those goods should remain the same but the exchange rate will have changed so that the foreign currency buys more of the local, inflated and depreciated currency.

Thus if there is 10% inflation in the UK and none in the US it follows logically that the value of the £ should fall by 10% relative to the value of the $US. People in the US will pay the same price in $ for the goods bought from the UK. The sellers in the UK will get more £ than before but will only be able to buy the same amount of goods in the US that they bought before with those increased £s.

Unfortunately that is too logical and has turned out to be too simplistic for the currency traders. In recent times currency traders have come to believe that inflation leads to an increase – the precise opposite of what should happen – in the value of a currency. Why? Because the response to inflation in recent times

187

has been to increase interest rates and the currency with the higher interest rates is more attractive monetary investment. Why? Because they hope to make a capital profit from buying long term securities at a higher rate of interest and then selling them when interest rates fall. This is an extremely naïve faith in the ability of interest rates to control inflation, of which there is little empirical evidence. Nevertheless it is how the markets behave and what has happened in recent times. It is of course nonsense, but that is how markets have behaved of late. They fail to see the other side of the coin. They focus on one side alone and there is no logic to the side upon which they will focus.

How does a country finance its trade deficits. It does so by issuing paper securities for sale to surplus countries. Again pursuing the example above the US exporters who have not been paid will not wish to be simply owed money by the UK importer for many years. The UK importer can pay the US exporter in £s. The UK importer borrows the £s and pays the US exporter. The US exporter takes the £s and buys UK bonds or other securities. If they are new securities nothing will happen immediately. If the securities are existing securities inflation will take place in the bond market, if the sums are substantial enough. The US exporter might buy UK government bonds or corporate bonds. He might buy shares in UK companies. He could also buy real estate or whole companies if he has sufficient funds. Buying long life assets such as companies and real estate is a good way of balancing the books but it is something that can only be done once. The next time that there is a surplus in the US there will be fewer long term assets in the UK for sale. The US exporter will then have to buy existing assets which causes inflation in those assets.

As night follows day the same principle outlined in this book occurs. The bank in the UK will have created new money which ends up indirectly in the purchase of UK bonds or property. The result is inflation in the price of those assets.

Of course the net result for a country such as the UK and indeed the US – the US started running trade deficits some time ago, the UK has done so since the end of the second world war - is that they are suffering surpluses by importing and consuming goods from abroad and in return they are selling their infrastructure and country. This is unsustainable in the long term.

The British government has not set a good example. Since the Thatcher administration it has gradually sold state assets – mainly the utilities - and used the proceeds to give tax cuts. This is unsustainable because one can only sell assets once. When you run out of assets to sell government income falls.

There is only one asset that any country possesses that is perpetually renewable and that is its labour force. Only by hard work can living standards be maintained and improved. Selling existing goods and property achieves only one thing – redistribution of wealth.

Of course all politicians hope that the process will be reversed as the deficit countries "grow". There is no evidence that this "growth" has resulted in any reversal of these trade deficits. The reason is that such growth has itself been funded by more borrowing. While there has theoretically been economic growth over the past 50 years the trade deficit too has been growing larger and larger.

It is often claimed that the solution to economic problems is devaluation of the currency. Indeed even now there would appear to be attempts to devalue the Yen, the $US and perhaps the £. Others call for devaluation in the €. Many ask the Chinese government to revalue its currency because it is giving rise to unfair competition in the countries that buy Chinese goods.

This approach is again pure fantasy. It is the result of thinking that complex problems can be solved with manipulation of some key financial instruments. It is the belief that wealth can be achieved without hard work. After all we have so much education we deserve to be richer just by thinking about a problem and then changing something or other from the comfort of our air conditioned offices.

These masters of the universe explain that we can export our way to wealth. This is delusional.

Certainly on the face of it devaluing a currency will have the immediate impact of reducing the cost in foreign currencies of all the goods in the country that has devalued its currency. However it makes imports from other countries more expensive by the same proportion. Thus suppose for example that the price of a Jaguar car manufactured in the UK was £30,000 and it sold in the US for $45,000. As a result of the devaluation of the £ from $1.5 to $1.3 the UK manufacturer was able to sell and did indeed agree to sell the car for £30,000, or $39,000. Suppose that US consumers who previously would have bought a Ford in the US for $45,000 and they now decided to buy a Jaguar for $39,000 the result would be greater demand for British cars in the US.

The UK production of Jaguars increases to accommodate the US consumer. UK production increases by the vast increases in sales of new Jaguars. We get richer. The US consumer is better off because he has paid $39,000 instead of $45,000 for an equivalent car and everybody is happy. That at least is how our economic experts see the process of devaluation.

That however is not quite what tends to happen. Firstly this completely ignores the position of the US producer, who might indeed retaliate if he sees his consumers buying British Jaguars instead of US Fords. He could lower prices to compete and the result would be a return to the status quo.

It also ignores the position of the UK consumer who buys foreign cars. Let us assume for present purposes that the foreign cars that the UK consumer bought previously for £30,000 (or $45,000) were Fords. These Fords will now, at the new rate of exchange of 1.3 cost the UK consumer £34,615. It is quite likely that the UK consumer who would previously have purchased a new Ford for £30,000, seeing that the price of the new car has increased by £4,615 as a result of devaluation will decide to buy a UK made Jaguar for £30,000. If he does so and Jaguar UK does not manage to build any more new cars nothing will have been achieved.

It is not so easy for manufacturers to increase production. It may take time. Jaguar UK might decide – this is the most likely scenario - that since it was able to sell its cars in the US at $45,000 it can now make additional profits in £ by merely selling its cars for that same price and pocketing the additional £4,615 of profit that results from the devaluation.

If the desired result occurs and production at Jaguar increases and UK consumers who would previously have bought Fords from the US react by buying Jaguars in the UK the result on the US producers will be material. The US will retaliate by devaluing its currency.

The normal reaction to devaluation is to do nothing. The UK producer will merely profit from the increased price in £ and will still sell at the previous $ price. Exporters therefore merely make additional profit in the domestic currency. Importers if they are consumers might defer buying from overseas. Many importers however are producers and have no option but to buy from overseas. Their imports will increase in price in terms of £. The result will be that their costs will increase, leading to inflation in the UK.

There is no panacea. Manipulating financial instruments does not lead to wealth. It can lead to redistribution of wealth as would happen if the UK consumer just goes ahead and buys a Ford car at the increased £ price of £34,615. That is what normally happens. The exporter gains and the importer loses.

If goods cannot be sold abroad because they are too highly priced there is no reason to wait for a devaluation of all goods and services. The price of those goods can themselves be reduced in price. Market theory says that they should be in any event.

The recent financial crisis in Greece has given rise to an interesting debate about foreign currency and the ease with which Greece can get out of its financial problems.

The theory is put forward by those who are opposed to the single currency. Once again it indicates ignorance of how foreign exchange markets operate.

This is the scenario as it has been explained by one of the most ardent opponents of the Euro – Michael Portillo, a one time Treasury minister.

The Greek government is technically bankrupt. It cannot repay its borrowings on the due date.

The solution is simple. So say the economic experts. If Greece exited the Euro zone and reissued the Drachma it would do so for example at an exchange rate of – say – Dr1 = €1. Greek homes that were previously worth €100,000 would now be worth Dr100,000. In $US terms these two sums are equal at today's rate of exchange to $130,000.

The Greek government would immediately set about devaluing its currency so that Dr1 is no longer equal to $1.3but to $1.00.

The result, so the pundits say, would be that those Greek homes that are on the market now for €100,000 will fly off the shelves at Dr100,000 because foreigners would see a discount in the sales price of $30,000.

This is fanciful and naïve. The property – any property – has a market value. If the true market value of the Greek property is €100,000 and it could indeed be sold at that price today, there is no conceivable reason why after converting to the Drachma the seller would agree to sell it for less than €100,000, or $US130,000. If the sale was in Drachma the owner would sell if for Dr130,000, making a nominal profit in Drachma of Dr30,000. Of course if the seller wants to buy something in foreign currency he will find that he made no real profit at all because the foreign goods will cost 30% more in Drachma.

There are theoretically two kinds of goods for sale in Greece or any other country. There are goods that can be sold at their current price in foreign currency and those that are too expensive. Devaluing the currency and maintaining the sale price in Drachma will result in those goods that can be sold at the pre devaluation price giving money away and those goods that could not be sold without a devaluating being sellable.

It does not need a devaluation to make goods that can be sold sellable at the pre devaluation price. There is no reason for selling at a discount. Those goods that cannot be sold just need to be sold at a reduced price.

Surely if price changes are all that is necessary those who cannot sell their goods and property at the current price merely have to reduce the price of those goods and services in €.

Unfortunately it is not that simple. Greece needs foreign goods. It needs to export in order to import. If the price of its exports falls as a result of devaluation (or price reduction) it will have less with which to buy goods from overseas.

There is no substitute for hard work. There is no substitute for producing real goods and exporting at a competitive price. If prices need to be adjusted in order to be sold overseas then it is not necessary to have a general devaluation because that will affect the price of goods that can be sold overseas and are properly priced. The result would be that the latter goods are sold at sub optimal price thereby causing more damage to the Greek economy.

13.   GLOBALISATION

This topic has been around for some time and has given rise to numerous protests and riots around the Western developed world.

Globalisation is just the name given to the principle that we all live in one world and one market place and therefore we all have to compete with one another.

This principle ignores the important question of development. When today's advanced Western industralised economies were developing they did not have to compete with other less developed countries. They were siege economies and they used tariffs and laws to prevent competition from afar. Of course there were not the means of transport and information that are around today.

In theory globalisation can make poorer countries rich. India, Brazil and China are examples.

Globalisation has resulted in whole industries in developed Western countries being exported to poorer countries. Thus for example whereas the UK was a successful manufacturer and had a thriving clothing industry during the 19th and earlier part of the 20th centuries manufacturing in the UK is now considerably smaller as manufacturing and the associated jobs have been exported to places such as China, India, Indonesia and other countries where goods can be manufactured more cheaply.

The result of this competition has been the impoverishment of those who lost their jobs in the UK and more jobs in China and India and the other countries.

India has also become a centre where other back office jobs are carried out more cheaply. Some accounting functions and many after sales services for anything purchased in the UK leads to a call centre in India where the job can be carried out more cheaply.

Those in the UK who have lost their jobs to their colleagues in India and China of course have suffered losses of income and are displeased. Those in India have benefited.

The approach that has led to this transference of wealth creation across the world needs more careful examination than has been accorded to it. The approach that has permitted the export of these activities, whether of manufacturing or of services, has been based on the simple and simplistic principle that we live in a competitive world and there is nothing that we can do to stop activities being carried out more cheaply elsewhere and the consequent loss of jobs at home in the developed world.

At first glance the uninformed observer might be led to believe that if an item of clothing can be manufactured for £1 in India whereas it costs £10 to manufacturer it in the UK then the UK consumer will profit by £9.

That is a mistake of course. Firstly the UK manufacturer would not be selling direct to the UK consumer but via a retailer. The UK retailer might have been buying for £10 and selling for £12.

The Indian manufacturer will not sell the goods to the UK retailer for £1. He will sell at a price that makes it marginally worth while for the UK consumer to buy from India. Let us assume that the UK retailer will buy the goods from India for £8 – a 20% reduction in his cost.

The Indian entrepreneur will have made a profit over and above his normal profits of £7. His workers might have jobs that they would not otherwise have had and are pleased by the export of the jobs from the UK.

So the UK retailer profits by £2, the Indian businessman profits by a massive £7 and the UK consumer pays exactly the same price as he did before.

It is true that the Indian businessman can afford to be squeezed should it be necessary to do so. However until he is squeezed he will become vastly wealthy. That accounts for the rather large number of billionaires in India and China despite all the poverty that surrounds them.

Of course underlying all this is a vast redistribution of wealth amongst a small minority. The massive wealth of the Indian and Chinese billionaires tends to be spent buying up businesses and properties in the UK and other Western countries. If the trend continues many large Western businesses will end up being owned by Indian and Chinese businessmen.

That, we are told is the price of progress. Yet the consumer profits not at all. He is charged the maximum amount that can be extracted from him. There is the possibility that because the Indian or Chinese businessman can afford to be squeezed on pricing the UK consumer gets some small benefit from time to time as the profits of the overseas producer are reduced. However this argument is false because if it was necessary to reduce prices to consumers marginally in the UK it is likely that the UK manufacturers would have been willing to suffer small marginal reductions in their pricing and eventually the wages of their workers. That would have been preferable to going out of business.

It is therefore reasonable to assume that the consumer gains very little as a result of globalization. The country loses out because many of its workers are unemployed. China and India profit but the UK loses out. The only people who gain are the UK retailer, much if not all of the profits from the savings going initially mainly in bonuses rather than in profits to shareholders.

Considerable misery is caused in the UK as a result of this transference of manufacturing and services to developing countries, and it is all for the benefit of a few wealthy individuals.

Whereas one might approve of businesses buying goods and services more cheaply in developing countries it is not so easy to understand why the government of the developed countries should accept this clearly detrimental effect on the national economy. Surely it is precisely the management of the national economy that is the responsibility of the national government. Should such important matters as the employment of a large sector of the UK population and the destruction of a large section of a nation's GDP not be left to the whims of a few rich men who want to become richer. Surely this is something that should be the subject of negotiation and perhaps of a treaty between two countries.

We are told that this is the price for progress. It is of course a redistribution of wealth and there is no doubt that the developing countries profit as a result. However the hardship that is suffered in the developed countries cannot be ignored. It certainly should not be ignored by the government of the Western countries.

There is no doubt that the removal of tariffs makes foreign trade easier. That of itself however cannot be necessarily a good thing for an economy. It might make it fairer that if somebody in India who is unemployed and is willing to do a job for a few pence should get the work that the UK worker is only willing to do for several £s. However it does cause serious disruption the effects of which are still being discovered.

The low wages in India and China and their foreign trade have given rise to a dual economy in these countries and doubtless other developing economies. You can still get a restaurant meal in India for £2, but it is impossible to do so in Britain. Medical care and transport are extremely cheap. They have their own prices. We have ours. There is no competition between their medical services and ours, or between their transport or restaurant businesses and ours. Yet their clothing is the same price as ours. We have created inflation in those countries. Why? Because any goods that can be sold to the UK will only be sold in

India at the same price at which they can be sold here. Cars are similarly priced.

Strangely property prices in India and China are at international levels.

Perhaps it was inevitable that this would occur. However the effect on world economic activity was minimal. It was merely a redistribution of wealth and jobs. The final chapter has not been written. The benefits are grossly overstated. The benefit has been to vastly enrich a small number of businessmen and women.

14. MECHANISATION AND ITS MODERN EQUIVALENT – INFORMATION TECHNOLOGY

When mechanisation was introduced on the shop floor blue collar workers were alarmed. They thought, rightly, that they would lose their jobs as a result. How would they earn a living.

Mechanisation was a great benefit to the world if not an immediate benefit to those who lost their jobs. Fewer people were needed to build cars, washing machines, houses, TVs. Consequently more of these items were made available to the rest of the population. They were "mass produced". They became available to and affordable by the masses. The economy undoubtedly grew richer and most were better off as a result.

Who would argue that a washing machine did not improve the quality of life of the housewife, or that the car not only improved the quality of life of the driver. The motor vehicle or at any rate the internal combustion engine was also an aid to industry and commerce as goods as well as to the people who were more able to move freely around the place.

Farming was made more efficient and we were able to produce more food with fewer workers, and no animals to pull a plough. More clothing was produced as weaving and spinning became easier, quicker, cheaper and more accurate. Most importantly production was cheaper. There were many reasons for this. Machines worked faster than humans. They did not go on strike. They did not fall sick or get pregnant, or ask for higher wages. They could work round the clock. They did not require personnel departments to manage them. They can be replaced without any litigation or disagreeable scenes.

The cinema became a great source of entertainment and considerably cheaper than live plays. One could go to the cinema and be entertained for a few pence. Live shows cost substantially more because the actors were only remunerated on the basis of those actually present. Movies could be copied very cheaply and sent to far corners of the world. Later movies shown in cinema houses were delivered to us in the comfort of our homes through the medium of the TV. This was even cheaper than going to a movie house as there was no need for a special building and staff.

The radio was invented and we were able to listen to people speaking and music being played over great distances. The telephone was created and as a result individuals were able to communicate with one another over large distances. One did not have to wait for the post to be delivered.

The internal combustion engine was able to deliver to us not only engine propelled ships that were faster and cheaper to run than sailing vessels but more comfortable, so much so that shipping became a pleasure. Later the airplane became a means of transport and is now widely available to everybody with a modest amount of money. We were able to travel large distances faster and cheaper. Goods from afar could be transported over great distances relatively cheaply and quicker. Thus fruit grown in one country could be sold in another far away the same day.

The goods produced were cheaper when the cost of the machinery was compared to the cost of labour that the machines replaced. That is the most significant economic feature of the forms of mechanisation described above. In short the machines that changed our lives in the 19th and 20th centuries had one thing in common - they paid for themselves. If I bought one of those machines it not only improved my life but I would afford it because it meant that my cost of living was reduced.

Take for example the movies. They were cheaper than going to the theatre. There was no need for the cast to travel. The cast gave their performance once and that performance was screened all over the world. The TV was even cheaper in the long run. The motor car meant that people spent less time travelling and more time producing goods and services. It meant that the cost of transportation was lower than before. Machines used to make clothing were cheaper than the labour that they replaced. The combine harvesters that replaced the horse drawn plough paid for itself several times over.

Most of these innovations paid for themselves. It was easy to reciprocate because the manufacturer of the motor car was able to buy washing machines and TV sets in return. The manufacturer of TVs was able to exchange his TV sets for trips abroad and new clothing. The farmer was able to exchange his food for washing machines and trips abroad. Each of these manufacturers benefited from the internal combustion engine. There was substantial domestic manufacturing and office workers were a small part of the cost of manufacturing.

Machines were used to build houses and other buildings making them quicker to build and more efficient in terms of heating, resilience and efficiency. Supermarkets were built that took advantage of the economies of scale that were available for large scale buying and delivery. Large trucks going to one supermarket were cheaper than a large number of small vans delivering to small local groceries.

The cost of these innovations was almost always in terms of reduced labour costs. However the improvements in efficiency and reduced costs were such that the economy at large was better off because the goods being produced and delivered were the same as before. They were produced and delivered more efficiently. The problem was merely one of finding work for the displaced workers.

The important point is that these innovations all resulted in a larger amount of goods being produced, not less. There was real growth in GDP. So long as the economic produce was shared fairly and equitably all could participate. As I explained above the

201

displaced workers had to become innovative in order to participate in this increase in wealth. They found the solution in office work. Through their work in offices they became part of and parasitic upon the factories and farms that produced the new wealth. So long as the office workers were not too large in number and so long as they were not paid excessive amount the economy was able to sustain them in their new jobs even if they were unnecessary to the production of the new goods.

There was some employment created by the machine manufacturers but nowhere near enough to employ the displaced workers.

Towards the end of the 1960s mechanisation had come of age. There was practically full employment and a state of comfort and prosperity existed in the advanced industrialised Western world.

The 1980s saw the introduction to the consumer market of the micro chip and the personal computer. This was an advance on mechanisation but it was not such a significant advance. Electronic equipment was introduced on to the factory floor but its benefits were not particularly evident at least not in terms of a reduction in the price of cars or their quality. The big revolution occurred in the application of the PC to the army of office workers. The PC was intended to revolutionise office work. It was followed soon after by the mobile phone and the Internet together with all the attendant gadgets.

What those who promoted the introduction of the PC never appreciated was that office workers were dependent upon and merely participated in the proceeds from sale of the end product. Office work did not assist or indeed inhibit the production of the end product. In most cases the end product could be produced without office workers. The office workers were sometimes imposed upon the entrepreneurs by statute. Often they sold their services in order to protect the entrepreneur from competition. Assessing the value of these office workers was not easy because their benefit was never immediately clear. By and large they

202

participated in the proceeds of production because they could be afforded. There were not so many of them and they were not expensive.

Economists rather naively assumed that these electronic items would make office work more "efficient". They had forgotten that many if not most office work was intrinsically not only inefficient but could easily be eliminated and that office work was created - admittedly serendipitously - in order to enable the workers that were displaced by the industrial revolution to participate in the undoubted benefits created by industrialization and not because they added value. They continue to make this mistake.

Efficiency in an activity that itself is inherently a waste of time is a rather incongruous concept. If the whole job could be eliminated without any impact upon the wealth of the nation there does not seem to be much point in making it more efficient by introducing mechanisation.

Take tax law as an example. This has increased hugely in volume since the 1960s. The amount of legislation and anti avoidance legislation as well as the army of lawyers and accountants continuing in their endless war of defeating the tax man achieves absolutely no additional revenue for the government. The law for granting allowances and tax deductions is so complicated one imagines how it could have got to that stage. Cases go to the House of Lords for a decision as to whether a light bulb is deductible for tax purposes if it is stuck to the wall or not, and armies of lawyers and accountants give solemn judgments on the matter. Yet the objective of tax legislation is the collection of tax. This can be achieved in a very much simpler way than these unnecessarily complex regulations. Few would disagree and arguments from learned scholars and practitioners from time to time advocate precisely that. Yet nothing is achieved except more rules and regulations.

Why is this system maintained. The simple answer has been that it was affordable.

Staying with the tax theme one wonders why it is necessary to have so many taxes. There are taxes on personal income, taxes on companies, there are taxes on living in a home and taxes on death. There are taxes on spending and taxes on alcohol. There are taxes on drivers and those who own a TV. There are local taxes and there are national taxes. Interestingly the local taxes are not enough to fund what the local governments are supposed to do, so the balance of taxes comes from central government which somewhat defeats the purpose of local taxes. Of course local taxes are a curious departure from the principles of national taxes. Poorer councils have more to spend but less to collect. Richer councils are in the opposite position. So the richer have to contribute to the poorer. There is no need for more than one or possibly two taxes if the intent was to provide for national income. It would be simple to abolish most of the taxes except for taxes on income and taxes on spending although even that seems to be overkill. Taxes on employees is also rather wasteful since the taxes are paid by employers who are much smaller in number than the employees. If employers were to pay tax on their payroll leaving the employer to decide how to distribute wages without any tax it would be far easier. Yet nothing of the sort is proposed. One could be forgiven for thinking that the whole purpose of the tax system is to make it inefficient and soak up excess employment through office work. The same principle exists in the private sector.

Lawyers for example are able to write a contract in a few pages. They can also do so on thousands of pages. There is no evidence that the latter is better than the former but the trend as more and more people come to work in offices has been to increase the volume of work. That is inherently inefficient. Yet it is regarded as an increase in GDP. It is of course nonsense. It is merely a way of redistributing the proceeds from sale of goods towards lawyers and away from the others in the production line.

Then there is social security and pensions, unemployment pay and the massive legislation connected with redistribution of wealth. There are allowances for one parent families, for the unemployed, there are housing allowances and there are pensions. There are child allowances and free meal allowances. Some old people get free care, others do not. All this could be simplified just by ensuring that everybody's income cannot fall below a certain minimum - a minimum tax all operated by the tax department and for those who are not employees.

These inherently inefficient activities are now apparently going to become more efficient by the introduction of the computer. Although their function could be easily abolished without any impact upon the economy except upon those who lose their jobs, and I do not dismiss this as unimportant, they are going to become more efficient and some will lose their jobs and be replaced by an answer machine or a computer. This is economic nonsense.

If economists were to appreciate that these functions, useless as they are, came into existence merely because it was a means by which the benefits of mechanisation and industrialisation could be shared then these insane attempts to introduce efficiencies would cease.

But what about the computer and the Internet. Is it really such a revolutionary concept that could improve our lives as did the internal combustion engine. Most importantly can it really pay for itself and still maintain those whose jobs were replaced by machines. For reasons that are not clear this is what we assume. Nobody asks the question or analyses the issue. It is merely assumed that all forms of mechanisation, including those that displace office workers can pay for themselves. There is no doubt that the introduction of certain forms of mechanisation in offices do reduce the work force. However that merely redistributes the wealth produced by the production of the end product amongst fewer persons. The displaced workers get less and those who remain employed – including the army of IT persons, get more. There is no evidence that the PC and mobile phone and the fortunes spent on these items pass the test of mechanisation - that they pay for themselves.

There has undoubtedly been a euphoria about the introduction of IT over the past 20 years. One can hardly turn on a business programme or read a business journal without reading about the prospects for IT, which invariably and mistakenly is assumed to represent the future for economic growth. So widespread is this belief based only upon assumption, that IT will enable us to maintain perpetual growth that the government has set itself the task of automating as many of its functions as possible.

There has been massive expenditure of fibre optic cables that cover the world. Satellites have been sent into space. Huge contracts for televising sports events have been made. Microsoft and its owners are amongst the richest in the world. Other businesses that used the Internet such as Google, Facebook and Twitter to name a few are worth vast sums of money. Yet nobody seems to have questioned in general whether this euphoria is based upon justifiable predictions of wealth creation or purely assumption.

I shall try to overcome this deficiency now.

As with all technology or mechanisation one has firstly to distinguish whether the item or service is quality of life improving or productivity enhancing.

In both instances it is essential to decide whether the item pays for itself. If it does then it is probably economically advantageous. If it is productivity enhancing and pays for itself then that merely leaves one question to be addressed and that is how displaced workers are to be employed. If the displaced workers can be employed earning not much more than they earned before then the product pays for itself. The item must produce more goods and services than before. That is a tall order.

The Internet is by and large a toy. Google, Facebook and Twitter and the other giants of the business are ways of doing things that we were all able to do before, differently. The mobile phone together with the stream of new inventions that are merely variations on the same theme - electronic wireless communication - are toys. So is the supply of cable and satellite TV. They are quality of life enhancing goods and services. They do not pay for themselves. They are sold as toys – "have fun with such and such" is the encouraging sales pitch when one buys a new gadget. They do not replace some other more expensive way of doing the same thing. They are themselves more expensive ways of communicating with one another and finding out facts and information. It is of course convenient to find out the price of an air ticket to New York and to book it at 3 AM but it is not revolutionary. The benefits of these instruments is marginal at best. The number of flights has not been increased as a result. All that has happened is that the travel agent on the high street has been replaced by the IT agent. That is classical redistribution of wealth, and not wealth creation.

Of course there are exceptions but by and large these toys are merely items of leisure. From the consumer's point of view he is able to get information from an infinite number of sources. Unfortunately the number of hours in the day are still only 24 and the reading speed has not increased. Indeed the obsession with texting has made communication by text and email instead of voice slower.

Is there a business advantage to these technological advances. Does the answering machine make a business more efficient. Perhaps it does so. It certainly reduces the need for receptionists. However no business that replaces a person with an answering machine takes into account the cost to its customers. Customers are invariable inconvenienced when they have to listen to a long list of options on an answering machine, most of which do not apply to them. It is certainly slower. Suppliers assume that the consumer's time is free. It is to the supplier of course but not to the customer, who is probably an employee of some other business and whose time is being wasted having to wait on the supplier whose sole interest is in reducing his own costs. Of course the supplier has employees and they too are having their time wasted in this way.

Yet nobody questions that these machines are good for the economy. Like lemmings business after business follows the trend, because others are doing so and it must make sense. I have news for them. It makes no sense at all. That is why people are spending more time at work than before. They are less efficient.

The real test of the Internet, the PC and the mobile phone is whether they pay for themselves. Nobody has performed that calculation. Most of the expenditure on new technology has been funded with debt and much of that debt cannot be repaid. That is no evidence that these toys pay for themselves.

To the extent that people stay at home communicating on the internet instead of going to the pub there has been a redistribution of wealth from pubs to the IT companies. However there is no evidence of real economic growth because the internet does not pay for itself.

Those who were asked and who had some responsibility for unemployment and economic matters speculated in line with market economic theory that the unemployed would find jobs making the new machines. This of course did not happen to a great extent because the machines were already being produced by those employed to produce them and they too were being replaced by other machines in any event.

We speculated that there would be more leisure time so the unemployed would find work providing leisure activities. This has proved a forlorn hope as people put in more and more hours of work. Indeed an attempt by the French government to reduce the working week was greeted with serious disruption and protest over there. Certainly there are more gyms around but these have taken over from other leisure activities as I shall show later.

Nobody appears to have considered reducing the working time of all their employees by 50% instead of dismissing half the work force at a factory that was to introduce mechanisation. The true test of efficiency is that more can be produced as a result of mechanization, whether industrial or IT. If a factory can produce more goods as a result of IT, why dismiss existing employees. Why not give people the same wages, which clearly can be afforded, and give them all more leisure time. Nobody has addressed this concept.

The reason is probably that so many people – the vast majority – are involved in redistribution of wealth that reducing the number of hours worked means that somebody else will redistribute wealth to themselves and away from those who are not at work. This therefore requires government action to reduce the number of working hours.

Instead mechanization resulted in large scale redundancies. The IT revolution has done and is doing the same, except that with IT the redundancies are in the office and there is no effect upon the end product, because office workers by and large have no influence on the production of the end product.

It was of course the government's job to consider the effects of mechanisation upon the stability of the workforce and the economy. Having a large unemployed workforce with no means of support is dangerous to the stability of the nation. In the event aside from minimal provision by way of the dole and some form of welfare little was done for the unemployed. They were expected to innovate, retrain and become more enterprising. They were expected to develop the new machines that would make us all richer and richer for ever more. It is curious that those who lost their jobs were, one must assume the least worthy of continued employment relative to the better qualified and more educated employees, yet it was those least qualified who were expected to innovate and not those who had the benefit of the better education and more skills.

So the position from the point of view of the labour force as a result of mechanisation was negative. Their standard of living dropped, some permanently. Many never worked again, and their familles lived and died in penury.

So how was mechanisation good for the economy. Hopefully the machines did two things. They reduced the cost of the finished product. This enabled the factory owner to make more profit, assuming that he sold the goods produced at the same price as before. What did he get back in return. Initially of course he got money. The money that would otherwise have gone to the now dismissed labour force was retained by the factory owner.

If the erstwhile employees were able to build a house for the factory owner or some comfortable furniture or a car they would sell him the car and all would be better off. The economy was better off because the same number of goods were produced by the factory owner. The erstwhile employees would be busy building a bigger or second house for the factory owner. They would get the same income as before except that they would not be paid for working at the factory but on a building site. The economy had a house that previously it did not have or a house that was larger than before.

That is probably what would have happened in a barter economy. Of course all economies are barter economies. We merely use money as an intermediate form of barter before ending up with the finished product.

I conclude that the industrialization did produce more goods than before, it did displace employees, but perhaps should not have done so because industry could have afforded to keep them employed. Eventually these employees or their children found a way of getting back to work and participating in the goods manufactured by the entrepreneurs by working in offices. The IT revolution operates largely in offices, where its benefits are not particularly clear if at all. Workers that were previously involved in accounting are replaced by machines but also by IT workers many of whom are paid more, yet the number of end products upon whom the office work depends remains the same. That is a recipe for large scale redistributions of wealth, not economic growth.

What about the consumers. Is all mechanisation good for them. The products of the factories is measured in terms of money. If a car previously cost £5,000 in 1950 and that was out of the reach of the average person and the same car was reduced in price to £1,000 as a result of mechanisation so that the average person was able to afford the price nobody could argue that the acquisition of the car was beneficial to the customer. Even the customer who could afford £5,000 who, following mechanisation was offered the same car for £1,000 received a benefit. There is no doubt that he was better off.

However one cannot ignore two facts. Firstly reductions in price are rarely so dramatic. The vendor of the machines would have done his sums. He would have calculated the marginal savings that would persuade the factory owner to replace his men with machines and would have priced his machines accordingly. The additional profit resulting from cost savings were therefore unlikely to be substantial. The reduction in the price of the end product was likewise probably even less material.

How many of us have noticed the price of goods falling following mechanisation. They hold up but they rarely fall.

Airline prices are a good example. They have fallen in real terms for many years but they have not fallen much in nominal terms. The same is true for most goods produced. The price of grain, sugar, wheat or other commodities did not fall materially when the farmers introduced machines to replace their workforce. The commodities were sold at the price at which they could find a willing buyer and that was much the same as before.

So the benefits of mechanisation to the consumer were and are generally modest. Nevertheless there was an undoubted benefit but it accrued over several generations.

It is important to appreciate the interaction of the forces that occur when some new machine is introduced into a process that makes it more "efficient". The golden rule is that the new machine must pay for itself. In a factory the calculation is easy. The factory owner calculates how much he will save on labour and compare that with the cost of installing and operating the machine. If the machine costs less he buys it.

However for the economy to grow two additional things must occur. Firstly those who are freed up must create some new wealth. They must invent or be employed to create some new consumer goods that will make us all wealthier. Secondly the goods produced by the newly mechanised factory must be greater in number and be affordable to more customers than before.

If the dismissed factory workers do not produce anything new and his goods are not cheaper then the factory owner will merely have the same income and more profit but the economy will not have grown at all. That is by and large what has happened with IT at least in offices.

That deals with mechanisation on the factory floor. What about mechanisation as a consumer item.

When a housewife decides to buy a washing machine instead of washing by hand she does so because of the obvious benefits of the washing machine. It will make her life easier. What however are the consequences of her action.

Firstly there is the question of how she pays for it. Does it pay for itself. Clearly not, because her labour is in theory cost free. It will give her more leisure time. But what will she do with the added leisure time. Perhaps she will just go for a walk in the park or spend some time gossiping with her friends and neighbours.

That there is a benefit to her cannot be denied. Her quality of life will improve. However economically she has to pay for the machine by giving up something else. There is here a classical redistribution of wealth.

This is what happens with the new internet gadgets. They are used for leisure and have to be paid for by the user foregoing other pleasures. Other businesses die out and new ones appear. There is zero sum growth.

With those electronic items that are business efficiency enhancing such as for example business networking sites, or the technical libraries that mean that you do not require to go to a library to get information but can obtain it in your office there is a benefit. However it is small and means that transportation loses business and so do libraries. The number of books read remains the same. There is no evidence that new businesses have failed to be created at the same rate because their engineers could not access technical books or because seller could not find buyers for their goods and services the old way. Most relationships are personal and using an electronic rather than a paper phone book does not get the sale done any quicker. Indeed the availability of phones and call centres to so many people mean that personal contacts are so much more important for doing business.

There will of course be cases where a deal does not get done because the right buyer and seller could not make contact, and now they can because of the internet. There is a taxi gadget that now enables taxis to be hired using a phone. Certainly there will be taxis that get more work as a result but that could be at the expense of some other driver who would have got the fare, so it is a redistribution of wealth. If that is what happens then the number of taxi rides remains the same. It is merely the few who have the gadget that are better off. The result – that is what the gadget sponsor wants – is that all taxis have to have the gadget. The end result is that the benefits of the gadget are eliminated but the cost of operating a taxi has increased. This may be simplistic but the question needs to be addressed. It never is.

As regards the information that one is able to obtain on the Internet these days the ratio of good to bad information is the same as it has always been and our ability to forecast is just as poor as it has ever been. Much information is designed to enable people to do the same thing as before so the supply of the end product does not increase.

Google is apparently now worth about $200Bn. It is a telephone book, a good electronic telephone book but a phone book none the less. Is it really worth that? There was a time when Yahoo and Expedia were worth vast sums of money. AOL was merged with Time Warner with a theoretical value of about $140Bn. In reality it was worth considerably less.

The stories of businesses who tried to sell goods on the Internet are numerous. Many have failed. The stories about buying things on the Internet to find that there was a problem are also too numerous to mention. There is no evidence that more goods are produced as a result of buying on the internet. High street sales fall and internet sale rise. People still have to pay for these goods and will only buy what they can afford. Producers also have to produce more if more is to be made and sold. There is no evidence that producers are not selling more goods because they cannot communicate with consumers through the high streets.

Yet nobody subjects the process to analysis. Nobody asks. They just assume that the novelty is economically beneficial.

The Internet is nothing more than a different way of doing the same thing as before. It is not necessarily better. Sometimes it is worse. There are many more ways through the Internet of deceiving people.

The fundamental point is that the Internet does not produce a single additional grain of rice. It does not build a single additional house. Estate agents are just as plentiful in the high street as before and their costs are just as high. Nobody has claimed that prices in the high street have fallen as a result of efficiencies.

As regards the mobile phone the supporters of this new technology claim for example that fishermen - this was their best claim for efficiency - are able to discover the market where the best price for their catch can be obtained. Suppose that is true. Firstly the best price could be much further so they would have to calculate the price of fuel for getting there and back. Secondly that price could change while they are sailing there. Finally even if they do succeed in getting a better price since not a single additional fish is caught as a result (they catch all the fish that they can) that merely means that either the profit made by the buyer is lower and the fisherman is better off or the price that the consumer pays is higher. In short no additional wealth is created, there has merely been a redistribution of wealth without wealth creation.

An old friend of mine who is an architect informed me that his work is now so much easier with the PC that he can produce 10 times as many plans as he once did with pencil and paper. I asked him how many more houses he built as a result. He looked at me with astonishment "none, of course" he said. So the additional wealth produced by the PC in his case was nil.

When considering the benefits of mechanisation we considered the enhanced production of goods. It was simple. More goods were produced and at a cheaper price. So they were wealth producing.

When considering the wealth creating nature of a machine that aids office workers the dynamics to be considered are different.

Office work is generally not an end in itself. It is usually subordinate or corollary to the production of some other goods or services that the end user requires. Few people want or need the services produced in an office. Certainly a doctor or lawyer may deliver services in an office that are the end product but generally this is not the case.

In a production line one must consider what is the slowest moving part. That is the speed at which the end product will be produced. It is no use whatsoever increasing the efficiency of part of the production process that is not the slowest moving part.

Take a car manufacturing plant. If the brake installing per car only takes 20 minutes but the gear box installation takes 2 hours and it is the item that takes longest then the factory will only be able to produce one car every 2 hours. There is no point reducing the brake installing process to 10 minutes because the car will still take 2 hours to come off the production line. It is just that the logjam at the gear box installation site will be greater.

It is the same with office work. There is no point increasing the efficiency with which one processes the paperwork in the car factory. The number of cars produced will not increase.

Unfortunately experience shows that office workers have an unlimited capacity to create work - Parkinsons law. All the efficiency produced in offices has not resulted in cheaper goods or services even to the producer. Show me a law firm whose costs have fallen following the availability of information on the Internet. Show me a doctor who charges less because he does not have to visit the medical library to do his research.   Show me an office anywhere in the world where the number of hours worked has reduced because of the PC and the Internet. Office workers have an unlimited propensity for inventing work. They can stretch a document out and make it twice as long thereby filling in the time they should have saved.

None of these questions were asked by or are asked by the numerous pundits who give their opinions daily on financial media programmes. They all merely assume that electronic toys including those that assist those of us in our office work will pay for themselves.

The real scandal however is the banks. Bankers do not ask rigorous questions. They assumed that businesses that produce these electronic goods will continue to increase profits for ever. They place ridiculous values on them and lend them vast sums of money or invest in their shares. They are betting on future profits. When these do not materialise they have massive losses to suffer. We know what happened then.

However the problem stretches wider than straight investment in or lending to these entities. What do these entities do when they receive a large loan from a bank. They invest it of course. Investing means creating an asset of lasting value. However the entity spends that money by paying their staff vast salaries, they pay consultants, bankers, legal advisers tax advisers and a host of others huge fees. They take a bet that they will get that money back and more.

Those who receive all those payments however have received income. It is profit to them. In a zero sum gain economy - which is what happens in an advanced economy where most people are involved in recirculating wealth without producing wealth - where there is a profit there is a corresponding loss. Not the way company accounts work. The recipient of the payments from one of these electronic behemoths is showing the payment that they make to him whether in return for an item of software, hardware or advice is receiving profit which he may spend. That same payment is not a loss to the company paying it but an investment. Magic. Everybody is a winner. The recipient of the payment is a winner. He has received pure profit. The expenditure is not a cost or a loss, it is an investment, an asset that will continue to exist for ever.

If the "investment" turns out to be similar to the valuation placed upon AOL by Time Warner it will be a disaster. Who will lose. The banks of course. That means savers. Wealth has been redistributed.

The trail is difficult to follow but there can be no doubt that this procedure of accounting for expenditure as if it was an asset, the lending of banks to support and enable that expenditure and them showing these sums as assets, have all helped to raise property prices, create vast inflation busting pay awards for a host of professionals and fee earners and have contributed to the most massive redistribution of wealth based on nothing more than a bet that the various valuations placed on these huge investment, many of which run into the 10s of billions of dollars, are right. If they are wrong then the system will collapse as it did in 2007.

The infatuation with technology is perhaps the most dangerous assumption that we make for the future. There is no substitute for rigorous analysis of any investment or loan based on first principles. If this is done we may yet survive. Otherwise we will suffer repeated collapses, and all because of redistribution of wealth facilitated by the use of money.

There are several examples of technology that make no sense. It is also impossible to lay out a series of questions that need to be addressed by any banker or investor who considers some new form of technology to be a good risk. One has to be rigorous in analysing the risks and rewards.

Take for example a bank that rightly in the event concludes that some new electronic toy will be extremely popular. He backs it with vast sums of shareholder or depositor money. Yet he fails to ask where the customers are going to get the money. If he did so he might conclude that the customers will stop going abroad. If that is the case the banker should sell his investments in holiday or airline companies because what the new toy company gains will be lost to the holiday firms.

There are all kinds of considerations that are ignored when backing some new technology. The problem is that banks throw vast sums of money at them without considering that there are consequences. The banks assume that if a business is going to do well that is good for all of us. It is not. It is only good for all of us if the item pays for itself. I do not know of many technological devices that pay for themselves. Certainly the huge number of applications that are invented almost daily do not do so. They are merely an idea.

Another aspect of technology is that it has led people to believe that it is easy to become an entrepreneur or business person. It is not. To become a businessman or woman you need to develop something that is worthwhile. You also have to price it right. Customers may fall into line and buy the new idea but sooner or later the consequences will appear, unless it pays for itself. Nobody with new ideas think about the consequences if it does not. If it does not then money is merely redistributed. Banks have a responsibility for considering   the consequences of throwing money at a business that will merely take business away from one of the other businesses in which they have invested.

What has changed in the Western world that has made us all so prosperous. After the second world war the Germans and Japanese worked very hard to change their economies. They produced cars and ships, computers and televisions, radios and washing machines. They were the true engine of the manufacturing age. It was easy to see why the German and Japanese people were able to live so well.

Now is it the turn of the British. We apparently are the miracle economy. People are extremely prosperous. They go on holidays four or five times a year. They buy houses here and abroad. They have cars for each member of the family and they spend money redoing perfectly good kitchens just because some manufacturer of kitchens tells them that fashion has moved on and they must replace their old kitchens. They have extensions even if they have 6 bedroom houses. They have more bathrooms than people living in a house. And how are we paying for this consumption. I frankly do not know. The only difference that I see is what is called technology.

The technology revolution has also occurred in Japan and Germany. Yet they apparently are basket cases. The technology has affected the British and American economies to such an

219

extent that we are now the envy of the world whereas in the 1970s we were the sick man of Europe. But has there really been a dynamic change in behaviour. As far as I can see the only dynamic change is that more and more people seem to want to live for fun and to have fun. I do not see of hear about people building new factories. I hear of lots of people being in the house building business and starting or working on Internet ideas, all of which have come to nothing. But that is it. As I see it the explosion in wealth is the result of the Internet and the mobile phone. Everyone has a mobile phone and although not everybody has a PC with Internet access many do and the numbers are increasing.

All technology these days is IT technology. Nobody bothers to analyse new technology. So long as some new idea can be considered a "good idea" people apparently will buy a new product. That is what we all assume, without asking question such as the ones I have outlined above.

But all this is foolish and will end in tears.

The use of the term "technology" is misleading. Firstly it makes whatever is being discussed sound as though it is not only new but better and more efficient than the alternatives. Often it makes things take longer. Those of us waiting in a queue on the phone to ask some simple question will testify to that. Sending emails instead of simply talking to a person takes longer. Sending texts takes longer. It is not more efficient to use the new gadgets it is merely different and different does not always mean better. Yet that is what is assumed. There are many examples of things taking longer with new technology. Yet nobody analyses the effect. They merely assume that if it is IT based it must be better.

It is impossible to mechanise all human activities. The human brain is vastly more flexible than any machine. I can ask a question directly of a person at the other end of the line in one minute. Automating answers requires me and millions of other like me to wait while irrelevant questions are read out to me by a machine. Is that really economically efficient. Yet that is what all businesses and government assume to be the case.

Nobody can explain to me why it is that when mechanisation is introduced in factories the result is that manpower is reduced with corresponding savings in cost, whereas when mechanisation is introduced in offices the opposite seems to be the case. The reason I suspect is that many if not most office personnel are mainly involved in redistributing wealth and that activity can go on for 24 hours a day. We are now in a period of 24 hour trading in financial markets. There is no room for improvement. Yet the securities traded are exactly the same. They just get recirculated more quickly.

15. CAPITALISM, FREE MARKETS, STOCK MARKETS AND PRIVATISED SOCIALISM

The misuse of certain terms has compelled me to define these terms for the benefit of those who use them, often indiscriminately these days.

Capitalism is the economic system that recognises that there should be a return for the use of capital as well as a price for labour. It is the rewards that are due to the person who provides the capital compared with the rewards that are due to the labour force that have given rise to such controversy in the past. The socialists / communists considered that goods were produced by labour and no reward for capital was necessary or desirable. They consider that the only real form of capital is land and that has been given to us by God and should be shared. All other raw materials are the product of the earth and are turned into consumable goods through the intercession of labour. The socialists make no allowance for the accumulation of capital by some who perhaps either produce more than others or perhaps consume less than others. The question as far as the capitalist was concerned was how much should be paid for labour and how much for the use of capital.

The communists did not consider that it was possible either to produce more than one needed to consume – saving - because they believed in the principle "from each according to his ability, unto each according to his needs". There was therefore no place in their philosophy for savings or accumulated wealth. The principle was similar to that of a tribal or itinerant community that consumes all that it produces.

The capitalists of course recognized savings and the possibility that capital could be accumulated through thrift or zeal. Such capital – particularly if in the form of land – meant that those who used the land or its fruits should pay for it. The accumulation of capital meant that the owner was able to receive a share of any goods produced as a result of the application of labour to the fruits of the land indefinitely. The communists could not accept that for the reasons set out above.

The capitalist claimed that since he risked his capital, which might have been accumulated over many years of generations, and the workers risked only their jobs he should get the lion's share of any income and the workers should get what the market determined was the going rate for the job. In practice this was the minimum possible because there was a hierarchy in which the capitalist employed the workers, was their boss and during working hours for practical purposes owned their labour. He paid the workers who could easily be replaced and was their master. It was for him to decide how much to pay the workers and if they declined he would replace them. He was of course subject to market forces in determining what he could pay but when labour was practically unlimited such forces placed little pressure upon wages.

If the enterprise was successful the entrepreneur made a lot of money. If it failed he lost his capital. The workers get paid the going rate no matter what happened.

The essential difference between the two systems is not as to whether or not capital is necessary but how the fruits arising from the combination of that capital and labour should be shared between the owners of the capital and the labour force.

The irony of the difference between the two systems can be seen when comparing the different economic units that are found in different countries that use the different systems.

The smallest economic unit in any community - the family – is run in all countries – capitalist or communist - along communist lines. Parents want all their children to end up equal. They will give unto each according to his need and expect from each according to his ability. They will spend more money on a child who is ill than on one who is healthy. They will spend more money giving extra tuition on a child who has low grades than on one who is gifted and gets good grades. They want their children to end up equal, so they treat them unequally. This is not considered unreasonable even in the US, where the term communist is a term of abuse. Indeed American families will be criticized or perhaps sent to jail if they do not take care of their family along communist lines. Americans do not recognize the irony of this. The family capital is used for the benefit of all.

Trade between the largest economic unit - the nation states – is on the other hand carried on entirely along capitalist lines even between businesses in communist states. No country gives its produce away to others on the basis of need. Those with large resources of capital – land – keep it for their own people. Russia is a vastly rich country but it does not give its capital wealth away, even to those who need it. Their charity begins and ends at home.

One of the problems with the communist theory that capital cannot be owned by individuals but was available for the good of all was that ownership by nature meant care. It is said that if something is owned by all of us then it is owned by none of us, and we treat it accordingly. There is no doubt that we take more care of our own goods than of goods that we own collectively.

Nevertheless even in a capitalist economy there is considerable public ownership of land and other assets and although there are instances of neglect of publicly owned assets this is not universally true. Many state owned assets are very well maintained at public expense.

Although land is the most durable form of capital much capital these days is in the form of money or monetary rights. Land has a use value all of its own and although it changes ownership it does not disappear. Money not only has a variable value but can disappear as I showed in an earlier chapter about money and banking.

Money gives its owner the right to claim the ownership of various assets including land and in the capitalist system it became acceptable for the owners of money to demand a return for lending it to somebody who uses it to buy capital assets.

We are all familiar with the risk that a capitalist takes when he invests his money in a project and nothing more needs to be said about this.

One of the essential principles of capitalism is the control of market forces. Indeed a definition of capitalism is generally in terms of market forces that determine how any profit made from the conjunction of capital and labour ought to be shared. Indeed the way in which different forms of capital and labour are shared is said to be governed by market forces.

It is these intangible market forces that determine the price of goods and services. Market forces however require elasticity of demand and supply. The UK has since the 1980s experimented in putting into private ownership certain utilities whose produce is not amenable to the forces of supply and demand. Such an arrangement is a recipe for the producer to hold the consumer to ransom. The government reacts by imposing regulators to determine the price that can be charged and indeed many other activities of the producer, such as his return on capital. Since pricing is the whole reason for allowing market forces to operate it makes the principle of allowing utilities to operate in the private sector questionable. It is the same with medical care. There are many advocates of private medical care. However if a doctor tells me that I must hand over my house for him to save my life I have no real choice. There is no elasticity of demand for medical health, at least critical health care. No activities that are not amenable to the forces of demand and supply should in a civilized society be exposed to the forces of demand and supply. The result is inevitably chaotic or at best nonsensical.

In capitalist systems many businesses are owned through collectives. The managers take the risk with the capital that is owned by the unit or shareholders of the collectives. The unit holders can be outvoted and are in most cases by other collectives such as large funds which control the underlying companies so the individual unit holders have little power. Power is concentrated in the hands of a few members of the labour force that manage the collectives. Does that sound like a capitalist system. Yet we call this capitalism today.

Almost all manufacturing and service industries today involve a collaboration of various parties. The end product of any process however is usually a single discrete item whether it is a plane, ship, car or a computer. It is that item that is subject to market forces. The income that is received by the collaborators has to be divided between them in some equitable way. We are told that such income is also determined by market forces. But is it? In reality the boss of a large organization decides how the income from sale of the end product is to be shared. He acts like a dictator. He pays what he wishes to those over whom he has power to decide.

As regards outside third parties there is little evidence that market forces pay a part except to a very small extent – between bidders for a particular component of the business. As between one component and another there is little evidence that the real value is attributed to each particular component or process. Is the manufacturer of a clutch entitled to a greater profit than the manufacturer of a brake when making a car? The same question arises when valuing advertisers or accountants relative to those working on the shop floor.

When an investment is profitable the senior labour force determine how much they should take and how much should be given to the junior members. The managers of the collective

226

these days take 20% of the profits made with the money of the real risk taker. Is that because of market forces. Is that a fair reflection of the risks taken by the capitalist – the real risk taker?

If the investment proves bad the real capitalist (the members of the collective) lose their capital but the senior labour force lose nothing. Indeed they still receive their fees. They have had their rewards for taking the risk with the money that belongs to the members of the collective. So senior labour gets the rewards and the capitalist takes the risks. Not quite what capitalism was meant to be.

That is the system that we now have in the West. It is not capitalism at all. It is privatised socialism. The senior labour force these days with its emphasis on obscene bonuses gets the lion's share and the capitalist is disenfranchised, he has no vote in the businesses that he owns unless he is a major personal and direct shareholder which is rare in the larger companies that comprise most of the economy. Where the shareholder owns shares through a collective it is the managers and not the real owners who is enfranchised. He votes according not to the wishes of the owners of the collective but his own personal preferences.

It is said that the managers of the collective will always vote in favour of what will benefit his members because he gets remunerated on the basis of the profits that they make. In reality of course his personal income is of considerably greater importance. This is not a free market. It is rigged. The managers of the collectives sit on the remuneration committees of large companies and pay the board members vast sums for their work. The members of the boards of the large companies then sit on the remuneration committees of the managers and reciprocate. That is not capitalism. It is wealth redistribution or theft.

Of course the junior workers are not so well treated. Why not? They did their jobs as well as the senior members. Our elitist system in effect says that the profits are made by senior labour.

Junior labour should merely get the minimum reward possible. Indeed if junior labour tries to strike in order to get a larger share of the profits of their company they are criticized loudly in the press and invective is heaped upon them.

The capitalist owns just a share collectively of these companies and arguably therefore owns nothing. His position is not dissimilar to that of the citizen in a communist country. They bear the risks if an enterprise is unsuccessful. However they benefit collectively if it is successful whereas in our modern Western economic system senior labour gets most of the benefit leaving a small benefit for the members of the collective. There is no true capitalism just as there is no true communism. Both systems in their classical sense are dead.

There was a time when labour – senior and junior – received the market rate for their work and all profits went to the entrepreneur. Our modern privatized socialist economies have reversed that principle. Now the capitalist – the real risk bearer – gets the minimum return possible, as does junior labour. Senior labour gets the benefit of any super profits but takes none of the risk. And we call that capitalism.

The stock market is a really true market. Shares are sold and bought anonymously at the best price available. However the movements of prices are often irrational. The major problem however is that market prices are based upon only a small number of shares changing hands. This can give a very wrong impression about true value.

The problem with shares these days is that the dynamic of the free market and the return on capital based on capitalist principles has been destroyed. Whereas in the past management was part of labour and the entrepreneur got the profits now management gets most of the profits and the entrepreneur gets the minimum reward possible for the use of his money. The position has been reversed and the entrepreneur is now dead, certainly defeated by the forces of white collar labour.

Stock market values are influenced not so much by market forces but by interest rates which are controlled by commissars. These commissars – called central bankers – fix interest rates. The lower the rates they fix the higher the stock market rises because it makes the rate of return that can be achieved on the market look better. That is not capitalism but manipulation of prices by officials. It certainly is not an example of market forces.

The demise of true classical capitalism has gone unnoticed. Nobody even realises it. It is nevertheless true. Labour has won. The battle now is between white collar and blue collar workers and the former are winning decisively. The average chief executive now earns about 60 times the average wage when it used to be about 20 times and the multiple is increasing annually. There is no incentive to stop these rogues and thiefs from stealing more and more. Their theft is directed at their poorer paid workers and at their employers who have been disenfranchised. This has perhaps been the most serious contributor to the economic collapse in which we now find ourselves. Vast sums of purchasing power - money - have been redistributed to the white collar workers. These transfers have been camouflaged by bank loans and the accounting principles described earlier in this book. Those who suffer are the pensioners and other savers whose money is being used to redistribute wealth to the managers.

Huge imbalances have been created. The books now have to be balanced. As governments try to balance their borrowings with cuts those who have to bear to corresponding cost of the inflation busting pay awards to the upper middle classes over the past 30 years are revolting. Greece is erupting, there are riots on the streets of London and Italy and Spain are also experiencing large protests. Ireland is in serious trouble. Hungary is about to default on its debts. Belgium, Spain and Portugal are next in line for assistance from the World Bank, IMF and EEC.

Yet nobody is willing to say that this is what happens when imbalances take place. They are not willing to say that these austerity measures are the result of too much redistribution of wealth without wealth creation. Probably this is because those who run the world themselves were the beneficiaries of that redistribution. And they still want huge bonuses.

The arguments that these managers put forward is that they must be paid the market rate and the market decides. Yet the market is rigged by, you've guessed it, themselves.

There are countless talented people who can do the jobs of these overpaid wealth redistributors. Yet they are insulated from competition by the small cabal from which they are chosen and they play musical chairs. As one gets fired he gets compensation and another highly paid job from another company in the cabal. All that needs to be said is that this is the best person for the job. That means that there is no market because every individual is unique. We must have that man or woman and he or she is the only person in that market so they can name their price. This is of course boastful rubbish. Nobody knows who is the right person for the job. People are selected on the basis of human chemistry and self interest. The thought that the selection process is based on benefit to the shareholders is fatuous nonsense. Look how the shareholders are treated. The person applying for the job is doing so for his own self interest, to make as much money for himself from the appointment as quickly as possible. Thoughts about duty to shareholders to make them as rich as possible never enter the mind of the average chief executive. The only time when thoughts of the shareholder enter their mind is when there is a danger of being fired when their thoughts become how best to prevent the end of the gravy train. Their inevitable answer is spin. They will say whatever will keep the gravy train going. Truth does not come into the equation.

16.   PENSIONS AND SAVINGS

I have explained elsewhere that increases in the value of any asset above the trend rate of inflation will be offset sooner or later by a decrease in value of other assets.

The simple answer to the question where has the value that has gone into property prices come from is, at least in the UK – mainly from pension funds.

Pension and savings are the precise opposite of borrowing. Borrowing represents consuming more than one produces and carries the implicit promise that one can reverse the process later. It enables the borrower to enjoy something now instead of later. Pensions and savings involve the saver consuming less than he produces on the understanding that in future - in most cases when the person becomes old or infirm - that saver will consume more than he produces.

Both borrowing and saving are two sides of the same coin. For every £ borrowed there is a £ saved – a truism that seems to have eluded politicians and economists. At least they never mention it when they are busy manipulating interest rates. Margaret Thatcher once famously announced that she was keeping interest rates high in order to increase saving and reduce borrowing. That would have been a neat trick if she could achieve it. Nobody laughed. When this is recounted today still nobody laughs. It seems that the obvious relationship between borrowing and lending is not appreciated including by the authorities.

The explosion in borrowing is the focus of much of the financial world's attention these days. Yet nobody focuses on the equal and opposite accumulation of deposits that must be the opposite side of the balance sheet of the banks. These vast deposits represent were created over the past 30 years since Margaret Thatcher made her famous statement. Clearly her words were ignored – at least by the borrowers. To the extent that borrowers

231

cannot repay their borrowings they clearly bought goods or services that they could not afford. It follows that those who own the deposits should not have sold these goods or services. Alternatively they overpriced the goods and services that they sold. Yet the inability of the borrowers to repay the depositors is a source of concern. In an economy where borrowers borrow from lenders directly the problem is quickly resolved because the borrower becomes insolvent and the lender loses his deposit. He takes back the asset that the borrower should not have bought in the first place – assuming the borrowing is secured – and equilibrium is returned.

The current situation is complicated by the banks who cannot get repaid by the borrowers but still wish to repay their depositors, who probably profited unfairly from selling goods and services that they should not have sold or did so at an overvalue.

Both borrowing and lending involve exchanging the present for the future. They therefore implicitly involve the making of a bet. That bet only becomes a bet because of the use of money. In a classic barter economy if I sold a piece of land to a farmer in return for him supplying me with eggs and butter for the rest of my life I would know exactly what I was going to get for my land.

In an economy where the barter (we all live in a barter economy, we merely use money as an intermediate means of exchange) is through the medium of money the picture alters materially. Taking the example of land sold to the farmer in return for money I have no idea how much milk or eggs the money I have received for the sale of my land will give me because I do not know what the price of those commodities will be in the future. I might get more or less than I would in a direct barter. One thing however is certain the result will almost certainly be different. The value of land for example could increase in money terms faster than the price of eggs and milk or vice versa. Then there is the rate of interest to consider - I shall deal with this in more detail later because it is a fundamental aspect of the redistribution of wealth without wealth creation - this could compensate me for deferring my right to claim future goods or services or it might not. It could for example be less than the rate of inflation in consumables such as milk and eggs.

Pensions are an even longer term bet than most borrowings because in theory an individual will save and draw money from his pension for 60 years or more. Initially the employee saves for about 40 years, and later he draws his pension for another 20 or more. Many things can go wrong with the predictions as can be seen from the number of British pension funds these days that are insolvent.

Pension funds have for generations been the main source of funding for most investments. They have been the mainstay of the financial markets. They invested in and remain one of the largest investors in quoted shares, and bonds. They invested and continue to invest in private equity deals, bonds and treasury securities.

When companies make bad bets and perhaps overpay their executives it is money that would otherwise have gone to the pension funds and therefore would have benefited the pensioners, unless of course those vast increases in salaries accompanied increased profitability.

When we consider how and why the income of British executives increased at a substantially faster rate than corporate profits we can see the redistribution of wealth from pensioners to executives.

We have seen in recent years that high rewards do not necessarily accompany increased profits. We are told that high rewards are the result of market forces. In fact they are the result of individuals deciding what to pay a person with money that is not their own. When highly paid employees get huge bonuses that is money being transferred from pension funds that would otherwise have benefited the pensioners. When banks pay billions in bonuses that penalises the pension funds who would have otherwise received more in dividends to their shareholders.

It is true that in many instances pension employees do deliver increased profits and so perhaps are rightly rewarded. However two points need to be made. If these additional profits were merely a redistribution of wealth without any wealth creation then some other company or person will have suffered the corresponding loss. The chances are that the pension funds hold shares in the company that suffered such loss. So whenever a company makes profits at the expense of a competitor it is likely that the pension funds break even because what they gain on one hand is lost on their other investment. However their profits from their investment in the company that made a profit is reduced because a large part of it is paid in bonuses. No corresponding reduction in salaries of the company that was at the other end of this redistribution of wealth takes place. So the pension fund loses out. Pensioners suffer and executives and other white collar workers profit.

For generations pension funds at least in the UK were so called "final salary schemes". This meant that the employee was promised a pension after retirement that was equal to a percentage of his final salary. For generations most major companies were able to afford these final salary schemes. Even in the dark days of the 1970s when Britain was an economic basket case companies could afford to pay pensions based on the final salary of the employee. Typical terms were 1/60th of an employee's final year salary for every year in which the employee was in the employment of a particular employer. Thus if an employee joined the company at age 20 and retired at age 60 he would be entitled to 40/60 ths of his final salary.

Contributions were normally paid into the pension fund (paid to trustees of the pension fund) which invested the money in treasuries and equities and sometimes even property. The pension fund would be revalued annually to see whether its assets were sufficient to enable a pension to be paid for the expected remainder of the life of the pensioner. If the value of the fund was insufficient the employer would make up the difference and if the value was surplus to the requirements of the fund the employer would take money back. The employer remained the guarantor of the fund and remained ultimately liable to see that the employee get the promised pension at retirement.

Problems arose for a number of reasons. Firstly the 1970s saw serious disruption in the rates of inflation. In the UK inflation approached 30% at its peak. Interest rates increased to around 15% as a result and the UK had to apply to the IMF for a bail out. The stock market under performed and there was a collapse in property values. The adequacy of pension funds was calculated on the assumption that pensions could be paid out of investments yielding 10% or more, which was the yield on UK government gilts.

In the event inflation fell dramatically and so did interest rates until they are now around 3% for long term gilts (treasury securities) which is where a pension fund invests its money to guarantee its pension liabilities. To the extent that pension funds were expecting growth in investment values they were disappointed because the stock markets experienced huge swings in the past 10 years. The Japanese stock market for example peaked at a level of 32,000 in 1989 and is now still valued at around 10,000.

Pension fund deficits are now enormous. They are simply insufficient to pay the pensions for which the employer (the sponsor of the pension fund) is ultimately liable. If employers were to plug the gap in their pension funds they will in many cases be insolvent themselves. That of course means that they are indeed insolvent using the classic definition of insolvency - the value of their assets is less than their liabilities.

This is puzzling. The economies of the world have been increasing or growing year after year for a very long time. In

235

Britain we are told that the economy has grown year after year (with few exceptions to take account of very short recessions) at around 2.5% per annum in real terms. We are apparently so enterprising with all our information technology innovations that we are just growing wealthier and wealthier. In fact practically the whole of the increase in GDP in the UK over the past 30 years is equal to the increase in borrowing over that period. That means that only one sector of the economy has been growing. The other sector has been borrowing and consuming that additional growth. This is unsustainable. Nevertheless we are told that our economy has been growing at around 2.5% per annum for 30 years.

Since such wealth would, one would have imagined, show itself in the value of the shares which are held so widely by pension funds it is at first sight surprising that these pension funds are in such bad shape. Where has the money gone.

The commissars have a response. We are living longer. We should be proud of that. It shows how clever our doctors are. It is a success story. How dare we complain. That is apparently true. However unless we are living longer in such a way as to increase the years in which a pension has to be paid by more than 2.5% per annum (the rate of so called growth in the economy) something must be wrong. If we are growing older by less than 2.5% per annum the increased longevity is affordable. Unless, of course there has been substantial redistribution of wealth from pension funds into other sectors. The blithe statement that we are living longer does not explain the dilemma without calculating how much longer. Yet nobody seems to want to indulge in that level of detail. We are living longer, perhaps by only 2 hours every 100 years so we cannot afford any pensions. That is nonsense. Yet nobody questions these ridiculous assertions. Do the maths. Calculate how much longer. They refuse. They are satisfied with their explanation that we are living longer. That should be enough.

236

Well I will assist. The average life span apparently in 1980 was around 77 years and pensionable age was 60. The average pensioner therefore had to consume his savings over a period of 17 years. The average life in the UK is now around 85 years. If we were to retire at 60 that means that the average life span for a pensioner is now 25 years instead of 17, an increase of 1.18% per annum. That is well below the rate of growth in the economy and therefore entirely affordable.

The situation is far better if one considers the annuity that is payable over a person's pensionable life at the normal rate of interest on UK government index linked gilts – 2.5%. The annuity payable at 2.5% for a pension of 17 years is – for every 100,000 – 7,300 per annum – plus inflation. If that was to be increased to 25 years the annuity would fall to 5,400. In order to return to the same level of annuity – 7,300 - the amount of the fund would have to be increased to 135,000.

In order to accumulate 100,000 over a working life of 40 years the employee would have to set aside (at 2.5% per annum) 1,500 per annum. If that sum was increased by 2.5% per annum, representing the rate of growth in GDP over the period the size of the employee's pension fund would be 157,000, well in excess of what would be required to pay the annuity rate of 7,300.

So where has the money gone. The answer is that it has been redistributed. It has been paid away in vast salary increases to executives, bankers, footballers, TV presenters, film stars, lawyers, accountants and many others. They have profited indirectly in a way that would not have been possible in a simple economy. In a complex economy using fiat money and with vast inflation in major assets such as property and corporate assets this was easy. The process continues to this day. Pension funds have been and are being raided. The politicians however have managed to satisfy the public that it is because of our success. It is the price for living longer. What a success. What a scandal. What untruths.

How do we know where the money has gone. Who has profited from these massive and uncontrolled redistributions in wealth. It is relatively easy. All one needs to do is to compare the wealth owned by some people today as a result of doing the same job their predecessors did 30 years ago and those who profited from these redistributions will be apparent. The results will be startling. Many lawyers and accountants have huge houses abroad, and yachts in sunny locations. They did not have such luxuries 30 years ago. Indeed 30 years ago there were far fewer. Now with more of them they are all much richer. That defies gravity. If there are more of them they should earn less. Yet they do not. They earn more. Celebrities today have homes in many places and billions of investments. The sports people play the same number of hours (perhaps a few more per annum) as their predecessors. TV personalities are vastly wealthier than their predecessors and the length of their programmes is the same. Indeed there are many more TV stations so theoretically and according to market forces they should earn less. The city bonuses are a well known way of redistributing wealth to individuals. Is there anybody out there who thinks all this wealth can be obtained without any consequences. Apparently yes. Nobody complained when these vast sums were being paid. Nobody examined or questioned. The market will take care of things, we were told. It might but not until the horse has bolted. There is however no doubt that many people including in particular those who own property and have participated in the inflation in property values of the past 30 years are richer than their predecessors 30 years ago. There is also no doubt that the pension funds are poorer and cannot afford what they could afford 30 years ago.

There is a connection between these two results. Money has leaked away from pension funds into the pockets of a select and large section of the population.

It could be argued that pensioners are not entitled to partake of the increases in the productivity of the country. Surely they are entitled to participate in the productivity increases that occurred whilst they were working. This kind of argument of course is an argument by children against their parents. It is not made but actions are taken and being demanded that will penalize parents who have brought up their children.

If it was suggested that children should not receive the benefit of increased prosperity because their parents want a second home or car there would be an outcry. Yet the same does not happen when children wish to have a second home and car at the expense of their aged parents. It is a scandal.

It could be argued that the productivity of the country was created by the workers and they alone therefore should profit from growth in the economy. That might accord with some perverted socialist thinking that says that there should be no return for capital. As the owners of the capital in the economy the pension funds in our so called capitalist economy are not only entitled to participate in the growth but are also entitled to participate to a greater extent than the labour force because they risk their capital. That at least is capitalist theory. It would be strange that those who profited in the past 30 years and did so on the basis that they are employed in a capitalist economy were to argue that pension funds are not entitled to participate in growth. The reality of course is that the growth in the economy and some more has gone to a select few.

Compare the net worth of the UK's 100 richest. Every year the amount of increase in their wealth exceeds the amount of the increase in the growth of the economy. It follows that the rest of us must be getting less and less. Our falling living standards are camouflaged by money and borrowing. However there comes a time when this cannot go on. Cuts will be made, as is happening now with the UK and various other governments. People will lose their jobs. They will pay for the excesses of the rich who have transferred and redistributed wealth to themselves without creating very much if any new wealth.

Another way of showing the deception of governments who say that we cannot afford pensions because we are living longer is to look at the UK population. It has increased from around 50 million in 1960 to around 62 million today. That is an increase of 0.41% per annum, well within the rate of increase in GDP.

Pension funds are managed by fund managers who charge fees. The government also encourages people to invest in pension funds by granting a tax deduction for money placed in a pension fund. It also allows money accumulated in a pension fund to be accumulated tax free. What many do not realise is that when the pension is paid (aside from the first 25% which can be withdrawn tax free in the UK) the pensioner will be liable to tax on the whole of his pension. He will be liable to tax on it even if he moves to a tax haven.

Here is something else that many people do not realise. The fees charged by a pension fund manager are frequently greater than the tax reliefs that are given at today's low rates of interest. The tax relief is not really a tax relief as such it is in reality a tax deferral. Tax is paid later (aside from the 25% tax free lump sum). There is a benefit in deferring tax - which is too complicated to explain for a book like this - but that benefit is nil if interest rates are very low.

A typical fund manager will charge 1% per annum for managing the fund. Over 40 years and ignoring compound interest that will be around 40%. When a pension is paid the pension fund buys an annuity. At that stage the poor pensioner is ripped off once again. The annuity is paid by an insurance company. The insurance company takes a sum of money from the pension fund. It invests that sum in gilt edged securities, retains about 1% per annum of that sum and pays the rest to the pensioner. There is no justification for charging that 1%. The insurance company will claim that it may have to pay a pension for another 40 years. In fact the insurance company has the benefit of actuaries who can accurately predict how long a pensioner will live and they get it right more often than not.

In fairness there is a problem with pension funds that are based on a final salary, and that is salary increases.

Depending on the rate at which the individual's salary is increasing the amount of the fund that is required must also increase. Thus salary increases are a real problem for pension funds. An example will make this clear.

Suppose our employee who is to retire at age 60 is earning 50,000 at age 59. Suppose also that his fund was targeted to be (as above) 520,731 at retirement. He gets a salary increase of 5% in his last year of work, taking his salary up to 52,500. His fund will have to be increased by 5% to enable him to take the same percentage of his final salary as before. That is an increase of 26,036. Thus the increase that the employer will have to contribute to the employee's fund is 26,036 but his salary increase was only 2,500. It is this requirement to contribute several multiples of any salary increase to a person's pension fund that causes problems. Indeed as pensionable age approaches this adverse affect increases. Yet it is when they are closer to retirement that people's salaries tend to be highest and therefore the problem gets worse.

This problem does not affect the argument that we could afford it 30 years ago how is it that we cannot afford it now. It does mean that as people get higher and higher inflation busting salary increases the ability of the pension fund to keep up gets weaker and weaker. So the problem is salary increases. Nobody pays any attention to this mathematical relationship. Yet its consequences are and have been disastrous.

Should people invest in pension funds. My own view is that the fee structures and the effects of salary increases are so serious and deleterious that it is unrealistic to expect pensions to be affordable. They are a sinister way of redistribution of wealth.

241

People would be better off paying the tax and managing their own affairs.

If the government was serious about making people save for the future it should not have such complicated rules about pension funds. It should provide tax relief for any sums that a person designates as savings, without limitation, and charge them tax as they withdraw sums from their savings. That would make the system simpler and would eliminate all the unnecessary rules that serve only to enable managers to redistribute wealth in particular to themselves and their friends and associated in the financial services industry. Instead it supports a system that allows and indeed requires fund manager to participate in the system of pension fund management. This aspect has not altered as a result of the change from final salary schemes to the present pension schemes that depend upon not the final salary but on how much is invested in the fund - the defined contributions schemes. These pension fund managers provide absolutely no benefit whatsoever to the pensioners or their employers or indeed to the government. If the government merely allowed employees to designate what investments or savings were in their pension fund and which were not there would be no need for this massive drain of money from the pension funds to the detriment of pension funds and pensioners without creating any wealth whatsoever.

Of course the argument that will be put forward in favour of and by the fund managers is that they are there to prevent tax fraud. There would be no such fraud if any withdrawal from a pension fund were to be taxed. I cannot understand why the government does not allow people to withdraw whatever they want when they want it from their pension funds and to tax the employee when he does so. It is after all an acceleration of the time when the government will collect the tax, and such amounts would not benefit from the 25% tax free lump sum.

Another argument in favour of the masses of legislation is that the government wants to limit the amount on which tax relief is claimed. That is a specious argument because this kind of problem affects only those with very high incomes and the government has made clear - I shall deal with tax legislation in a later chapter - that they do not want to adversely affect the highly paid. If they really did want to limit the benefits to the very rich they could impose a limit to what can be claimed as a pension contribution. That would still not require policing by fund managers who charge fortunes and redistribute wealth to themselves without creating any.

Finally the government rather paternalistically argues that pension funds should not be allowed to return money to members because they do not want them to become a drain on the state. This is nonsense. The government pays a state pension to most employees when they retire and if an employee wants to withdraw all his employment pension and to live off the state pension that is surely his business. This kind of statement does not sound like a market or capitalist economy but a fascist one.

Pension funds have also been responsible for another insidious change and redistribution of purchasing power in the past 20 years of so. The move away from defined benefits to defined contributions schemes can be supported because of the huge additional contributions that an employer needs to make because of increases in salaries particularly in the final years of employment. Such schemes will of course limit the pensions that future pensioners will earn. That itself has resulted in a large redistribution of purchasing power without any wealth creation in the UK. However another problem with the new style of pension funds is the fact that with pensions now being left to the individuals most have decided not to save at all or to limit the amount that they will save. This has led to a dangerous redistribution of purchasing power as the employer has either held on to the money he would otherwise have contributed to the company's pension fund on behalf of his employees and handed it out to senior managers or in specious fees to professionals or paid it to employees generally. Well these sums have been spent on high living, going abroad mainly it would appear. Employees have felt better off as their salaries have increased. But the money that they have received for doing the same job and not producing any additional wealth or indeed profit for their employers should have been saved and spent when they retired. Well it has not been. It has been spent now, leading to a perception of higher living standards whereas in fact all that has happened has been spending or consuming today what should have been spent or consumed in the future. This the government enthusiastically called "growth" in the economy. It is nothing of the sort. The sums involved are massive.

A recent study into pension contributions advised that contributions of around 10% - 15% of salary should be paid into a pension fund to save for one's retirement. This is a gross understatement. If an employee wants to retire on 2/3rds of final salary his contributions would have to be closer to 30% because of the salary increase problem in later years that I identified earlier. The calculation of 10% - 15% is dependent on highly optimistic calculations of rates of return on the investments of the money in the pension fund. It should be invested in index linked securities so as to provide an inflation proofed pension. The returns on inflation linked British Government gilts is now a very low 1% per annum. My calculations assume that salaries increase at around 2.5% per annum, what the government sees as potential and perpetual growth in the economy.

How did pension funds come to be insolvent. How did the whole industry come to be in such a difficult position. Why can we no longer afford pensions. The answer is interest rates.

Pension funds were able to fund their pensions by buying index linked gilts. These yielded 2.5% above the rate of inflation. Now they do not even give an investor back the principal that he invests. It is nothing to do with longevity.

244

You might say that that is because of market forces. Market forces have no part to play in financial markets. They are dominated by the commissars, who set interest rates and in this way redistribute wealth without any say by the legislature or comment from the press, who do not understand basic maths.

If interest rates were set by the market they would be determined by the amount of borrowers. If there is more demand by borrowers for loans than there are depositors interest rates will rise until there is equilibrium. The demand by borrowers has been so excessive since the 1980s that interest rates would have to increase substantially above 2.5% for inflation linked gilts for there to be equilibrium. Unfortunately that ignores the dead hand of the central bank commissars. They can print money to equal and satisfy the demand by borrowers. This is what they have done.

They have shown an overt preference for borrowers over savers – despite what Thatcher claimed. They can of course be excused since all the increase in GDP over the past 30 years has been funded by borrowing. If interest rates had been increased in accordance with market forces we would not have seen any increase in GDP. But of course, as I explained earlier the increase in GDP is fictitious. The redistributions of wealth however are anything but fictitious. They are real.

The country can easily afford to keep its pensioners. It has enough food, housing and clothing for all. It cannot do so and pay billions to those who do not need it. The government is keeping interest rates low so that property values can be sustained. There is a cost that is being paid and that is reduced pensions for those who have brought up today's borrowers and worked hard for their retirement.

17.   PRIVATISED SOCIALISM IN SPORT AND LEISURE

Sports and leisure have experienced quite a revolution since the 1970s. Sport is popular and not particular elitist. Yet it has experienced perhaps the most radical and widespread redistribution of wealth of any sector of the economy.

In the 1970s Britain had three TV channels. All were terrestrially transmitted.

Now we have close to 100 TV channels all broadcasting via cable networks or satellite. The dominant provider is Sky, run by the Murdoch family. In the US there is CNN, a news provider and Fox. Other countries have their own channels including many in Italy for example controlled by Berlusconi, at one time Prime Minister.

What was the effect upon the economy of the introduction of all these different TV channels. Most will say "choice". Certainly there is a lot of choice, some may say too much choice, because it is often difficult to choose what to watch. New technologies are being introduced so that one can record programmes that clash. At other times there is nothing worth watching.

No analysis of the effects upon the economy were, as far as I am aware undertaken by the introduction of this massive number of new channels. Most operate on the basis of advertising. Many are pay for view channels. All suppliers however have in common a requirement to subscribe not for one particular programme, or for one particular channel but for a multiplicity of channels most of which one has no interest in supporting whatsoever. In short one's choice is limited. If you want to buy a Cable package you may have a choice of two or three bundles, each of which will have many if not mostly channels that you do not want. You have no choice. You pay for all the channels in the bundle or not at all.

When it comes to the sports channels or the movie channels the position is the same. The customer can order a particular sports channel but he cannot be sure that his particular sport will be shown on that channel. Even if he does get it right he is obliged to pay for all the sport in a particular channel. The viewer may have a particular interest in golf. If he does so he is obliged to subscribe for a channel that provides golf, tennis, football, hockey, basketball and tiddlywinks. And who decides how much of the income from the subscriber is paid to the footballers, hockey players and tiddlywinks players. Not the consumer. Not the market. The controllers of the channel do of course. Certainly there are some market forces at play in deciding how much the channel pays but it is certainly not determined by the subscriber. The only market forces that operate are between what one supplier provides and another. It is very limited. The sharing of the proceeds of the money received from the subscribers is determined by bureaucrats, using in most cases not their own money but that of others – the shareholders.

Perhaps the best example of the failure of market forces in determining the pay of performers is in the prize money paid to female and male tennis stars. The pay is the same. Yet the number of fans who watch women's tennis is considerably smaller than the number who watch men's tennis. The matter is determined not by market forces but by dictat, imposed by political correctness.

If the subscriber was allowed to pay per view for particular matches that would be true free market economics at least as regards that particular programme. Instead what we have in TV is privatised socialism. We have to subscribe as a society to a group or collective of channels and a group of sporting events, most of which are of no interest to us whatsoever. Yet we have to pay, no matter how little we view a game of tiddlywinks. The only true free market choices exist in the movie channels when one can pay for a particular movie. The rest are collectively supplied to the consumer.

However in movies the collaboration that is required to make a movie are considerable. Yet the way in which the proceeds are shared amongst the performers and producers is not determined by market forces but by dictat. There are stars who are paid fortunes. There are other actors, probably just as good if not better and who might give a better performance than the stars who would be willing to play the part for a fraction. They are not allowed to do this. As with sports stars the difference between the top and next string of players is very small indeed. Yet the difference in remuneration is massive. This does not reflect market forces.

Only if the consumer is allowed to decide who he would rather watch and at what price would market forces really operate properly. If I was offered a choice of seeing Pavarotti sing for £2,000 or some talented relatively unknown singer from the Royal School of Music for £10 and I chose Pavarotti could I really say that market forces were operating properly. I am not given the choice. The conglomerate who puts the show together decided that it is Pavarotti or nothing. If I cannot afford it I get nothing. Is this really how market forces are meant to operate.

Even if one subscribes to a particular sports channel one may be asked to pay a special fee to view for example a boxing fight that is very popular.

The point I make is that unlike in the case of live viewing of an event, whether it is a sporting event or a musical show, play or opera the individual has some control over what the performers and their acolytes earn. If I went to a football match and was told that the price of a seat to watch Chelsea was £2000 I would turn away. If that was the price that the club have to charge in order to pay their footballers £5mm a year each they would quickly get the message that the viewing public does not consider that they deserve such an income. The viewing public would have control. That is how a capitalist and market economy is supposed to operate.

That is not what happens now in our privatised socialism of the leisure industry. The money that is eventually received by the performers who are the end product of the payments by the customers goes through so many hands that there is little or no control by the consumer.

This is a typical flow of money from consumer to for example a footballer. The footballer is paid from two or three sources. Firstly he is paid by his club. Secondly he is paid for advertising. He may advertise underwear or some car fuel which have nothing to do with football. Thirdly he is paid by sports manufacturers who pay him to wear their equipment. There are other sources of income such as appearance money for particular events but these are not regular sources of income.

The club gets its money not only from the gate where spectators have some control and are operating in a totally free market. It gets most of its money from the Football Association. The FA pays huge fees to the clubs for allowing particular matches to be shown on Sky. The sums involved are massive. I understand that the FA receives around £500mm per annum from Sky for these viewing rights which are paid to the clubs. Sky gets its money back in the collective way described above from the viewers who buy one of their packages. Many of the viewers who buy a Sky package have no interest in football but as in a true socialist state they have no choice. Just as we all pay a license fee to the BBC we have to pay the same fee to Sky if we want one of the sports that we view. It matters not that we may only subscribe to the channel because we want to watch 50 hours of tennis per annum. The bulk of our fee goes to the footballers. Certainly with the BBC license fee the socialism is wider but the principle is the same. If we want one channel we get all the sports and the part of our subscription that is paid to the footballers is outside our control. It is decided by a commissar, working in the private sector, the controller of Sky.

The whole matter is determined by massive conglomerates. The consumer is given little choice. He can take it or leave it. He is not offered less famous players to watch, as for example with a car or a house. The team collaborate to win a match. The sponsors decide who to pay what with other people's money. They pay players who may be 1% better than others 5,000% more than those others. Why? There is no clear reason. It is certainly not market forces that led to this imbalanced in pay between the top players and the next tier.

Sky also gets advertising fees which interrupt all their broadcasts. The advertising world operates to promote particular products. In a later chapter I show that most advertising expenditure in an advanced economy is merely redistribution of wealth without any wealth creation. Nevertheless advertisers pay large sums of money to Sky to advertise their clients' products, many of which have nothing to do with sport. The effects of an advertising campaign are impossible to assess. It could be a complete waste of money. However the client estimates that by paying Sky several millions of pounds his profits will increase. He may get it wrong. He does not really care because he is using the money of his shareholders. It could be a complete waste of money. Yet the money is paid.

Aside from the vast sums that Sky pays to bodies like the FA (it pays to show tennis matches, boxing matches and other sporting events) Sky incurred a massive amount of capital expenditure on its equipment. Likewise the expenditure on laying cables across the world was massive. Laying cables and paying for satellites costs money, lots of it. The cable companies found out early on that their expenditure was excessive and could not be recouped from the subscriptions that subscribers were willing to pay. Many went into insolvency. This resulted in massive sums of money being redistributed into the hands of professionals, sportsmen and women, advertisers and such like. The manufacturers of the cables also make massive profits and were the beneficiaries of these redistributions of wealth.

So the showing of sport on TV involved the collaboration of a vast number of people and businesses, from the manufacturers of the cables to the manufacturers of the satellites, the manufacturers of the TV sets, the groundsman at the clubs, the physiotherapists, the teachers who originally taught the footballers how to play and may have initially spotted the talent. How are they remunerated. The simple answer is – indiscriminately. The cable manufacturer may have gone bust. One or two TV companies may have gone bust, and so will some football clubs. The groundsman is paid a pittance. The school teacher is paid just enough to keep his family. The sportsman earns a vast fortune, and it keeps increasing. Who decides? Is this really market forces?

Somebody was at the other end of this redistribution. In some instances it was the consumer. In some instances it was the banks who lost money that was lent to cable companies or football clubs. It is still too early to tell whether the capital expenditure by Sky and their massive costs that help pay for the huge inflation busting increases in salary and other income from which footballers now benefit was worth it. If it is not then further redistributions of wealth will occur. Certainly Sky is now apparently profitable. However their subscribers who pay on average about £500 per annum in the UK for one of their packages including the sports channels have benefited from the unprecedented increases in nominal value of people's homes and their resultant feelings of affluence. This may not continue indefinitely.

I do not doubt that for example football fans who pay £500 per annum to watch possibly 40 or more football matches consider that they are getting good value for their money. They are able to view matches when their previous alternative was to attend matches live and there was a limit to the number of seats in the ground.

That problem was overcome when the BBC used to screen matches. It is still possible for it to do so. Yet the contract price that Sky was willing to pay was much higher than what the BBC was willing and able to pay. So Sky got the contract. It paid huge sums of money to the FA. Subscribers were satisfied because they were able to view matches live for a small sum in the comfort of their homes. Finally the footballers were able to profit from huge inflation busting pay increases.

Could the BBC have done this? Certainly - possibly by charging to view. They were constrained by the amount of the license fee that was not set for football fans but for all viewers many of whom did not want to watch football. Was that license fee determined by market forces or by bureaucrats?

The huge sums paid to the clubs are however distributed in accordance with the negotiating strength of the clubs. That means that the top clubs get more. Even so we hear that Manchester United, the largest of them all, is insolvent. Other clubs have faced and face insolvency. What are the causes and consequences of insolvency. The causes are simply that income is insufficient to pay the vast wage bills that most clubs have to pay. The consequences are that money has been redistributed into the hands of footballers without any reciprocal creation of wealth. Somebody has to lose. Who will that be. The banks will lose initially. They will recover their losses from the rest of us by charging higher interest rates to all borrowers. That means that the general public have to pay for the redistribution of wealth to the footballers and their acolytes.

Another aspect of the TV programmes these days is the number of new programmes that there are. All report essentially the same news items, doubtless produced by some international agency such as Associated Press at least for international items. The newscasters have become celebrities. They are paid fortunes, considerably more in real terms than their predecessors 30 year ago. Logically if there are more TV channels showing the news it follows that there are fewer viewers per TV channel. It should follow – if the matter is controlled by the market – that the presenters should receive less. Yet they receive more and more. The number who are able to read the news is practically, particularly as education increases, everybody. So there is no limit to the possible supply. Yet we are told that so and so is the best TV presenter and people watch that particular programme because he presents it. Yet they never try using somebody cheaper. Is that really market forces or privatized socialism?

18.   PRIVATE EQUITY AND COMMERCIAL PROPERTY

This has been one of the more inventive ways of transferring wealth in the past 25 years. Private equity is a massive business today. It hardly existed in the 1970s. It did of course exist in one form. However Private Equity today has come to mean and be synonymous with "Leveraged Acquisitions". What do these terms mean and why do they concern us.

They concern us because for the past 25 years they have become the classic way in which vast sums of money have been redistributed to a relatively small number of people. Private Equity and the way in which the industry has operated has been perhaps one of the main reasons why we find ourselves in this financial crisis today.

There is absolutely nothing wrong with the provision of equity capital to businesses that want to expand or even start up. The issuing of shares to private investors is as old as the joint stock company.

This novel branch of the financial services industry started life in the 1980s when the first "leveraged buy outs" were introduced to the market. Leverage simply means borrowing to buy assets – in this case shares. This is a typical example of how a leveraged buyout worked and why it was considered so attractive to investors.

A company with a solid reliable and sustainable business that had probably been in business for a long time and that had no borrowings had a share capital valued at (say) £1mm. The business was therefore worth £1mm. A Private Equity firm would offer to buy the business for its market value - £1mm. The business would have been generating profits of (say) £100,000.

In market language it was said that the business was worth a multiple of 10 (its value was 10 times its profits). Alternatively it was yielding 10% (its profits were 10% of its value).

The PE firm would approach a bank and ask whether the bank was willing to take a risk on the business. Naturally being a solid long established business with a good track record and an end product that was in demand the bank would agree. The bank would offer (say) to lend £500,000 at an interest rate of 6%. That is £30,000 per annum.

If the bank lent 500,000 then the PE firm only required another 500,000 as equity. The business was about to be "financially restructured". Instead of having equity capital of £1mm it now had equity capital of £500,000 and bank loans of £500,000. However its profits were no longer 100,000 but 70,000 because it had to pay interest to the bank.

If the business was valued at a multiple of 10 time and its profits were 70,000 all of a sudden its equity capital was worth 700,000. The PE firm had paid 500,000 of its own money and through a process of fiscal alchemy that 500,000 was worth 700,000. The PE firm had made a profit of 200,000. Not a single additional widget was produced by the business. Its output remained the same, its turnover was unchanged, no additional wealth was produced for the benefit of the economy.

What happened of course is plain as a pikestaff. It was not, as the exponents of these financial restructuring claim "clever". It was not "brilliant", nor were those who invented the process talented. They did not deserve the billions of pounds that they have been able to pocket over these years. It was simple arithmetic. The 100,000 of profits instead of being the return on £1mm of invested capital was formally divided into two tranches. The first tranche was payable to the bank and earned a return of 6%. That meant that the second tranche was entitled to earn 14%. The two together earned an average that was the same as before - 10%.

Yet for reasons that are unclear the PE industry was able to claim that they had enhanced the return of the investment from 10% to 14% and they therefore were entitled to a large part of the additional profit that they had created through their cleverness. These apparently are the kinds of geniuses without whom the country cannot function. They are irreplaceable. They can hold us to ransom. We cannot tax them more because they will leave the country and where would we be without their cleverness. Of course it is all in reality rather trivial. It is not clever at all. It is in fact rather misleading and achieves in reality absolutely nothing except the redistribution of vast sums of money, the price of which has got to be paid by persons unknown.

One minute of consideration even for somebody not proficient at maths will realise that this cleverness is really nonsense. What was previously a business worth 1mm was still worth only 1mm. The fact that the 1mm deserved and earned a return of 10% did not mean that every £1 was at the same risk. The first £1 of the £1mm invested was probably as safe as the monarchy. The chances that the business would fall in value and be worth less than £1 was negligible. The last £1 of the £1mm of total value was a very hazardous part of the £1mm invested. It would only take a day of bad weather, a rise in wages, an electricity failure, some accident on the shop floor for the profits of the business to fall. If the profits were to fall that £1mm of value would fall to (say) 900,000. That meant that the last £100,000 invested was at extremely high risk of being lost. It deserved a very high return to compensate for the risk.

Thus in reality the £1mm of value was tranched. It was made up of several levels or tranches of risk. Each tranche carried with it a correspondingly higher rate of return. Thus for example if we were to divide the £1mm of investment value into 10 tranches it is possible that the first 100,000 was so secure that the appropriate rate of return was only 3%, the next 100,000 was slightly more at risk and therefore perhaps deserved a rate of return of 4%, and so on until we get to the last 100,000 of value which is at such high risk that it deserves a rate of return of (say) 20%. The average of all those rates of return on all the 10 tranches is of course 10%. If the markets have got things right then the appropriate rate of return for the first 500,000 of capital is on average 6% (the same as the bank debt). The appropriate rate of return on the last 500,000 of capital is probably 14%.

Viewed in this way the original capital structure, although nominally called equity capital was in reality made up of debt type capital worthy of a return of only 6% and real equity capital worth a return of 14%. In short the business was properly valued.

Yet for many years the PE industry flourished with massive bonuses being earned and paid from leveraging up existing businesses. Not a single additional grain of wheat or rice was grown, not a single additional shirt was made. Yet the PE members grew fabulously wealthy by simply reclassifying what was in reality senior debt (in terms of risk) but was nominally called equity capital into actual senior debt and maintaining the right return on the equity capital.

The size of deals that were done were massive, billions were spent releveraging businesses and formally reclassifying the capital of a business without changing the risk parameters or the proper returns at all. The returns on equity were allegedly enhanced. This was however done by means of increasing the risk to what was called equity. Previously safe equity was converted into high risk equity for which a higher return was required yet the consequent higher risk was ignored. The apparently higher rates of return were attributed to the "cleverness" and "brilliance" and "brightness" of these people in the city. It was nothing of the sort.

If the people in PE understood what they were doing then they were cheating. It was nothing more than legalized theft. Yet they now pretend that they create wealth and that the country cannot do without them. They are the mainstay of the British economy.

If they did not understand what they were doing then they were ignorant. The important point is that they did not deserve the fabulous remunerations that they received. They profited enormously by redistributing wealth to themselves. Somebody had to be at the other end of the transaction. Somebody else had to be making losses. The loss makers as is normal in the city are ordinary investors or risk takers. It is the pension funds who saw value flow out of their investments into the hands of the PE partners. The pension and other fund managers thought that they had been given a better return than they previously had. In fact they had indeed been handed a better return but they had been handed a correspondingly higher risk that made their return appropriate. That did not stop the PE firms from getting generally 20% of the increase in value. The pension and other fund managers (you and I) were consequently poorer by the amount of money that had flowed into the hands of the PE firms. Redistribution in a massive scale had occurred and continues to occur.

This kind of advantage from leveraging soon came to be understood and whenever a company was up for sale it first considered re-leveraging so as to increase the price. The old game of merely leveraging the purchase price was no longer possible in many cases. However such was the reputation of these "geniuses" that huge funds were entrusted to their hands and they continued to buy companies in the belief or delusion that they could turn water into wine. They had after all the Midas touch. Failures started to occur. Large buyouts such as Magnet, Le Meridien and EMI proved to be worth less than perceived. Losses were incurred but the PE partners did not suffer. The losses that were incurred were suffered by the fund managers who manage money entrusted to them by you and I. Pension fund suffered.

The PE industry is nowadays just another form of the Mergers and Acquisition business except that Mergers and Acquisitions are generally between trade buyers seeking to consolidate their businesses whereas the PE industry buys anything that they think is undervalued. Well that is a betting game. You will win some and lose some. It is no longer as simple and it was originally in the 1980s.

The same happened to commercial property. Commercial property in the UK is rented to businesses who pay a rent to the landlord. The rent, for many years, had been around 7% of the capital cost of the property. A valuer's job was easy. He would merely take the rent, multiply it by 100 and divide by 7. The result was the value of the property.

In the UK property leases are generally for 25 years. All leases allow the rent to increase with market prices but not to fall. Because rents do in fact fall it is possible that a new lease will have a rent that is considerably lower than an older lease.

There have been many property booms in the UK and a major collapse occurred in the late 1970s. Many investors went into insolvency. One of the main reasons for their insolvency was that they were not able to borrow at fixed rates of interest. Thus when inflation took off in 1973 interest rates started to rise but rents did not increase. Landlords who had borrowed were squeezed and soon were unable to pay the bank loans. The results were inevitable.

Fixed rates of interest through what came to be known as the interest rate swap had not been invented. The first swap was done in 1980.

Following the introduction of fixed rate borrowings some financiers came to realise that a 25 year lease was a series of receivables that had a discounted present value independent of the demand and supply of property. It mattered not if the property on which the lease had been granted was desirable, well located or not. The lease itself had a value that was at least equal to the discounted present value of the payments using the discount rate appropriate to the tenant.

Unfortunately the valuers had not yet come to terms with the brave new world of fixed interest borrowing. They continued to value properties as if interest rates were variable. Because demand for property had fallen as evidenced by the falling rents they concluded arbitrarily that appropriate yields were closer to 8% or even 10% depending on the location. City financiers valued the leases on a totally different basis, namely on the basis that the lease was an annuity of receivables from the tenant, who in many cases was a well known and rated company, sometimes it was the British government. They discounted the rents at the interest rate appropriate to the tenant - the rate at which the tenant could borrow. The result was that in many cases the value of the lease - valued in this way - was more than the value of the property placed upon it by valuers.

Financiers were therefore able to borrow on security of the lease 100% of the value of the lease, which meant that their leverage (borrowings) were more than the price that a buyer had to pay for the property. So the property market in the early 1990s was flooded with buyers who provided no money for the properties. The whole purchase price and indeed more in some instances, was provided by the Bank.

This enabled some property "magnates" to become fabulously wealthy without risking a penny. Many did not have a penny to risk. This particular part of the investment activity delivered not a single additional £ of new wealth to the economy. Secondary properties were bought and sold in this way. Those who profited did so at the expense of the rest of us. The properties were sold at the wrong value. Those who owned them beforehand - pension and other funds - lost money, and the investors made it.

19.   INTEREST RATES, INFLATION AND WEALTH CREATION OR REDISTRIBUTION

Listen to any business programme and it is likely that the discussion will directly or indirectly involve consideration of what the monetary authorities are going to do with interest rates.

Interest rates drive financial markets. When interest rates fall bond prices rise, because the income from bonds is fixed and the price therefore rises to reflect the new lower rate of return. When interest rates rise the opposite happens. It is the same with a real estate investment where the rental income is fixed. As the yield (ratio of rent to property value) on real estate rises, the value of the property falls.

Short term interest rates alone are controlled by the central bankers – the Fed in the US, MPC in London and ECB in the Euro zone. These committees are made up of unelected bureaucrats appointed by politicians and paid directly or indirectly by the government.

The manipulation of interest rates is the most direct and overt way in which governments directly interfere with market forces and carry out regular redistributions of wealth. Although these commissars only have control of short term interest rates their words and actions influence the whole market.

The bond market includes not only short term bonds, the interest rates for which are set by these committees but long terms bonds up to 30 years or more. The interest rates for these bonds are not set by these committees but theoretically by markets. However the long term interest rates reflect the market's views of what these committees will do in the future – yes 30 years into the future. All interest rates are therefore directly or indirectly influenced by the decisions of these unelected bureaucrats.

When the US went to war against Britain it did so because the US states were not prepared to tolerate taxation without representation. Taxation is – we all agree – to a large extent the redistribution of wealth.

The parliament of England had as one of its main tasks, the control over taxation. Parliament – or the people – alone can decide how much to tax, how much wealth to redistribute. The process is tortuous. It is subject to scrutiny in parliament and the press. Elections are won or lost and governments can be thrown out because of their taxation policies.

Yet the redistribution of wealth in far larger sums than is ever possible through the process of taxation, is carried out by stealth by unelected bureaucrats without anybody complaining through the central banking committees. Nobody questions what right these commissars have to take purchasing power from one sector of the economy and give it to another.

It is quite probably unconstitutional. Nobody to date has considered it worth challenging in the courts.

Yet this is what happens every month in all countries that have a central bank.

When interest rates are reduced money is redistributed from pensioners and savers who take a drop in their savings and future income to borrowers who receive a reduction in their borrowing costs. Nobody questions why the government permits this to happen. The matter of redistribution of wealth receives scant comment in the press as such, except for the occasional cursory remark that savers will get less as a result of interest rate reductions.

The interest rate reductions are now so severe that borrowers receive a negative real return on their money. In short they pay the borrowers – banks and government in most cases – to take their money. This is not a deal that any sane saver will carry out, yet that is what is now happening.

The stock market is even more sensitive to interest rate changes than the bond market. When interest rates fall stock prices increase simply because they are an alternative investment to bonds and if the return on bonds has fallen it is no longer necessary to give investors in stocks the same return as before. Stock prices therefore rise accordingly. Certain companies have borrowings and if their cost of borrowing falls then their profits increase. Other companies involved in retailing will sell more goods because consumers who have borrowings will have more disposable income as a result of the reduced interest rates.

That deals with the legality of wealth redistribution through interest rate manipulation.

What about the policy. Is it economically viable to manipulate interest rates in this way. Is it sensible economic management. Should the matter be left to market forces, and if so why do governments all over the world refuse to do so.

I have explained in the chapter on borrowing why governments keep interest rates low. Borrowing for the past 30 to 40 years kept advanced economies apparently growing, when in fact there was no basis for any real economic growth. Now the music has stopped and governments want to keep it playing. The only thing that they can do is reduce interest rates to allow borrowers more capacity to borrow. It might work for some time but sooner or later the borrowing must stop, even if interest rates are at zero.

Of course we all grow old sooner or later and have to rely upon our savings and if savers have had their returns depleted the expenditure by pensioners will reduce materially so the consequences of this wealth redistribution is temporary relief. Sooner of later one has to pay the piper.

Interest rates are said to be a way of controlling inflation and that is the basis for the manipulation of interest rates. Some central bankers are also responsible for unemployment and they consider that reducing interest rates reduces unemployment.

Interest rates have an important connection with the rate of inflation but it is doubtful that inflation can be controlled by interest rates. The relationship between interest rates and inflation can be seen when examining the rates of interest of different countries with different rates of inflation. Generally the short term rate of interest is equal to the existing rate of inflation in a particular country plus 1% or so. Inflation erodes the value of any monetary investment. The rate of interest on any investment should therefore compensate the investor for such erosion in value and provide him with a real rate of return. Thus if the rate of inflation is 7% as it is for example in India the short term rate of interest is around 9%. In the UK when inflation was around 3% short term rates of interest were around 4%. That at any rate is the theory.

This kind of interest rates structure ensures that the investor or saver is not prejudiced by the erosion in his capital as a result of inflation.

In reality Japan which has suffered from too much deflation cannot create inflation no matter how low its interest rates are. It creates new money and has had interest rates of around zero percent for many decades. Yet it cannot create inflation. The UK and US have interest rates that are below the rate of inflation. Yet there is no general inflation. So much for the alleged control of inflation. Of course there has been massive inflation in real estate and the stock markets. These have been caused by the printing of money by commercial banks, which I explained in an earlier chapter. Interest rates play very little part in this kind of inflation.

Unfortunately the impact of taxation cannot be ignored in these deliberations. If the rate of inflation was 3% and the rate of interest was 4% in theory and so long as the investor does not have to pay tax he will receive a real rate of return of 1%.

If the investor is liable to tax he will pay tax – at around 20% if he is a UK basic rate taxpayer – on the whole of his income. His after tax return will therefore be 80% X 4% = 3.2%, so that his real after tax return is only 0.2%.

The borrower is in the corresponding position. The borrower who borrows for the purposes of his business will pay a rate of interest of 4% (he might have to pay a margin on top of that) and will get tax relief at 20% (or perhaps 30%). His after tax cost of borrowing will be 3.2%. Since the loan that he receives is depreciating in value by 3% his real cost of borrowing is only 0.2%.

What is an appropriate rate of real return on savings? This can be seen by looking at interest rates at a time when there was no inflation. One can also look at index linked gilts which were introduced in the 1970s when inflation in the UK was approaching 30% per annum. The appropriate real rate of risk free return was around 2.5% - 3% per annum. This compares with the current nominal rate of return of 0.5% which when one adjusts for the rate of inflation of around 2.5% means that savers are paying around 2% per annum to the bank for keeping and using their money.

Borrowers of course receive the corresponding benefit of these record low rates of interest. A borrower who is able to borrow at 0.5% is effect is being paid 2% per annum to borrow money in real terms.

If interest rates were intended to compensate savers for the decline in the value of their savings it is clear that real rates of interest (nominal rate less the rate of inflation) should be around 2.5% to 3%.

If governments were serious in wanting to deal with inflation they would ensure that real interest rates were sustained at a level that makes inflation not worth while.

Milton Friedman the Nobel Prize winning economist of the 1970s advocated that most borrowing should be inflation linked. He was looking at the matter from the point of view of savers. In that way the erosion in the value of savings by inflation would be automatically compensated by borrowers. He also held the view that high interest rates were the result of inflation and not the antidote to it. That at least was what he said. He appeared to look at the position of borrowing and lending from the lender's point of view.

If Friedman's views were followed there would be no need for the commissars to decide on how much wealth to redistribute without any act of parliament every month.

The rate of interest would be fixed, possibly by parliament from time to time. It will be a real rate of interest and will change annually with the rate of inflation.

The commissars however say that their job is not to deal with inflation retrospectively but to anticipate the rate of inflation. This is of course nonsense because their job is always reactive. They wait for the numbers and then they react by changing interest rates.

Recently the trend has been to reduce interest rates. Hence the negative real rates of interest.

Anybody reading of the financial news anywhere in the world will quickly come to realize that the knee jerk reaction to an economic downturn is lower interest rates. Central bankers have been lowering interest rates for some time now until they have reached the levels they are at today.

This extraordinary situation is brought about because governments consider that borrowing is the source of wealth creation. This is a mistake. Borrowing creates a bulge in expenditure that sooner or later stops or has to be reversed. I deal with this in an earlier chapter. It is a temporary and illusory increase in GDP. However the commissars are convinced that increased borrowing will result in increased GDP and greater wealth for all of us and that this can carry on indefinitely.

The government of course advocates not consumer borrowing but greater borrowing by businesses, who they say will invest and create more jobs and more wealth and therefore more prosperity. Yet most borrowing is from people buying real estate which for the reasons given in earlier chapters gives rise to additional new money being created and inflation in property prices.

The commissars seem unconcerned about inflation in real estate. This is rather puzzling since inflation in real estate is considerably greater than inflation in the price of foodstuffs. They seem to think that inflation in the price of a house means an increase in people's wealth. This is of course nonsense unless we are going to sell our homes and live in tents. Homes have a use value and their nominal value is merely of value for information purposes. The real use value of homes is the same as it was 100 years ago.

Why do politicians and economists believe that lowering interest rates will give rise to greater economic activity. They believe this principle so strongly that they consider that lowering interest rates will cure unemployment. Lower interest rates, so the logic goes, will cause a businessman to build that factory that he could not afford to build before. He will hire people to build those goods that people did not have before. The result would be that everybody would be wealthier. This is nonsense.

I have never come across a situation in which a business has declined to expand a plant, factory or other income producing and labour employing asset because interest rates are too high. The interest rates in question are of course always real interest rates because if there is inflation the goods produced will

267

increase in nominal value. The real rate of interest that a credit worthy business normally had to pay on its borrowing was around 3%. Lowering it to a rate of around 1% will hardly make a project more viable because investors normally require rates of return of around 20% on their equity investments. Such a reduction in interest rates could easily be offset by incidental costs, exchange rate differences or inflation in some part of the cost of the proposed business including labour costs and the price of energy. Businesses are hardly likely to be deterred by interest rates of 3% and a reduction of 2% in borrowing costs is unlikely to make a project viable when it was not viable before.

There is one kind of asset that is very sensitive to interest rate changes and that is real estate. Lowering interest rates could make a property development viable when it was not viable before. However that is not what has tended to happen.

Lowering interest rates for real estate borrowing usually results in property prices increasing. That would suggest that higher interest rates kept real estate values lower. When interest rates are higher the rental cost is higher or alternatively the profit made by the seller is lower. In short real estate gets built if there is a need. Interest rates merely affect the price. No new or additional activity is created.

When interest rates are reduced there is no doubt that purchasing power is transferred from saver to borrower. The implication is that certain kind of spending is better than other kinds of spending. Certain kinds of spending lead to economic activity whereas certain kinds of spending do not.

The implication is that spending by savers – which will of course fall if interest rates are reduced – does not lead to economic growth whereas spending by borrowers leads to economic growth. There is no basis for this assumption.

There is a basis for believing that borrowers are more likely to spend all the additional income they receive as a result of reduced interest rates whereas very wealthy savers are likely to merely save any interest that they earn and therefore will not miss the reduced income. That is the only justification for reducing interest rates. However it does affect indigent savers as well as the very wealthy. Taxing the wealthy might be far fairer. And of course there is nothing to say that the borrower who benefits from a reduction in interest rates will not use the money to repay his loans or to save it.

Subject to that assumption there is nothing to suggest that reducing interest rates will result in additional economic activity. If an entrepreneur has an idea that is viable it will be viable at 3% interest rates or at 0.5%. No businessman deals with such small margins and declines to build something because real interest rates are too high.

Real economic activity requires hard work, a genuinely good product that pays for itself. There are few examples of such new forms of economic activity. The belief that transferring purchasing power from one sector of the population to another through the increase or reduction in interest rates will increase economic activity is naïve.

20.   EDUCATION

When Tony Blair was elected UK British Prime Minister in 1997 he declared that he had 3 priorities "Education, education and education". He was roundly praised for focusing on education. Education, it is widely believed - and this is true of underdeveloped countries perhaps more than developed ones - is the solution to all economic problems. If only we were better educated the problems of poverty from which we suffer both in the developed and underdeveloped world would not occur. Most importantly we believe, as do all the experts, employers, business people, journalists, politicians that education will make us all wealthier.

This belief is misguided at least of education as we know it. It is based on the superficial evidence that in developed societies those who are educated get paid more than those who are not. It is true that we pay people and promote people in jobs on the basis of their education. We often do not pay people for doing harder or more useful jobs. Neither do we pay them on the basis of market forces. We pay people according to the amount of formal qualifications that they possess at least when they start work. That is a form of competition but it is not market forces as we know them. It is an artificial test of limited ability and skills.

This principle is at odds with the economic principle that the price (for labour) depends upon the supply and demand for such labour. No matter how many candidates there are for a job, no matter how overprovided the labour force is the professions and those who work in offices continue to get paid more and more than those without formal qualifications. It is as if you can never be too educated. It is as if the demand for educated people is unlimited.

But what do we mean by education. Do we mean simply learning facts? Do we mean learning a trade for example? Do we mean that learning how to be a carpenter, mechanic or builder is education? It is of course in the true sense but most do not regard learning a trade to be education. Education – at least in the UK - is perceived to constitute solely academic learning. Many other types of learning are derided as being useless. We ridicule many of the more unusual degrees that are around today.

To most people, education means becoming a doctor or a lawyer, or perhaps an accountant or architect. Perhaps even an engineer or a chemist receives what is thought of as education. Education means having a profession. Learning how to teach and becoming a teacher is also considered to be education. In general most people consider that those of us who work in offices are educated, whereas those who work outside are not. Farmers can of course go to college these days even though they do not seem to be able to make the vegetables grow any quicker than their fathers who did not have the benefit of a classroom education.

The Amish do not consider education beyond the basic level important. They have all the skills necessary for living. Yet despite the evidence we continue to persist with our belief in education as being the source of all good and the solution to all economic problems.

Education can of course prepare us for nothing in particular as for example an education in classical languages. Those with classics degrees get to work in offices. What else are they able to do? Yet they tend to get highly paid jobs. Many might say that studying the classics is a sport but unlike learning bridge or tennis it is considered to be education.

Miners perhaps perform one of the hardest physical jobs around. Yet they are not paid more than for example lawyers who work in warm offices with all the comforts of home and do little if any, hard physical work. Doubtless they will say that they suffer great mental stresses but it is not clear why mental stress – assuming it happens – is as persistent or worse than the undoubted physical stresses or working in a mine and the mental stress that accompanies the relative poverty associated with that job. The fact is that our society is set up in such a way that those who have greatest knowledge about how the system that allocates wealth works get paid the most. Lawyers and accountants know how the system works. Their jobs are backed by the coercive powers of the state. Lawyers create the rules of society. The rules include two very powerful weapons, the rules that decide how your liberty is to be taken from you and the rules that decide how your money is to be redistributed either privately or through the tax system. Accountants are very familiar with the forms of redistribution of wealth through taxation and are a necessary if we are to avoid having our wealth redistributed by the state. In many instances the employment of an accountant is compulsory.

In a modern economy the goods and services that we need and want can be provided by a very small proportion of the population. The rest therefore have to find a way of getting their share of these goods and services. So a farmer who clearly produces goods that we need is compelled to fill in various forms to ensure that what he delivers to the consumer is of a certain standard. He is prevented by more and more bureaucratic rules from doing certain things and has to undertake many activities if he is to employ others to help him. These other activities do not result in more food being produced. These standards and other rules are devised by educated people, who purport to be improving the standards of what we consume and therefore protect us. They have however the ability to produce and invent regulations that protect us against dangers that are utterly fanciful and ridiculous. Their regulations could miss the target or perhaps be entirely counter productive.

If the farmer was to break one of these rules he would face the full force of the law and in order to avoid pitfalls he has to share his produce with lawyers, accountants, veterinary surgeons, government inspectors and a whole army of officials whose sole interest of course is purportedly in enhancing production of good quality goods for our tables. In reality the number of rules and regulations that they could invent are practically endless.

The army of educated people all form part of a production line that ends with the end product, which may be coal or oil, it may be a car or a vegetable. It may be a loaf of bread or an egg. The real difficult economic question is how are those in the production line to share in the proceeds of sale of this end product.

The matter is not decided by market forces. If it were then only those whose labour was indispensible to the production of the end product would be rewarded. Many are involved in the production process because of legislation backed by the coercive powers of the state. The law is full of restrictive practices. It is not possible to practice law unless you are approved, no matter what the consumer wants. Others like advertisers and marketing consultants are involved in the production process by persuasion. They may be entirely useless to the production of the end product but so long as they are perceived to be useful they will be rewarded. How much is only to a limited extent determined by market forces. Advertising is often an unnecessary burden because it is a cost that is the result of competition by suppliers. One supplier hires an advertiser and spends lots of money on an advertising campaign. The other retaliates and the position returns to what it was ante. Yet the two have incurred an unnecessary expense which merely cuts those involved in the advertising in for a share of the proceeds from sale of the end product.

How does one determine how much is to be paid from the process of sale of the tomatoes or cars to advertisers, accountants and lawyers. The matter is not determined by the buyer of these goods. It is determined by the lawyers and advertisers who set a price and compete amongst themselves for business. So long as one advertiser is cheaper than another the cheaper one will get the business.

But it is not as easy as that. The more expensive advertiser might claim that he does a better job, something that cannot be determined objectively. Market forces can operate in an opposite direction. One advertiser might increase his charges. The others will follow. Why not?

The real point is that nobody calculates the relative worth of the various parties who participate in the production of the end product. Each constituent sets its own market price. Relative contributory value does not enter into the calculation. This is not how market forces are meant to operate. Market forces depend upon an assessment of the various buyers of the intrinsic value of the particular item that they are buying. It requires proper understanding of relative value. No such assessment takes place in a complex production line in which various persons are involved.

One must sympathise with the problems faced by the entrepreneur. He has to determine how much to share the proceeds from sale of his goods. He has no way of assessing relative value except on the basis of the most powerful or most persuasive. Educated people are often more persuasive or are backed by the coercive powers of the state. The entrepreneur often has no choice but to pay the better educated more than the uneducated not because of their intrinsic worth but because of their powers.

The end result is that the proceeds of sale of tomatoes is distributed not in accordance with any sensible perception of value either by the farmer or the consumer but of the education of the various parties involved in the production process.

Of course when, as in the case of accountants who prepare tax returns or lawyers who are employed to obtain licenses or such like, the client is coerced into paying as much as possible. He has no choice. He has to pay and so long as the profession maintains its position their rates of pay will be excessively high and will not reflect true value either as placed on them by the producer who hires the accountants or the eventual consumer of the end product.

There are in effect two economies. One is the real economy that produces all the goods and services that the consumers need. Then there is the redistributive economy which involves people constantly striving to play a part, whether it is a necessary part or not in those goods and services that are produced by the real economy. The real economy works only when necessary and its output determines and controls the amount of work and workers that are required. The redistributive economy has the potential to work for 24 hours a day 7 days a week. It is constantly trying to play a part in the real economy. It insinuates itself into various processes sometimes by persuasion and at other times with the help of the legislature. It also spends a lot of time trying to claim for itself the lion's share of the real economy.

Education provides the backbone of and ability for those who participate in the redistributive economy to perform. It enables its members to devise endless bureaucratic and frequently useless techniques and uses the art of persuasion to obtain a position for themselves when the proceeds of sale of the end product are being distributed. Education enables people to analyse situations, anticipate dangers that are non-existent and to be persuasive. Most of all education provides people with the ability to be articulate. CEOs of large organizations and politicians tend to have that in common. They are articulate and they are assessed on that particular feature that is the by-product of all education. This skill enables the educated classes to persuade entrepreneurs and industrialists that their skills are required.

Some education does of course provide people with skills that are required by consumers. Doctors and teachers and those involved in technical work are an example. Those who do provide their learned skills to serve the consumer are however very small in number relative to the army who work in offices and provide services to producers.

Markets really operate only when the consumer determines the value of the goods he is purchasing based upon proper information. When a producer or entrepreneur has to pay for the constituent elements involved in producing the end product he makes choices as to how to distribute his costs. There is a constant tension between those involved in the production process for getting a larger and larger share of the sale proceeds of the end product and the winners are invariably those who are able to make their case best. These tend to be the more educated people. The reason is that the producer is usually not in a position to gainsay what they advise.

Educated people are assisted in their objective of getting a larger share of the economic cake by mantras such as that "education is essential". When this is repeated more and more often it becomes received wisdom and the entrepreneur finds himself accepting that mantra because "everybody knows that".

As more and more people get educated economic theory states that their pay should fall – in according with the principle of supply and demand. As there are more and more people able to do the office work they should therefore be paid less and less. Our educated masses have found ways around that problem. Firstly for practical purposes the amount of work that an office worker can produce is unlimited. Why? Because what he does is not governed simply by the necessity to produce goods or services. There is no objective standard that says "you have produced what you set out to produce and have therefore earned your fee". The office worker is constantly engaged in trying to get as much money from the rest of us as possible. He is engaged in this battle with other office workers. It is a 24 hour a day task. He creates unnecessary work and persuades the real producer to pay for it, or alternatively the producer is coerced into paying by law. He tries to take as much as possible from others and to prevent others also working in office from taking from him. The taking is of course subtle and does not involve anything so murky as holding up a bank. It takes place in one of the ways money is redistributed that I described throughout this book. Forms are filled in, meetings are held about the most ridiculous things. Papers on any number of irrelevant topics are circulated for discussion. Staff are appraised subjectively and psycho-analysed at length. Health and Safety rules are introduced and considered. Rules are introduced for any number of purposes none of which have anything to do with work. Conferences and staff training meetings are held off site. New systems are introduced that are no better than the ones that they replaced and staff and consultants are required to be trained to operate them. There is no evidence that this has any effect on the end product. All that is necessary however is that the real producer believes that it does so, or perhaps he does not care because it is not his money that is being spent but that of the shareholders. Of course if the person who pays the bills is himself an office worker of that kind little persuasion is necessary. The process is self fulfilling.

Dangers of computer hacking or frauds are anticipated in the most fanciful way. Analysis of adverse consequences are predicted in countless numbers of ways. The possibilities are endless.

The computer - the machine in the office that was meant to make life easier for all of us and to reduce the number of hours spent in the office - did not result in less hours being worked. It resulted in more and more as the PC has an unlimited scope for producing paperwork, introducing and fighting viruses and hacking, advertising, disseminating information, requesting more and more information from more and more people. I could go on. The evidence is all too clear.

The principle that we need more and more education is misguided. A visit to India will immediately make this clear. Adverts are to be seen everywhere offering education of all sorts. India turns out hundreds of thousands of well educated people every year. China is the same. Yet many of these highly qualified people cannot get jobs because their skills are not what is required. The needs of the real economy are very evident. The infrastructure is crumbling. The streets are covered with ordure. The real need is for unskilled workers to be organized to clean and repair the infrastructure. Nobody will do it. All want comfortable jobs working in offices at high pay. That is what they were promised.

If all people were to go to university and to work in offices and be unwilling to work the land or the trains and maintain the infrastructure and clean, what would we do. We would live in chaos. Well we have found ways of making sure that the avowed intention of governments to make us all educated and all of us to participate in the fruits of a prosperous economy where all work in comfortable offices pushing around useless pieces of paper is only achieved by very few. There are of course only limited places at Universities. That limits those who can attend. Although the Internet should make it possible for people to attend lectures at Oxford or Cambridge from their homes only a select few are allowed to attend and to go there. In addition we have increased consistently the fees payable for attending university.

Before the introduction of compulsory education being educated was synonymous with being literate. It was a sign of superiority. Now most people can read but we have not abandoned the view of superiority. We have merely raised the bar. Those of us who go to university are better people, superior people than carpenters and mechanics or bus drivers. They are "bright", and "smart", so they must be better. That is why they are paid more. Never mind that they in most cases do a useless job and nobody will notice if they went on strike.

Some administrative work in offices is to a limited extent necessary if communities are to be organised to co-operate in the production of goods and services. It is essential to account for profits and losses - a by-product and cost of using money incidentally which was necessary in a simple barter economy. Property had to be registered and legal work had to be done to protect ownership of property. However the proliferation of educated people now working in offices has resulted in not only useless but time wasting activities. There is moreover a complete imbalance in the economy.

As the children of those who previously worked in factories and fields now work in offices they get paid more and more. They demand and get more and more because they are educated. Whether what they do is worthwhile is irrelevant. Thus the cost of producing the goods and services increases since these office workers are part of the production line that ends with the farm and factory produce. This leads to losses. The balance is not wrong. If it is necessary to employ people in offices doing useless work they should be paid a very small amount, certainly not more than their parents earned on the production line.

Educated people take advantage of particular events and see opportunities that other cannot see. Nowadays it is security that has provided the educated classes with unlimited opportunities.

Security rituals are carried out to the annoyance and at the cost in time of their customers. Bureaucratic documentation that gets longer and longer take place constantly. It is perfectly possible to have a legal document drafted on 10 pages. Yet as there are more and more lawyers the documents get longer and longer. Are they better? Are they less likely to result in litigation and disputes. Nothing of the sort. The work expands to fill the time available.

The quality of people working in offices is now poorer than it was 50 years ago. Many do not know what to do or why they are doing it. They cannot deal with unusual situations. Rules proliferate on the basis of the "why don't we" or the "because we can" approach. Educated people sit around anticipating ways in which problems that have never arisen could arise and they devise complicated ways of preventing that which never needs to be prevented. Indeed the antidotes to many perceived problems whether these are in "health and safety" or "data protection" are far worse and ubiquitous than the disease.

The army of people working in offices dealing with security issues in order to protect us against fraud probably costs substantially more than the money that will be lost through the frauds. The matter could be overcome with insurance which would be far cheaper. Yet we have "bright" and "smart" and "educated" people who are there to protect us. Of course the truth is very different. They are there merely to participate in the fruits of the economy, not to make the cake any larger. And they are frequently backed by legislation to force us to comply with their paternalistic time wasting.

That is the effect of modern education.

One often hears people mentioning that some person - usually a child - is "bright". Brightness is considered to be desirable. Of course brightness would be selected rather than dullness if one were given a choice. However it is unclear why a person who is "bright" is better and more desirable than one who is strong or fast or has a good voice. Bright is the ultimate accolade. This is a unitary or totalitarian education system. Only one type of person is worthy and we should all aspire to be like that. We should all aspire to be professionals and to work in offices. That is our education system today in Britain. Those who have mechanical skills are despised. Good cleaners are doing a worthless job. They are paid less. They are condemned to being regarded as inferior.

That is the kind of education system that we encourage. If possible it is considered to be a success if all were to work in offices and to have professional qualifications. Such an economic system would be a disaster. Yet the nonsense of having a system the success of which would be a disaster and that can only really succeed if most fail to achieve the desired goals is never even questioned. Yet that is the system to which we aspire. Parents all want their children to become professional unless they are not "bright" in which case they are condemned to second place for ever.

Strangely economic principles seem to go out of the window in these considerations. Economic theory is that if there are many doctors and few electricians then electricians will get paid more than doctors. Somehow the system is manipulated so as to defeat this economic principle, and it is manipulated by those who claim to support free market economics.

If the free market was allowed to decide these matters there would be a balance and there would be a time when electricians and brick layers were paid more than doctors and investment bankers. I consider the way in which the system is manipulated elsewhere in this book.

Educated people have found ways of defeating market forces. Power is everything. They are able to articulate policies that are designed for their own benefit and make them look as if they are doing something for the benefit of the rest of us. Bankers argue very cogently that their bonuses should be larger for the benefit of the country, not themselves. Higher rates of tax are argued down on the basis that less tax will be collected. It makes them sound as if they want to pay more tax rather than less.

The art of dissembling is learnt at colleges of higher education. Public speaking is highly valued. Indeed our national and business leaders all have to be good at it. It does not matter so much if they are good at running a business. If they are articulate and can speak well publicly they are admired and regarded highly by analysts and journalists and that is what matters. That is what determines the amount of their pay.

It is educated people who devised the corporate system that we have today in which the real owners of public companies are not allowed to vote. It is educated people who set up the system that provides that only the fund managers can vote the shares of a company that was purchased with the money of a pensioner. It is those same educated people who argued that allowing trade union bosses to vote all the votes of their members instead of asking the members themselves was wrong. It is educated people who argue that trade unions and restrictive practices for blue collar labourers is wrong but for lawyers and accountants it is right. Inconsistencies in principles such as these abound. Yet the arguments are made so cogently and so articulately that the inconsistencies are ignored.

There is no reason why an incompetent lawyer should be paid more than a good cleaner or taxi driver. Yet that is the system that we have devised. Even if there are scores of qualified lawyers waiting for a job the rate of pay for lawyers does not fall. They have unlimited ability to introduce new laws and regulations through their friends in parliament.

The number of laws does not reduce, it keeps increasing. The number of lawyers will therefore continue to increase. Yet no legal work produces a single additional grain of wheat or an additional car off the production line.

Market theory should intervene to pay more for those activities that are in greatest demand. Yet it does not out of homage to the God of education, who must not be upset at any cost.

The legal profession manages to keep qualified lawyers out of work by simply refusing to allow them to practice. Why? For the good of the rest of us of course. They do so to protect us. It is better for a litigant to be denied justice than for him to be assisted by an ""untrained" lawyer who has passed his exams but cannot get a job with a law firm for the requisite training period.

Reading the press I am often struck by the number of lawyers who are referred to as "top lawyers". It is the same with medical consultants. One's friends who are receiving treatment for some serious ailment are always treated by the "top man" in the field. It is of course nonsense but it shows ignorance of real worth and without knowledge of actual worth it is impossible to measure market value.

Professionals often charge by the hour and once one hires a professional one has no control over the number of hours that he charges.

There is too much education. It is too totalitarian. There is no substitute for on the job training – apprenticeships. That should work for doctors, lawyers and accountants as it should for skilled craftsmen. More importantly there is no justification whatsoever for paying educated people more than formally uneducated ones just because they are educated. The matter should be controlled by market forces. It is not.

Unfortunately demand and supply for personnel tends to be very personal and biased. The formally educated employer, using the money that belongs not to him but to his shareholders who do not get a say in the matter, thinks he is a good and worthy person and so he hires persons like himself. It is time to break the habit and to revert to market forces. People will be paid more or less demanding on demand and supply for their labour. Their education qualifications should not determine how much they earn. Only their usefulness.

So the foundation for the belief that education will cure our economic problems is based upon the principle that because professionals are able to redistribute more wealth to themselves, by whatever means, we would all be better off if we all became professionals, and we do so through education.

It is a misguided principle. Any principle the success of which leads to by economic collapse must be wrong. If we all worked in offices there would be no food to eat and nobody to clean the streets.

Education has a use value. It should not be overrated. Those who work in offices are parasitic upon those who work in fields and factories. If there are not enough of the latter the former would starve.

Education became of use as a means to enable those whose labour was no longer required because of the introduction of machines to participate in the proceeds of sale of real goods through persuasion. It enabled those who would otherwise be unemployed to re-enter the production line. The process was so successful that those who were educated found ways of not only getting paid what their fore fathers would have earned in the factories and fields but far more. They achieved this unfair remuneration by virtue of their knowledge which was superior to that of the farmer and entrepreneur. Whilst their numbers were small the cost of employing the educated classes was manageable. As the number of these educated people increased however it became impossible to sustain their wages. Now with the advent of computers the position is even more serious. Those who operate computers tend to be ex office workers. The computer has come to replace office workers with computer experts. The computer experts together with all the equipment, anti-virus systems and the other items of expenditure however cost more than the jobs that they replaced.

The kind of distribution of costs that involves replacing the uneducated with the educated at higher costs with no effect upon the end product is clearly unsustainable. It is probably a root cause of the current economic problems and the persistently high level of unemployment that has now stretched into the highly qualified and educated masses.

Education these days costs a fortune as more and more people think that the costs are worthwhile. In the US tertiary education is funded with loans. People will subject themselves to massive debts in order to get that college degree.

It is easy to sympathise with those who do this. They see their more highly educated friends getting better jobs so they assume that if they could only get a university degree they too will get the better job. That of course is nonsense. Yet the vast majority do not know this. They are not told by anybody. Indeed their illusions are encouraged.

The reality is that in most cases education does not give rise to more value. It might give rise to higher wages in the short term but in the long term the real value of much tertiary education will be found to be illusory.

Accounting firms are now going back to the training on the job arrangements that existed before they abandoned their principles to the universities. They are hiring school leavers and training them. There is no substitute for on the job training and there is no evidence that those with university degrees can be trained more quickly or more effectively than school leavers.

It is the same with banking. There is no evidence that bankers hired from school or from fruit markets do any worse than those who are hired from universities at vastly higher salaries. The reason is probably that banking is really very simple. Most banks train their employees for 6 weeks. That is all it takes.

Education as a tool for employing personnel is the refuge of the lazy employer or head hunter who does not want to properly assess applicants himself.

Most jobs involve selling and common sense. University training does not make those who use common sense or sell goods or services any better. There is no objective criterion that indicates that a university education equips people better to do most jobs – other than ones that require considerable technical expertise – than a school leaver.

Yet the delusion persists. Why? It may have something to do with recruiters who have an interest in paying more and more because their fees are a percentage of the wages of the new recruit. When the adequacy or excesses of wages are discussed guess who is asked to give an opinion. The recruiters of course and like all educated persons they provide eloquent self serving arguments that back their point of view. Nobody indicates that their arguments are self serving. Their comments should come with a health warning but they do not.

Life is so easy for the recruiters and the human resources departments of most employers who can afford such a luxury. In order to assess the multitude of applicants for a job all they have to do is to see who get the best degrees or pass grades. That is an objective criterion. Who could possibly blame them for that.

Yet the real employer – the shareholder or entrepreneur – only wants to know who is likely to add most value at the lowest price. His human resources department backed by the self interest of the recruiting firms tell him that the best results for his business are achieved by hiring those with the best school grades. In fact those with the best school grades have merely proved that they are good at passing exams. That is not what most businesses want, even technical ones like law firms. They want some body who can give the client what he wants.

So education has become the panacea that makes the lives of recruiters and human resources departments easy. The interests of their employers is ignored and the interests of the country and the economy are irrelevant.

Such is the state of education today. It is in effect an epidemic. It is like a drug. We all want it because those who have it seem happy. Yet the nation is worse off. It wastes money. It re-circulates wealth through useless formal education. Wrong decisions are made as to whom to recruit into a job.

A friend of mine who is a lawyer once told me that he gets 500 applications for training programmes every year. He hires 3. How do you choose? I asked. "I just pick 3 at random", he said, "I do not want anybody who is unlucky".

Education is based not upon real value to the economy but merely the ability to get the better jobs. This is the result of going to the better universities. The system says nothing about what is put into the economy, merely what people can take out of it and that is how education is assessed.

Education in the UK is either private or public. The latter is a far larger part of the system but it is also the less successful. Schools like Eton are of course private.

St Paul's in London is another highly regarded private school.

Everybody wants what is best for their children. If your children can get into a particularly prestigious private school such as St Paul's they are pretty certain to get to Oxford and get top jobs in the city earning the big bucks, whether they deserve to or not. They will do so because of the unofficial old school principle. Those who run the city have that particular background and will select young people to succeed them from similar backgrounds to their own. That is understandable from their point of view but not particularly far sighted. It is also not best for the economy. But parents do not care about the economy, they only care if their child is doing well. In fact they want their child to do better than their neighbours. They would rather their child earns £10,000 per annum on graduation when everybody else's is earning £8,000 than that their child earns £20,000 when others are earning £25,000. That is the nature of our envious selves.

In order to achieve what we want for our children, or perhaps for ourselves, who get a feeling of importance through our children, we operate, at least in England a system of educational apartheid. We make sure that entry to particular universities is best achieved by going to particular schools and that our children enter those particular schools. We also make sure that their entry precludes and prevents others entering those schools. How do we achieve this? Simple, we boycott the state schools. We also make it more difficult to get into private schools through a system of payment which leaves the indigent out no matter how talented they may be (there are token scholarships given in order to lessen the charges of elitism) and exam results.

The latter restriction is perhaps more insidious than the first because it ensures that late developers are excluded from sharing the benefits of the economy. It ensures that only exam results rather than economic input are the only basis for assessment. It also ensures that mediocre teachers get rewarded for teaching pupils who in many cases do not need teachers.

I often hear people talking about a good education and good or bad schools. This is how we achieve educational apartheid. I try, generally without success, to analyse these comments about good education and good schools by inviting people to consider what elements make a school. A school consists of pupils, teachers and a building. The aim of all schools in the UK, and I suspect in other countries is the same, a final examination set by an independent board. Each school tries to achieve the highest number of passes at the highest level possible in these final exams.

The primary means of achieving this aim is learning in a classroom by means of lessons given by teachers. So what about the teachers? There is absolutely no evidence whatsoever that the teachers at the elite private schools in the UK are any better than the teachers in the state schools. They come from the same colleges or universities. Certainly the private schools may pay higher wages but they are not usually substantially higher, and the job security in the state sector tends to be better so there may be a price to pay for the additional money. But how does one assess a teacher. The usual, and in my opinion mindless way is by the results of the pupils. Thus it becomes impossible to assess the quality of teachers without taking into account the pupils. But certain pupils do not really need teachers. Indeed many are smarter than the teachers. So if a smart pupil is taught by a stupid or bad teacher and that pupil gets good results we say that the teacher was good. That of course is nonsense.

There is only one way to assess a teacher and that is by comparing him or her with another teacher and getting them to change classes with one another and then examining the results. I should like to see the teachers at Eton spending some time at a school in inner London and vice versa. The results would be interesting. I suspect they will show that there is no difference between the quality of teachers. I suspect also that the teachers at Eton will be unable to cope with the discipline or lack of it in a central London school. I have person knowledge of teachers in both the private and state sector and I cannot tell the difference between them in terms of ability, knowledge, dedication or any other basis.

That leaves the buildings. Well some state schools are in a bad state of repair and lack facilities. So do some private schools. I consider this to be a moot point. Children can learn in a garden, if the weather is fine. Certainly they need facilities like libraries, laboratories, music rooms and instruments, IT rooms and facilities and playing fields and the state sector is strapped for cash and fails to provide these facilities in many instances. However this failing is insignificant compared to teacher pupil interaction and is nowhere as widespread as we may be led to believe.

So the real issue is pupil teacher interaction. Now there is no doubt that a compliant pupil who reacts well to discipline is easier to teach than an unruly one who considers life hopeless and education pointless. There is no doubt that private schools provide pupils who want to learn and whose attitude to learning is positive and supported by their parents. There is also no doubt that learning in a state school is harder because of the number of pupils who just do not want to be there and want to cause disruption. The environment is different. Why should middle class parents send their children to state schools where they will find it harder to learn. I suppose the answer is that life will be like that and if we want our children to be protected from nasty working class people we will insulate them in the private sector. What happens when these future captains of industry enter the real world. They find it equally impossible to interact with the working classes and the system of apartheid is perpetuated. Yes what starts off as educational apartheid continues throughout life, where the class barriers are as high as they ever were. Working class people should know their place, if they have not learnt that at school they will learn it later on.

You cannot blame parents for wanting to see their children achieve the best results from the best Universities. After all employers choose their employees on that basis. That may be why so many employers are so useless. They choose their workers not on the basis that they are best able to do the job but on the basis that they are best able to pass exams. What possible correlation there is between passing exams and performing a job diligently where in most instances there are no questions on an exam paper I do not know. Most work involves thinking with a blank piece of paper. Students who have passed exams are generally faced with a question paper. They cannot think without one. They know the answers but do not know the questions. I cannot imagine why exam results are so important. I know people who can pass any exam just be memorising the facts on which they will be examined. They are however unable to think for themselves. These are our future professionals, who are used to receiving questions but can rarely make suggestions.

Likewise employees are rewarded not on the basis of their value to the economy but their exam results, in short their ability to repeat what they learnt. This is wholly inappropriate yet it is what happens in real life.

I frequently come across lawyers and accountants who if you ask them what the consequences of a certain proposal are will produce perfect answers. However when told that you merely want to achieve a particular result they will merely tell you the problems. No solutions. Yet these incompetent professionals demand the highest compensation, based on their school and university results.

We have an economic system that rewards incompetent lawyers more than competent plumbers. That is a recipe for economic downfall.

The real problem is that schools select their pupils. Naturally they will select those pupils who in reality do not need good teachers. Indeed some need no teachers at all. All they really need is a book. These "good" schools are the equivalent of a hospital that only treats healthy patients and then boasts about its low mortality rate.

Around September time our children go off to university. One only has to go down any high street in England in August when the A level results are out. There is one topic of conversation. My child is going to University, one parent might say. The other will point out that hers (they tend to be mothers) is going to Oxford. Not some low standard ex polytechnic, but Oxford. That of course makes the parent a finer example of middle class Britain than the other and she puffs herself up accordingly. But not to be outdone another will point out that hers if going to medical school. Not some nondescript degree in languages or history but something that will equip her child for not only a guaranteed job but one that will give the child power and authority. During the years of training at medical school the parent will often boast about her medical school student child whilst the parent of the child at Oxford will make every effort to steer the conversation round to her child and the word Oxford will occur so frequently until you are forced to ask "is your child at Oxford". Yet it is possible that the car mechanic or computer technician adds more real value to the economy than the Oxford graduate. What one puts into the economy however is not what determines how much a person takes out of it. Only one's education determines that and having gone to one of the prestigious universities is one of the most important factors.

I was astonished to find that even the great and celebrated TV personality David Frost still boasts about have gone to

Cambridge. There are approximately 13,000 students at Cambridge at any one time so there must be about 500,000 Cambridge graduates in the UK and about a similar number from Oxford. There is only one David Frost. Yet he will boast about his University.

A French colleague of mine once remarked that in France mature people rarely talk about their universities and talk more about their achievements since then, "yet here people of 50 years old" he said "still want to tell me about the school that they attended or their university". It's as if that is the pinnacle of their achievement.

The system in the US is more like that of the UK than France. People boast about have gone to an Ivy League university. Pupils or their parents will suffer great hardship to ensure that their children get that particular degree. The graduates leave university with massive borrowings that they hope to be able to pay off because they will get better paid jobs.

Unfortunately the economy simply does not work in a way that can accommodate all these graduates. As more and more graduates come on the job market the economy finds itself unable to cope with the influx and more and more are finding themselves unemployed.

There is a limit to the amount of excessive pay that can be handed to the products of our top universities.

There are now over 100 universities in the UK. Many, if not most of them have the same courses in languages, law, science, history and many other subjects. Nobody has been able to explain to me why it is that each of these universities have their own examining board. I have asked many vice chancellors and educationalists why not have one single examining board called The University of the UK. Never having considered the point, they are astonished by such a suggestion and they respond in the usual way, with suspicion and an attempt to justify the status quo. One would have expected more from academics whose main task it is to push forward the boundaries of knowledge and to be imaginative. No such chance when their self interest is at stake.

Yet there is probably a good reason why many Universities do not wish their students to be assessed at the same examination. What would happen if, heaven forbid, a student from Slough University was to obtain higher marks than a student from Oxford University. It would undermine the whole basis of British society and the British economy. It would start to ask why it is that a person with a 3rd class degree from Oxford will get a top paying job in the city whereas a person who gets a first from Slough will not even get invited to an interview. It may also mean that people, having been given a place at Oxford may have to start looking over their shoulder and can no longer rest on their laurels. It may mean that they may have to work harder and fulfill their potential.

Every year there is a boat race in London between Oxford and Cambridge. When these were the only universities in the country this was understandable. Since the introduction of other universities it is difficult to understand why the race is always between these two only to the exclusion of the other UK universities. A friend of mine whose son was at Oxford said to me when I asked him the question "because they might lose". And there we have it, these elite universities must be protected from any suggestion, that they are no better than many others. Even if this is true. That is a frightening thought. It means that we protect the status quo at all costs. We will carry out these deceptive tricks in order to pretend that there is a good reason why the elite are in fact an elite.

There is an annual rugby match at Twickenham also between these two elite universities. The principle is exactly the same as for the rowing match. They dare not let others join in because they may lose. They myth would be damaged. The fact that the myth does not accord with the truth of the situation is irrelevant. It is, as a boss of mine once pointed out, a matter or perception.

Perception is more important than truth. And why would we want to perpetuate a myth that is not true. Because it supports those in power and maintains the status quo. But what if the status quo is bad for the country. After all surely we want the best sports people to represent our country. No sir. Those who represent out country do not do so for the benefit of the country. They do so for their own benefit. They would rather they represented their country and came fourth than lose their place to somebody who could come first. That is the nature of man. We really are not very nice, or honest.

Recently I heard a broadcast from one of our ministers, Patricia Hewett who was being interviewed about equality of opportunity in higher education. The discussion was about working class people going to university. She made an outrageous statement saying that she wanted the working class people of her constituents to get university degrees instead of middle class people doing so. "Let them (the middle class people) go off and become plumbers". This statement, reminiscent of Marie Antionette's famous statement about eating cake, gave the game away. It made clear that our politicians, including labour politicians considered being a lawyer or accountant superior to being a plumber or electrician or a builder. A trade is inferior to working in an office. And of course the remuneration reflects this prejudice.

So Patricia Hewett wants more people from the working classes to go to University and then to work in offices instead of becoming plumbers or electricians. It was clear from her statement that she also wanted fewer middle class people to go to University. After all we cannot all go to universities and work in offices. Patricia Hewett ignored the fact that it was implicit in her statement that electricians and plumbers were not as useful or at any rate as deserving as lawyers and accountants. Nobody picked up on this insult. Our spineless and unthinking press ignored what she had said. After all they did not have a judge to reach a conclusion. Nor did she give them a punchy headline, although you can bet that it she had it would have been a very favourable one, thought out by the spin doctors that put words into our politicians' mouths.

So all these debates about improving the standard of education in the state system is designed to increase the number of lawyers and accountants working in offices earning the big fat salaries and to reduce the number of people able to mend out drains. Clearly not, because it would be impossible to live without people who do useful work for us instead of pushing round useless pieces of paper. So the objective is to have more working class people working in offices and more middle class people mending our drains. Unless that produces more real wealth it is a complete waste of time. Yet most wealth is not produced by paper pushers but by innovative and hard working businessmen many of whom have never been near a university.

Education could be a deterrent to innovation. It leads one to believe that by answering questions and storing knowledge one can receive the lion's share of the economic cake.

That is the problem with British education. Some of the problems in Britain are of course unique. The obsession with education is not as widespread elsewhere. The truth is that education provides a false market. It enables us to select certain people on the basis of one factor alone - academic ability - to get a larger slice of the national cake, merely because of their superior education and knowledge in some areas. The fact that these areas are of little practical use and do not results in a single additional loaf of bread being baked or a single additional pair of shoes being made is irrelevant. It is a way of manipulating the market and dividing it into a number of smaller ones.

21.   SOCIAL ENGINEERING - THE NEW BRITISH PHENOMENON

Closely connected with the concept of education is that of class, certainly in Britain and probably most countries outside the New World (America, Canada, Australia and such countries). Even in those countries the concept of class does present itself, albeit in not such a clearly defined way as it does in Britain.

A new term has recently crept into the lexicon of English politicians and commentators - "social mobility". Nobody has defined it with any clarity. It is assumed that the term itself is clear. I will try to make up this deficit.

The term in the British context is clear. Britain is a society that is built on class. If one ignores the aristocracy there are essentially two classes, with many sub classes in between. There are what are called the "working class" and then there are the professionals, who also work for their living but who are nonetheless not working class. They are distinctively "middle class".

The term social mobility is designed to emphasize this distinction. It is not politically or indeed socially acceptable to describe working class people as inferior to the middle classes. Nevertheless in private it is assumed to be the case. Sadly even the working classes probably regard themselves as inferior. They most certainly have a lower standard of living.

Social Mobility is process whereby working class people can become members of the middle class. There is nothing complicated or obscure about it. Nobody apologises for this. Practically everybody who mentions it as a desirable aim is safe in the knowledge - at least in the UK - that all, no matter what their background and to what class they belong, will approve of the process.

In theory of course one could move from being middle class to being working class. However Social Mobility is not intended to make people worse off. It is intended to make people better off. The concept represents one way traffic only.

Implicit in this concept is that it is better to be middle class than to be working class. Of course since middle class people normally have a higher living standard than working class people few could argue that moving up a class is beneficial.

It is however a ridiculous concept. Middle class people usually work in offices. Working class people usually work with their hands and use their brains less. Office people use their brains more and their hands less. Aside from the fact that it is more comfortable to work in an air conditioned office there is nothing to suggest that the so called work of the brain that is carried on in offices is superior to the work done by hand. Yet that is the underlying concept to which the people of Britain subscribe.

Social mobility is an insult to the working classes. It effectively tells them that we - the middle classes - have out of the goodness of our hearts, have a policy to take you out of your miserable lives being electricians, bus drivers, brick layers and such like and find jobs for you in air conditioned office where you will earn more money.

So who is to do the real work if this policy is successful. The question will not arise because we will always make sure that membership of the middle class will be strictly limited. We can employ the examination system of education to determine who should be allowed to join and then limit the number qualified to apply so as not to prejudice our own living standards.

The concept of social mobility with its connotations with social engineering is a particularly insulting concept. It assumes that being middle class is better or more worthy than being working class. The financial rewards that accrue to the middle classes might appear to be an incentive and a barried. However the rewards that are apparently available to the middle classes can and should not make it necessary to indulge in this odious concept. If the middle classes really were in favour of raising living standards of the working classes they would operate free markets so that if there is a shortage of waiters or bus drivers but an excess of doctors or lawyers then waiters and bus drivers would earn more than doctors or lawyers.

The work done by those who are skilled with their hands is just as worthy as the work done by those who work in offices. The market should be allowed to determine remuneration without manipulation and coercion. If they did so there would be a balance of work and mutual respect of those who carry on one activity towards another. That would be a just society.

Instead the middle classes who have the levers of power in their hands manipulate the system to make sure that those who know the rules get paid most. We all live in a society and all participate in providing the necessary goods and services. Yet those who control the money and know the rules - the professionals - are always able to take care of themselves and to manipulate the rules so that their incomes increase and are always higher than those of the manual worker, no matter what the respective value of what they produce.

22.   THE PROFESSIONALS

"Every profession is a conspiracy against the laity". So said Bernard Shaw.

Much of what I said in the chapter on Education applies equally here so I shall not repeat it.

Professionals are of two kinds. One provides services direct to consumers. The other provides his services to a producer and is part of the production process that leads to the production of the end product.

I have said enough about how professionals who are rewarded for their part in the production line. The price of their services does not reflect their real value, and is inflated either because the requirement for their services is imposed upon producers by the coercive powers of the state or alternatively by their persuasive abilities.

Professionals who provide services to consumers directly are theoretically more subject to market forces than those who are part of a production line.

However many professions are not subject to normal market forces. A doctor providing medical services to a patient is not really subject to market forces. Market forces are the forces of supply and demand. There are usually more than one doctor so the supply of doctors is not generally in dispute. The demand however is not elastic at all. Where my health is at stake I cannot refuse to pay what is demanded.

It is the same with other professions such as the legal profession. If I wish to stay out of jail and protect my liberty if I am improperly charge with a criminal offence I have no real choice. I have to employ a lawyer. I am not free to choose. I am free to choose a lawyer but he has to be one who is acceptable to the courts and the legislature.

It is the same with accountants. I am obliged to file a tax return so I have to hire an accountant. I have no real choice.

Likewise if I carry on business through a limited company I have no choice. I have to – if my company is large enough – have an annual audit. I do not have a choice.

Many professionals charge by the hour so that although I am able to enquire as to their hourly rate before hiring one I cannot control the number of hours worked. If I find that some item of work took too long I am told that it is very complicated and of course as a lay person I am not able to argue.

Professions are often controlled by statutes. Their membership is controlled. Theoretically they are set up as learned professions in order to protect the public. In reality they protect their members.

The General Medical Council is meant to discipline doctors. In fact it acts as another leg of the British Medical Association and protects doctors except in the most egregious of cases.

The statutory provisions prevent people entering the profession without the sanction of the governing body.

It does not matter what the consumer wants. If I wanted to be treated in the UK for some incurable illness that I believe only a Ukrainian doctor can provide I will not be permitted to do so. It is said to be for my benefit, but of course it is nothing of the sort. It is for the benefit of the profession, which wants to protect the income of its members as high as possible.

There is no reason why an audit should be forced upon companies. The matter could be left to any third party wishing to deal with the company. The justification for this practice as well as the practice of requiring annual accounts of a company to be filed is that anybody doing business with that company – a potential creditor – will be able to tell whether the company is credit worthy. The number of people who deal with companies in that way must be very small indeed. If it is important to the potential creditor he can require a set of audited accounts to be produced. Bankers do this all the time. Most sets of accounts filed at Companies House are never seen by anybody.

And of course those who rely upon audited accounts do so at their peril. Various ways have been found for protecting negligent auditors from the risks of litigation. Even shareholders cannot get compensation from auditor for negligent work.

Doctors who are sued for negligent injury to patients claim that they should be protected because otherwise they will carry out defensive medicine. Defensive medicine is an unnecessary medical procedure that is there to make sure that the doctor cannot be sued. It is nonsense of course but yet another example of the eloquence of education being used to serve the interests of the educated than of the consumer.

Many professionals provide little true value and if they were not involved in a production process nobody would notice any difference. We would still eat the same food, and drive the same cars. We would still wear the same clothes. The amounts of real goods and services are in many cases not affected by the intervention of the professionals.

I exempt from criticism all those professionals involved in actually essential to the production of the end product such as for example the engineer or designer who made the machines that makes the goods or the architect who builds the factory. I also exempt those professional who provide a service direct to the consumer.

My criticism is mainly directed at those professionals whose contribution towards the production of the end product and to its delivery to its eventual market place cannot be justified on either a sine qua non basis or the basis of value added. In general these professionals work in offices and produce useless pieces of paper.

Most lawyers draft legal agreements that never see the time of day. They can be a few pages long or many hundreds of pages long. None are perfect and cover all eventualities. Both short and long documents are as subject to potential disputes, litigation and uncertainty. Yet as the number of professionals increases the tendency has been for longer and longer documents.

The control of the customer, who is supposed to instruct them is particularly noticeable if one tries to sell something in a different jurisdiction. The seller and buyer will require two sets of professionals, neither of which is expert in the laws of the other country. Hours and fees multiply needlessly. Yet the professional is able to point to legal requirements that could result in serious losses if more and more legal fees are not incurred.

Surprisingly, despite their dubious or limited value, professionals involved in production frequently take the lion's share of the sale proceeds of the goods at the end of the production line. You will find that the management consultant and the auditor get paid far more than the engineer who built the machinery that makes the goods. The lawyer who draws up an unnecessarily long legal document covering the agreement to sell or produce the relevant goods, is paid far more than the architect who helped build the factory where the goods are manufactured. Compared to the worker who stitches up the clothes that we wear or who weaves the fabric or puts the sports shoe together, the lawyer and accountant gets several times what these poor unfortunate people earn. This is not a reflection of the value of the professionals. It is merely the result of coercive and persuasive powers of the state and the trade unions of the professions.

How do we justify this apparently unfair sharing of the proceeds from sale of the goods that we consume. It is all done by money and a manipulation of the mechanism of supply and demand.

We can manipulate the demand for lawyers and accountants just by introducing more and more complex legislation that compels us to hire lawyers and accountants. As the demand increases their price goes up. And we can restrict the supply of lawyers and accountants just by making them join an institute. There is no free market in lawyers, even if they are competent. Either they join the trade union or they cannot practice. And if they join a trade union they must behave in a particular way. Their union will protect them and make sure nobody can break their monopoly. And of course they will tell the public that it is for their own protection.

Accountants have a bit more freedom and theoretically anybody can be a tax adviser. Only qualified accountants however can be auditors. That limits the scope for fees falling because just as with lawyers you cannot practice unless you get hired and undergo a training programme for a number of years with a firm that is a member of the learned profession. You may have all the necessary knowledge and have passed the exams but you cannot help anybody of compete with other professions unless you undergo that training programme.

It does not matter what the consumer wants. If he is willing to take the risk of hiring somebody who is not a member of the professional body and who is willing to provide services at a lower cost than a member of the learned body the consumer cannot do so. He is not free to choose.

Professionals are meant to act in the best interests of their clients. Here they face an immediate conflict because their client's interest is to be charged as little as possible. The professional's interest is to charge his client as much as possible.

In order to understand how professionals operate we must first accept that professionals are running a business. Whether they are doctors or lawyers, architects or accountants, bankers or advertising executives, they are running a business. Their aim is to make money. They would all appreciate a good reputation but

303

making money comes before almost everything else and a good reputation is only wanted as a means of making more money. Certainly there are lawyers who give up a profitable career at the bar to become judges. In doing so they tend to take a large drop in salary. However they tend to make this sacrifice when money is no longer a problem and they can afford to take the drop. There are benefits in becoming a judge. These are obvious. The self importance, rank and position will in most cases outweigh the loss of income. However their financial security is guaranteed and so is their job position. Nobody can fire them except for the grossest forms of misconduct. Few suffer this fate.

Many lawyers advise in favour of or against proceeding with legal action depending upon the ability of the client to pay. If the client is rich he will pursue the case on the flimsiest grounds. If he is poor no lawyer will take on his case, even on a contingency basis.

Certainly there are obvious cases where it would be foolish to take a case without any merit. Even lawyers do not want to look foolish in front of a judge or one of their colleagues. However for money they would be very willing to look foolish. It is of course possible to fight a case that is totally without merit without looking foolish.

I am told for example that most cases settle on the steps of the court. That means that the lawyers acting for the party that is settling want to earn as much as they can from their clients although they know they do not have a case. Of course they do so on the basis that the other side could give up. Honesty and truth never come into their consideration. All they want to do is to make money for themselves.

The vast majority of legal disputes proceed on the basis not of justice but of power. The party with the deepest pockets effectively terrorizes the other party with financial death as a result of the massive legal fees that he will have to pay if he loses. The weaker party often gives in even if his case is entirely just.

Doctors likewise frequently act in their best interests. That does not mean that they will operate without cause. In the UK they mostly work on salary and get paid whatever they may do or not do so the temptation to undertake unnecessary surgery does not present itself. It does however in the private sector and it is for that reason that I steer clear of the private sector whenever possible. The temptations and rewards are too great.

Doctors in the UK generally moonlight. This was a condition upon which they insisted when the National Health Service was introduced. You can visit them in their state jobs only to be told that there is a very long waiting list for the surgery that you require or that it is not available at all under the NHS. However if you care to make an appointment with their private secretary you can have the operation next week. In short if you pay for it we have the facilities.

This is a scandal that has never been properly addressed because bureaucrats are afraid of upsetting the doctors. It shows dishonesty.

The best way of seeing doctors operate against their duty towards their patients and in their best interests is when something goes wrong. They falsify medical records, invent excuses and situations that did not or could not possibly exist. When asked to examine what one of their colleagues did wrong they will invent all sort of circumstances that could have led to the situation, despite the fact that no such situation occurred or even been suggested by the negligent doctor.

The hierarchy is such that when something goes wrong the nursing staff are far more likely to be blamed than the doctor.

There are fortunately a small number of honourable doctors who do not behave in that way but they are in a minority.

Accountants pretend that they are acting in the interests of the consumer. It is they who prevailed upon the government at the time to compel every company to have a set of audited accounts.

Yet when something goes wrong and a third party loses money they deny any responsibility.

How often do you hear that when you go to court the lawyers get the lion's share. It is not always so but it is often the case.

Professionals talk pompously about taking instructions from their clients or of working with their patients. Try arguing with them about their "advice". It will not get you very far but will get you a larger bill. Unless you know as much as they do they will have the upper hand because they can always invent some technical argument to back them up.

Undoubtedly the worst professionals for wasting time and not producing value are the lawyers. The largest profession in parliament is the legal profession. Many politicians continue practicing whilst they are MPs. They spend their time introducing new laws. Rarely do they remove laws from the statute books. The size of the laws gets larger and larger.

When I started practicing tax law 30 years ago the tax code was about one inch thick. Now there are 5 volumes, each of them 3 inches thick.

The tax rules are so complex that the administrators have no chance of knowing and being able to administer all the laws. It would need the whole of the population of the country to administer the tax code properly and to audit all the transactions that take place. The tax system operates by lottery. If you are caught that's tough. Most will get away with the most blatant tax evasion. The reason is that there are so many rules, so much case law and so many statutes. The tax code is the tip of the iceberg. Behind the acts of parliament there are long and detailed tax cases with judgments, often by up to 9 judges. There are extra statutory concessions, statutory instruments, statements of practice, Revenue interpretations and press releases. I defy anybody to be familiar with all this.

In the US successive Treasury Secretaries and politicians advocate a reduction or simplification of the US tax code, which is more complex than ours, to a far more abbreviated document. Nothing happens. If anything it will get longer and more complex. No professionals want a reduction or simplification in legislation.

I shall deal with taxation in another chapter. For the time being however I merely want to concentrate on the professionals and their attitude.

I remember when working for a well known, distinguished and wealthy Australian accountant, when the Government there was contemplating introducing a wealth tax. My boss, to my utter surprise was very much in favour of it. Not because he wanted to be taxed on his vast wealth but because he thought it would bring him more fees. None of our clients wanted the proposed tax and they lobbied hard against it. They would have been astonished to find that their accountant was lobbying in favour of it. Was this a conflict of duty and interest. Surely his duty was to his clients. But of course he had a higher duty. To the poor who would benefit from such a new tax. Not if he had his way. He would spend all his time trying to make sure none of his clients paid any of the tax but of course paid his fees. Was he not doing his duty to his clients. That depended on the audience and the time of day.

As far as the complexity of the rules and regulations are concerned the more complex the better it is for the professional because the more likely it is that he will be hired to sort out the client's problems.

Millions are spent every year arguing whether the words in a certain tax code mean one thing or another. Here are some examples.

The tax rules allow a trader to claim allowances for certain capital expenditure referred to as "plant and machinery". The principle is that certain expenditure that costs the taxpayer money should be allowed as a deduction. That makes sense. Yet you should see the rules relating to what is plant. Well it depends on whether it is fixed to a building or not. And whether it is a moveable part or not. It also depends on whether is constitutes the setting or not. And each of these rules depend on the business of the taxpayer. Thus what is plant to a certain business is not plant to another.

The case law on the subject runs into millions of pages. The lawyers and accountants who have represented their clients in arguing their cases have made fortunes from these serious arguments. The Inland Revenue argues the case vigorously and employs highly paid lawyers to represent it in the courts. And what for. They have forgotten that their purpose it to collect tax to enable the government to function and fulfil its obligations to the country. They win some and they lose some cases. And what do they achieve. If they decided to allow all capital expenditure on the basis of the depreciation of the asset and saved all the money from arguing whether a light bulb is part of the building or a functioning part of the business they would probably make a profit. But that is not their purpose. Their purpose is to dip their beaks in the trough and take a large chunk of the proceeds of sale of whoever produces the food and clothes and other consumables that we require.

There are many arguments where absolutely no value is added by professionals yet they earn a fortune for their work. What is plant is just one example. If the Inland Revenue were to realise that their purpose is to collect tax and that the taxpayer would rather pay 1p more in tax and have all his capital expenditure allowed the whole country would be better off, except of course those who create no value at all and who would otherwise be spending thousands of days in court arguing what is and what is not plant. If raising tax by 1p is not acceptable why not just say that all light bulbs are plant. Just have a list of all items that are deductible and have done with the arguments. That would mean that the villas in the South of France for the accountants and lawyers may have to go. That would not do of course. The system must remain in place and these people must be allowed to participate in real goods and services without adding any real value. What they do is the equivalent of ploughing through water or of digging holes and filling them up again. They are working hard but delivering nothing.

And what chunks they take out of the proceeds of sale. The market is rigged. I hear that one barrister charges for a conference of one hour about some argument like what is or what is not plant £25,000. That's right £25,000. And the number of additional t shirts or loaves of bread or cars that are produced as a result of his efforts is nil. That apparently is how the so called free market works. If that is a free market I shall eat my hat.

This is pure redistribution of wealth. Who is to pay for such redistribution. The answer is that we do not know. It could be all of us through inflation. It could be somebody in Africa who might starve as an indirect result of the lawyer being over paid.

Professionals create their own market. They are theoretically just as amenable to the rules of supply and demand. However they participate in the produce of the economy on the basis not of the value that they provide because this in most cases is doubtful or worthless. Their participation or the size of the chunk they take out is proportionate to their knowledge about spurious and useless rules, whether that is of any value or not.

23.   TAXATION

Why are there so many different taxes. There is an income tax, NHI, capital gains tax, corporation tax, stamp duty, duty on petrol, liquor and tobacco, there are local taxes, vehicle licenses, TV licenses, VAT, import duty. There are probably many others.

The local rates notice that comes from our local authority sets out how local taxes are spent. It shows how, in percentage terms our local council spent the money we gave it. It also shows how much it collects from ratepayers and how much it received from central government. In our borough about half the income of the local authority comes from central government, in other words from taxpayers around the country.

If such a large percentage of the money spent by a borough in London comes from the taxpayers of the whole country, it is difficult to understand why the local borough bothers collecting the rest from the local population on a basis that is different from that on which central government raises taxes. Why not dispense with local taxes and collect it all centrally.

There is an argument in favour of this approach. Local authorities, in the UK are subject to the duties imposed upon them by central government. They simply cannot turn around and say that they cannot afford to do something, like providing for education or welfare. They cannot argue that the local population do not want them to do something. They can simply be overridden by the will of central government. That has the duty of providing uniform services throughout the UK. This does not however explain why we have a local tax. If the services provided by the local government are uniform why should two residents in different borough whose circumstances are identical in terms of income and wealth pay different amounts of local tax. Nobody can answer this question. There is no answer. The only one that makes sense is that abandoning a tax will put people who collect the tax out of work. But they are doing a job that has no value. They are participating in the proceeds of sale of real products, food, clothing, cars, homes and other goods without providing anything of value. The same goes for other taxes. There is no justifiable reason why there should be so many taxes. There is no justification for the complexity of the tax rules. They only serve to keep the professionals in work, doing a job that adds no value to the products that they consume.

The claim for efficiency in government that occurs from time to time is spurious because it ignores why people are employed both in government services and elsewhere. They are employed doing what is inherently inefficient because otherwise they would be unemployed and it is a way of allowing them to participate in the economy. The coercive power of the state requires them to be employed in that way. Nevertheless from time to time politicians ask for efficiency in what is after all an inherently inefficient activity. There seems little advantage in doing something inherently inefficient efficiently.

Before capital gains tax was introduced, around 1965, there was a distinction between capital gains and ordinary income. When the government decided to introduce capital gains tax it did so at a lower rate than ordinary income. There was a reason why people would rather classify their income as capital than ordinary.

Why the difference. Why not just tax people on all gains and profits at the same rate. The rules for the two classes of income are very distinct. One still has to distinguish between income and capital. Why. There is no good reason. The reliefs are complex and different. Why. Nobody can say. Who gains. Only the professionals and the tax administrators. But they add no value to the economy, they just take large chunks out of it. It is pure wealth redistribution that carried to extremes will result in economic catastrophe.

311

I can see a reason for imposing a tax on income and a tax on spending. The latter will collect tax from those who do not earn income here. Aside from that however any sensible use of resources would abolish all taxes except one or two of them. That would raise the question what would we do with all those people who now participate in the economy without adding anything useful. The answer is that they would have to produce something useful. That would be unacceptable in this allegedly capitalist economy. There is an alternative and that is more leisure time for all. We could share the few jobs that are available and have a lot of leisure time. That alternative has not been considered. Doubtless it would result in those earning vast sums have to accept less and they would object.

If this is a market economy then I do not understand simple English. The market is rigged. The largest spoils or share in the production process goes to those whose knowledge is greater than others. The more restrictive and opaque their knowledge the more they get paid and the greater the chunk they take out of what genuine workers produce. They create a sub market of their own and since few can join the supply and demand factors work in their favour.

During the 1970's Milton Friedman, the Nobel Prize winner in economics argued that he could see no reason why there was a tax department and a social security department. Since the tax department knew exactly how much income everybody had they could abolish the department of social security and have a system of positive and negative tax. Those below the minimum level of income would receive a cheque monthly from the Inland Revenue to take them to that level. Those above the minimum level of income would pay tax.

I believe Mrs Thatcher looked into this possibility and formed a committee made up mainly by people from the department of social security. Guess what they found? It was not possible. Of course it is not. They would lose their jobs, which add nothing to the economy. If they did not exist not a single less t shirt would be manufactured. Not a single less loaf of bread would be baked, not a single less car or TV set would be manufactured. These officials add nothing to the economy. Yet they participate in the produce as do the tax accountants and lawyers who operate this increasingly unnecessarily complex set of laws and regulations. The officials argue whether a child should get a clothing allowance and what the rules say or do not say. They argue whether a person should be on supplementary income or some other benefit. There are benefits galore. The poor really need only one benefit - money. Just give them the money. No we have to humiliate them and ask them to queue up and fill in a 20 page request for a pair of shoes for their children. We have complex rules to provide some with rent allowance and others with council homes. And for what purpose? There is only one that I can see. It keeps people in jobs producing nothing of value, no additional bread or cars, you know the rest. Yet the chunk that they take out of the economy is substantial and depends not on market forces or value added but on education. The more complicated the rules and laws the more education one needs to interpret them and therefore the more one gets paid.

There is no doubt that taxation policy can influence behaviour. I have often wondered whether most people, faced with the alternative would not prefer to pay tax on death than during their lives. I certainly would. However and more importantly, and I shall discuss this subject in more detail in a chapter on corporate governance, if the government really does want to encourage entrepreneurs and wealth creation, they should tax high salaries at punitive rates so as to discourage executives paying themselves vast sums of money and eliminate tax on capital gains. Thus executives would have every incentive to increase the value of shares, of which they will hold many. However their incentive to increase the value of their shares would mean that they would benefit the entrepreneur who invests in shares at the same time.

313

The self serving arguments regarding taxation particularly of the rich are astonishing. There is an old theory of taxation known as a bell curve theory for reason that will be clear. The theory is that no tax is collected by governments when tax rates are 0% but no tax is collected when tax rates are at 100% because nobody will consider it worth their while working. That of course is just common sense although it has never been tried in practice. In between those two extremes it is assumed that there is somewhere in the middle when maximum tax is collected. It may be 50% but it might be less.

When the Thatcher government was elected in the UK in 1979 income tax rates were 83% for top earners. This had the result that both employers and employees considered it not worth their while receiving either large remuneration or dividend income. The latter was taxed at the top rate of 98%. The money was best left in the businesses. Capital gains were taxed at 30% so a corporate investor could pay a rate of 30% on increases in the value of the underlying business. Clearly the value of a company would increase if cash was left in the company instead of being paid out in dividends and high salaries.

Companies paid a tax rate of 52% but there was a so called imputation system that effectively reduced their tax rate to around 30% if they paid dividends.

Although the higher tax rate for dividends was 98% most investments in companies was through pension funds that not only paid no tax on any dividends received but were able to claim back part of the corporation tax paid by companies – the difference between the 52% and the effective 30%.

Thatcher immediately set about reducing the top rate of income tax and did so in two dramatic moves to 40%. Once the income tax rate was reduced in this way there was an explosion in salaries and fees of wage earners the effects of which we are still seeing today. The result naturally was that income tax collected increased materially. However that was not without cost.

Firstly capital gains tax at 30% which also had the benefit of relief from inflation and which was an encouragement to real entrepreneurship ceased to be so attractive. The result as I show in other chapters, was that there were less and less real entrepreneurs and more and more businesses the purpose of which was the redistribution of wealth. The effects of these redistributions are still being felt today. Capital gains tax later came to be increased to the same rates as income tax and additionally the inflation relief was withdrawn.

Corporate taxes fell as a direct result of payment of those substantial salary increases. It is true that corporation tax was only around 30% whereas income tax for the higher paid was at 40% so there was effectively an increase in tax collected.

This is now put forward as evidence that the reverse will happen if tax rates are increased. What is the reverse? The reverse is the following process.

Those earning salaries of 1mm per annum who were paying 40% tax are now to be taxed at 50%. On the face of it this will increase the amount of tax collected by 10%. Not so say the highly paid. Increasing tax rates will reduce the tax collected. Look what happened under Thatcher. We are apparently to believe that the additional 10% of tax which will reduce the take home pay of the employee earning (I use the term loosely not in the classic sense that implies that he deserves that pay) 1mm from 600,000 to 500,000 will result in that same employee saying to his employers "please reduce my salary to a level where I am not liable to the additional 10%. This level is 150,000. The employee is therefore willing to accept a reduction in his take home pay from 500,000 to 90,000 (60% of 150,000). Not only are we expected to take these arguments seriously but the press and media accept the assertions and claim that "everybody knows that increasing tax rates reduces the amount of tax collected". This kind of self interested double speak is something we have had to get used to. Truth however requires these falsehoods to be exposed.

Of course there are some who will leave the country if tax rates are increased. However the vast majority will remain and there is nothing to suggest that those who leave cannot be replaced with better people, assuming that they are real wealth creators rather than wealth redistributors.

Those who create real wealth in the UK will have no option. Those whose skills are UK related will stay. Those with licenses to practice in the UK will stay. There are in reality very few who would leave. One only has to look at what happened when the UK was in serious economic difficulties after the war. Emigration to Australia was possible. Many left, yet the population did not fall. Those who leave can be replaced.

Ultimately if there is a material brain drain it is possible to offer jobs to foreigners with tax advantages.

24.   CORPORATE PROFITS

Many people believe that drugs companies are in business to make them healthy. I have no doubt that their mission statement will reflect this view. One only has to think coldly about their size and profits as well as to consider the fight they put up to hide the evidence whenever one of their products is found to be faulty to begin to doubt their good faith.

Drugs companies are just like any other company. They are in business to make money. That is their primary purpose. They make money for their benefit, not ours. Certainly the way in which they make money is by providing a service to the public. However whenever there is a conflict between their interest in making money for themselves and our interest in recovering from our illnesses guess who will win the day.

Of course whether one is buying a drug from a drugs company or groceries from a supermarket or whether one is considering dealing with a bank the advertising is cleverly aimed at making the consumer think that they are altruistic organizations. At no stage do they ever say what really motivates them. One only hears how the customer comes first and how they are in business only to please the customer. The reality is that pleasing the customer is an inconvenience that they have to overcome in order to make money.

Consider for a few minutes what you would do if you were the head of a drugs company whose mission is to make as much money as possible. You have at your disposal untold millions to spend on research scientists. You have the most sophisticated laboratories and scientists at your disposal. The general public are your customers and are ignorant of what is contained in your drugs and how they work. The public who use your drugs are, unlike in other markets, ordered, by their doctors to take particular drugs.

First and foremost of course you would get the doctors on side. This is done quite overtly. Drugs companies wine and dine doctors. They invite them to conferences, all expenses paid, to fancy resorts. They recruit them to their teams of advisers, paying them for their services. They keep them informed of all developments so that they will appear to be at the cutting edge of medical technology. Nothing much wrong with all that you might say, aside from the freebies but that is not a mortal sin.

The drugs companies however also have another hurdle to jump, and that is the regulatory bodies that authorise the use of particular drugs. These bodies we take on trust. We have to assume that they have our interests at heart. Of course the drugs companies would want to be friends with those who approve their drugs for use.

Relying on other people to push your drugs is not that easy, and may not be too profitable.

What would you do with the large knowledge you get from your laboratories. Suppose for example that one of your scientists discovers that instead of using an expensive drug to cure or control a particular disease the patient would be better off eating the rid of a melon. He reports this to his CEO. What would the CEO do. I guess you know the answer to that. He would suppress the information of course. Arguably he would be in breach of his duty to his shareholders if he revealed the truth. There is a lot of evidence of cheap and effective cures sometimes of very serious illnesses being available. Yet the drugs companies will do everything in their power to stop this knowledge getting out. If it does get out they will ridicule it, lie about it, disparage its sources and do whatever is necessary to prevent their expensive even if useless drugs being displaced by something natural that works.

It is simply not credible that some of the simple remedies that are available nowadays have not been examined by the drugs

318

companies. And have you ever heard of a drug company taking a drug off the market and informing the consumers that they have discovered something more effective and cheaper that you can buy at your greengrocer.

And what if one of your scientists discovered that one of your drugs that makes a substantial profit contribution to your bottom line could be killing people or is useless, or has nasty side effects. Have you ever heard of a drugs company voluntarily withdrawing one of its drugs and coming clean with such a revelation. That sort of information usually comes from patients who put two and two together. And when that does happen just watch the drugs companies fight. They will use every trick available to discredit the evidence.

Perhaps if you were the head of a drugs company you would think more laterally. You might think that in order to sell more drugs people need to be sicker. After all healthy people do not need to take drugs. Something must be done to make people less healthy so that they can buy more drugs. How about finding ways of making people sick and then selling them the drugs that will make them better. All that is necessary is to have some nasty illness introduced into something like the aspirin or some useless cough mixture that will have the patient running to the doctor who will give him the antidote, manufactured by, you guessed it, the same drugs company that introduced the illness in the first place.

And how do we know that drugs companies do not have some special laboratory, possibly situated somewhere far away from civilisation that is busy finding out ways of making us ill and them coming up with the antidote. Or perhaps they are merely contributing funds indirectly towards other companies that produce products that make us ill, such as for example tobacco companies, oil companies that pollute the air.

And what would you do if you were CEO of a drugs company if somebody outside your control discovered some simple cure that was better and cheaper than one of your expensive drugs. Why you would discredit them, prosecute them, throw an army of lawyers at them. You might even kill them.

Beware of the drugs companies. Their motive is to make profits. It is not to make you well. That is an inconvenience that is necessary to get us to part with our money.

The NHS is the biggest consumer of drugs as it pays for most of them. We only pay a small contribution.

I am astonished that nobody at the NHS has set up a laboratory whose sole aim is to discover drugs that are cheaper than the ones being manufactured by the drugs companies. The industry rapidly needs an injection of disinterested advice as to what should be used. There should be a system for remunerating medical staff on the basis of their savings. Every time some new drug is introduced it costs the taxpayer more. Rarely do we discover some alternative form of treatment that could cost less. There should be a special department whose sole purpose is to discover cheaper ways of doing what is currently being done.

Drugs companies are not alone in their approach to customers. Banks have been in the public eye since the great economic collapse of 2007 /08. Their profits are enormous and their balance sheets are the size of a small country. Because much modern investment banking takes place on the phone telephone conversations of staff are recorded. The public statements of banks would suggest that they are benevolent organizations there with one thing only in mind and that is being of service to their customers. Their charges and the profits that they make, well that is just an unfortunate necessity. The salaries that bankers earn are of course anything but necessary reaching into the stratosphere. Bonuses are paid to bankers that run into millions and several multiples of their annual salary. Yet the conversations on the trading floor about customers that have come to light in some court cases indicate a contempt for customers and are about how to take advantage of their customers.

Banks are notoriously profit redistributors. Only about 5% of banking on the trading floors, which is where much of their profits are made and where much of the higher bonuses are paid, is spent in financing international trade and real economic growth. The rest has properly been described as a casino.

These profits of course belong to the shareholders. Yet nowadays much of these profits are paid to the white collar labour force in ever increasing amounts. The aim of this part of the labour force is merely to make as much money in the short term as possible. That is how their bonuses are calculated. I shall deal with executive compensation in another chapter but for the time being merely point out that there are many businesses – the two that I considered in this chapter are merely examples – that are in business mainly to redistribute wealth and not to create new wealth or make our lives better.

25.   EXECUTIVE COMPENSATION – MARKET FORCES AND CORPORATE GOVERNANCE

In the 1970s when higher rates of tax in the UK were 83% on earned income and 98% on unearned income such as dividends and interest, directors of major public companies like Marks & Spencer did not pay themselves large sums of money. A salary of £50,000 was unusual. There was little point in paying large sums because the government got most of it. Companies provided benefits in a tax efficient way. These included cars and home loans. Companies provided lavish entertainment for their staff and often provided meals. The cash payments to staff however were limited because of the disincentive of taxation policy.

I do not know many people these days, now that tax rates for the very well paid, have been reduced to 45%, who are not outraged by the undeserved payments that many company executives pay themselves. These payments are not deserved. They are merely taken from the company, or rather from the shareholders because of the biased way in which companies are allowed to operate.

During the days when people considered that the only way of making money was to create real wealth business people would risk their money to develop an idea and create a business. If the business failed the business man would lose his money. The business man was generally both the manager and the entrepreneur. Henry Ford comes to mind as typical of the entrepreneurs of those times. Those were the days of the railway companies and of real mechanisation that created real efficiencies that were noticeable, as opposed to the so called efficiencies that nowadays result in merely more paper being produced. The introduction of mechanisation in those days made travel easier and far quicker, it made communication over vast distances possible by the use of the phone. It meant labour saving machines in the mills and factories. The benefits in terms of efficiency were unarguable.

Because of the large sums of money that were necessary to equip a factory with new machinery or to build a railway across a continent it became necessary to split the function of entrepreneur and manager.

However the principle was the very sensible one that the entrepreneur risked his money whereas management was paid for its time. If the project failed management lost their jobs. The entrepreneur lost his money. The very sensible basis for remuneration was that since management got paid for its time if the project succeeded any super profits went to the entrepreneur. That is what was called capitalism. The return in the form of profits to the person who risked his capital.

Management of course were regarded quite properly as part of the labour force. The split between labour and capital and the rewards to each were never clearer.

Senior management got paid more than manual labourer. Exactly how much more remains a difficult question but the difference came to be based upon the educational standards reached rather than the real relative value of the two. However the consequences to both were the same if the project succeeded and if it failed. They lost nothing except future income for which they would not be required to work. The consequences to the entrepreneur were vastly different. The entrepreneur actually lost money if the enterprise failed and made profits if it succeeded.

In order to control the operation of the company there was a board and above the board there were the shareholders, the real entrepreneurs. The shareholders controlled everything ultimately. They could appoint the board and decide their remuneration. The board controlled the day to day operations of the company. The shareholders could decide how the company and the board operated, so long as they had the necessary votes.

Things have changed significantly these days. The major shareholders are now the large fund managers that hold the money that belongs to the ordinary worker who hopes to retire on a pension and to savers who have decided to invest their money through a fund manager. Of course the fund managers are not the real beneficial shareholders. The real beneficial shareholders are the savers, including mainly the future pensioners.

These fund managers are part of the labour force. They get paid a salary for their work that often involves nothing more onerous than attending meetings and discussing the progress of and prospects for shares.

The operation of a company is now split into several parts. There is the management, who are definitely part of the labour force. There is the blue collar labour force if the business is a manufacturing business.   There is the entrepreneur, or the shareholder who is beneficially entitled to the shares. These are the future pensioners, who are frequently unaware that their money has been invested in particular shares and the savers who probably are aware of the shares in which the fund managers have invested their money. They take the risk if the enterprise fails. But do they get the reward if the enterprise is successful. You've guessed it. Not any more, aside from very exceptional circumstances. Then there are the fund managers, who are definitely part of the labour force and not entrepreneurs. Yet it is the fund managers who decide how to risk the money of the real entrepreneurs – the savers.

In the old days the entrepreneur took the decision as to how he would risk his money. He suffered the loss if the enterprise failed and made profits if it succeeded. Now the decision as to risk is taken by professional managers. In theory the risks and rewards go to the real entrepreneurs, the shareholders. In practice this rarely happens.

In theory the fund managers are obliged to act in the interests of their clients. As I have said these managers get paid very well for doing very little. They are often referred to as "whizz kids" or "the brightest and the best". The implication is that they are very clever indeed, in fact rather exceptional. In fact they are not at all clever. The most complicated thinking that they do does not go beyond calculating compound interest and percentages over a number of years and understanding the basic rules of company operations. Many fund managers have no background in finance or banking. They would have trained as chemists or engineers. They found it very easy to take up a new career in banking and finance because it is very easy. It should take the average fund manager about 6 weeks to learn his trade. What he gains later is experience and memory of facts. Those who manage their own investments all have that skill. Many who manage their own investments perform better than the "brightest and the best" fund managers.

There is no doubt in theory that these fund managers are supposed to procure for their clients the maximum returns possible. Taken to its logical conclusion these fund managers are supposed to ensure that the rewards that are paid to labour are as low as possible whilst the return to the entrepreneurs, their clients, are as high as possible.

The problem here is that being on the side of labour themselves these fund managers are in an impossible position. Their duty to their clients conflicts with their self interest. Of course we know that the rule governing the behaviour of professionals is that where duty and interest conflict they must do their duty and ignore their self interest. However in practice only lip service is ever paid to this principle. I can think of no situation where this principle has been applied in practice. When duty and interest conflict the latter is generally the victor, and duty the victim.

The fund managers, being part of the labour force are meant to keep the wages of themselves, who charge outrageous fees to their clients for "managing" their money, as low as possible. That is an illusion. They overcome this problem of conflict by agreeing with the benighted investor a fee in advance of taking his money. Has anybody read the book that was a best seller on Wall Street some years ago entitled "Where are the clients' yachts". The title says it all.

However these fund managers are also meant to keep the wages of the labour force - including the wages of the executives of the companies in which they invest their clients' money, as low as possible. This should not be such an onerous duty. Unfortunately it appears to be.

The fund managers are individuals. They often sit on boards of companies. They often sit on remuneration committees. They are very close to and friends of the executives of the companies. They are entertained regally by them. Moreover fund managers are also companies. Many are parts of large banks, with boards and shareholders. The executives of major companies are often invited to sit on boards of companies that are part of the fund managers. They will often participate in decisions regarding the remuneration of the fund managers themselves and their colleagues. The system is so incestuous that it is often difficult to tell which company board meeting is being held since many of the same faces appear on several boards. The idea that a fund manager will overtly take any action that will reduce the amount that an executive pays himself is absurd. It will never happen, except is wholly unusual circumstances, such as for example when an acquisition is in contemplation.

There is accordingly a real conflict, not for the first time, between the forces of labour, in this case management of the company and the fund managers, on the one hand, and the entrepreneur, on the other. In a real capitalist society the latter could be expected to win that battle, or at least the law would protect him. Not in today's society. The tables have turned. The white collar labour force have gained control over the entrepreneur's money and not unnaturally claim most of it for themselves. The entrepreneur now risks any losses but has to share his profits with the fund managers, who often take 20% of such profits. When losses are made the fund managers take their fees, which are not insubstantial.

There is a very simple solution to the problem of executive greed. The entrepreneur should be given back his power to decide on management compensation. That does not mean the fund managers. Only the real entrepreneur should be allowed to vote on such an issue. The ordinary shareholder is the real entrepreneur. It is he who takes the risk if a company becomes insolvent. It is he who should decide how the profits of a company should be shared. It is he who should decide whether the management should get a bonus for doing their job.

Some time ago I wrote to the British government minister responsible asking her why she did not introduce a short bill stating that fund managers would only be able to vote shares according to the directions of those who beneficially hold those shares. I did not receive a reply. I wrote to one of the national newspapers and was told that they considered such a proposal to be "too radical". Giving shareholders real rights is "too radical". Now we know that labour has triumphed over capitalism.

Now the European Union, incensed by the damage that has been done to the banking system by massive bonuses has reacted by introducing legislation that limits the size of bonuses to 100% of base salary and 200% with shareholder approval.

The reaction of people in London to this outrageous suggesting that the brightest and the best would have their greed curtailed is to threaten to leave the UK for Switzerland. The Swiss people have reacted by deciding that they do not approve of the bonus system either.

Yet the legislators miss the point. The fund managers will still vote with their friends. They will still support massive executive bonuses because they want them too. The real entrepreneurs are not allowed to vote.

Banks – particularly investment banks – make profits from trading. In this they use the money of depositors, who are unaware that their deposits are being risked in that way. Indeed the depositors would be horrified if they found out what really happens with their money.

It is likely that the shareholders are also unaware what is being done with their money too.

So armed with shareholders and depositors money the intrepid bankers take risks on the same basis that the croupier at a casino takes one's chips. If the bet comes off he gets 20%, if he loses money the depositors and shareholders lose 100%. In addition of course the banker gets a rather generous salary. Heads the depositor and shareholder lose tails the banker wins. Not an example of a level playing field.

This sharing of profit without any risk attached is one of the aspects of the new market economy. Take no risk with your own money. Risk money that belongs to somebody else who is unaware of the risk being taken. If the risk results in a loss that other person suffers. If it results in a profit take a percentage of such profits.

That is the game currently being played out in the corporate sector. The management receive a bonus if things go well and suffer no loss if things go badly.

But how did these large bonus payments come about? How were they authorized. Are they really necessary. Are they really, as those who benefit from them have claimed, brought about by market forces, that ubiquitous phrase that is trotted out to justify the most unfair and unreasonable compensation packages?

The simple answer is that the market has been rigged. Those who decide the pay of these executives are not using their own money. They are using shareholders' money. Employees tend to be employed by other employees who will be senior to the new employees. If a senior employee hires a junior employee and pays him a huge salary and bonus it follows that the more senior employee will be able to justify a larger bonus and salary for himself.

Bankers have also manipulated the compensation system for professionals. They pay lawyers and accountants whatever the lawyers and accountants demand. Yet these costs are passed on to the borrower, who cannot complain to the lawyers and accountants because they are not employed by him.

The real truth is that compensation is not determined by the free market at all. There is only one really free market and that is the market of an end product where the consumer is using his own money. Other markets such as the market for individual employees is not free at all.

There is a way of overcoming the anomaly and that is for the senior employee to be given a budget for his activities. Every £ more that he pays an employee is a £ less that he will retain. Only in that way can the compensation of the junior employee be said to be subject to market forces.

I suppose there would be nothing wrong with paying people a share of profit if their salaries were small. There are many jobs where people get remunerated on a commission basis. Often there is no salary. The commission is an incentive. However the bonuses being paid to people in the city of London and on Wall Street, as well as to corporate executives and the army of professionals is on top of a very generous indeed often extravagant salary.

I wonder what Henry Ford would have said if he had been approached by one of the professional managers who proposed to the ageing entrepreneur that he should put his feet up and play more golf and let him manage the company. Henry could have asked how much the manager would want. If it was one of today's managers the answer would have been about $1million basic salary and a bonus based on the profits made to be determined by a remuneration committee. And who would sit on this remuneration committee. My friends of course, would be the manager's reply. Henry would have shown the manager the door. And so would anybody faced with a deal based on what is acceptable today in the corporate world.

Suppose I was to propose a deal in which I manage your money, invest it as I please, charge a fee irrespective of whether I make a profit or not and if I make a profit my mates and I will decide how much of it my associates and I should retain and how much should be paid to you. We will work out my share of profits on the basis that you should receive a return equal to a certain percentage acceptable return. The rest will go to me. This is the deal that we do daily with our pension money and other savings. Nobody in their right mind would agree to such an offer. However the majority of us accept this arrangement through ignorance. We simply do not know what is going on. The complexity of the system and this ignorance as well as the disenfranchisement of shareholders amounts to legalised theft.

The system could be easily replaced with one that is firstly a real capitalist system and secondly one that encourages enterprise and hard work. Yet the government will not do anything. All that they see is the scandal of what they call executive payment for failure. This is a small tip of the problem. If an executive gets paid far above what he deserves but the company makes profits he is stealing just as much as if he is paid a large sum when the company loses money or its profits fall.

Executive pay these days is running at around 70 times the average wage. In the 1970s it was around 20 times. What has given rise to this vast real increase in wages. Is it their sheer brilliance. Far from it. In the 1990s Marks & Spencer made profits of close to £1billion. Then their CEO was earning about £100,000. Now their CEO is making millions yet the company is making around £500million. If that is not rewarding failure I do not know what is. I fear we must not look at whether CEOs deserve their rewards. They pay themselves these vast sums simply because the system allows them to do so. There is no sound reason behind these payments. And what is more, these payments will continue to increase until companies are nearly bankrupt. Certainly executives will continue to squeeze company profits for their own benefit so long as the company can afford it. The share indices will continue to drift so long as the amount left to shareholders continues to stagnate or indeed fall.

When the first £million directors took place in the 1980s I remember wondering why it is that directors of Woolworths for example can get increases of 30% - 50% for doing the same job as the previous year whilst their shop staff only got 5%. The implication was that the contribution made during the year by management was supererogatory whilst the contribution from the shop staff was not. And how are we to identify this devotion to duty. There is no answer. After all the board is meant to do its very best in the interests of the shareholders.

Unless and until real shareholders are permitted to vote on executive pay the system will continue to cause large redistributions of wealth.

There is another possible system – aside from high taxation – that might be introduced at least to cope with the bonus system. Employees should be asked to nominate the bonus that they should receive as a percentage of their salaries on one condition and that is that if they make losses or do not meet their budget the same percentage will be taken from their wages and other assets as compensation. Only in that way can the trader at the bank or the investment manager be said to be taking a real risk. It is only those who take entrepreneur's risks that should be permitted to take entrepreneur's rewards.

331

Failure to deal with the issue of excessive pay is the root cause of the economic crisis that has fallen on the developed Western industrialized world. The problem will recur as more wealth redistribution occurs and at the core of this redistribution are the wages of highly paid employees.

26.   OF POLITICS AND POLITICIANS

Why is there such disillusionment with politics? Why do politicians lie? Why do they avoid questions and rant on in their public broadcasts as if they were making a statement rather than answering the question. I have often wondered whether the habit of politicians of answering not the question asked but the one they want to be asked has not contributed in a large way to the decline in educational standards.

Young children taking exams are always instructed to answer the question. They are told for example that if they are asked a question about the Battle of Hastings they should not write all they know about William the Conqueror. But politicians do exactly that. Young children must surely be confused when their leaders who are also in a way celebrities, answer any question by picking something associated with any word in the question and saying anything that is in some way connected with that word. Of course we all know why politicians do that. The true answer to the question they have been asked is embarrassing at best or would lead to an admission that the politician has behaved corruptly at worst. So the politician avoids the question and answers a completely different one. Often the politician starts his answer with the words "that's not the question" before posing the question he wants to answer and proceeding to answer that question instead.

The word political is often used to describe certain behaviour. What does it mean. I believe that if rather than using a devalued word that has lost its meaning the true meaning was used the effect would be greater. The word political means that something is done in order to get the actor re-elected.

Politicians have behaved in a political way for ever. Machiavelli lived in the middle ages. It was politicians who killed Julius

Ceasar. Mark Anthony was a politician. Christ was crucified by politicians.

It is not so long ago that the Soviet Union represented to us in the West a form of dictatorship that was the antithesis of western democracy. There a small number of officials decided who was to be leader and the leader was imposed on the people. The leader's word was law. There was a show of support from various meetings and congresses and these were always unanimous. Ordinary people who stepped out of line were severely punished. Yet surprisingly from time to time there were changes when ordinary people revolted. There was a revolution in Iran. The Soviet Union itself was the result of a revolution when the Czar was deposed. Modern China too is the result of a revolution. These revolutions happened because there were sufficient numbers of ordinary people who were willing to risk their lives to overthrow their oppressors. Nevertheless it remains illustrative to me that the majority of people in countries that are not democracies seem quite content with their lives. This is probably because economic matters are more important than the right to challenge the ruling elite. Indeed it is only to those who aspire to political positions that a dictatorship is oppressive. To those who wish merely to get on with their lives and accept the status quo elections are of little importance.

In the west we had elections. This means that when we find that the government is behaving oppressively we can overthrow it without bloodshed. That is the one great benefit of democracy. Perhaps it is the only benefit.

Leaving the issue of a change of government aside are we really able to claim such superiority for our system of elections, particularly when there is not so much as a cigarette paper between the two parties who may form a government.

The so called Arab Spring that resulted in the overthrow of the Libyan and Egyptian leadership are depicted as revolts in favour of democracy. We are told that the people who are revolting want freedom. They want freedom of speech.

This is nonsense. The people want jobs. They want fair distribution of wealth. Money is more important than free speech. Indeed enough money buys free speech and free speech without the means of living is not worth very much.

Even dictatorships go through the process of holding elections. These appear to be rigged affairs. People are kept in check however not by these phony elections. They are kept in check by apathy. Those who try to overthrow or to participate in overthrowing the existing regime are treated brutally, even killed so long. That is not unusual. Even in Britain which has abolished the death penalty for most crimes there is still a death penalty for treason. However no government or system can survive if there is a groundswell of popular opinion that is willing to march against it and man barricades. The people must therefore be either brainwashed or kept apathetic. This rule applies to dictatorships as well as democracies.

The Western democracies have elections but in reality nothing changes. The rich and powerful stay rich and powerful. There is considerable apathy and for good reason. The faces may change but the underlying principles do not. Yet many people still believe in politics and vote with fervour. They also speak glowingly about the wonderful characteristics of the most roguish politicians. Why is that?

Politics does not only take place in the national or government arena. It exists wherever there are people who have to act collectively. A good example is the large corporations. Most people working in a large, or even a small corporation will talk about office politics. I believe we can learn a lot about politics by examining the phenomenon of office politics.

By politics, in the corporate sector, people mean quite simply back stabbing, lying and conspiring in order to get promotion and a greater share of the corporate cake than before. Sometimes it means holding on to ones job. There is no attempt as there is in governmental politics to pretend that it does not exist. Everybody knows it happens. It is explained away by saying that there is politics wherever there are people. That may be true but politics is the act of realising ones self interest. When a potential chief executive tries to get the top job he or his friends will do everything they can to destroy his competitors for the top job. If appointed the new CEO will reward his friends for helping him to get the top job. And why does he want the top job. For himself of course. That however is not what he tells the appointing committee. They will announce with all the eloquence that a top class education equips them to do, that they have appointed the best man for the job, the one who can lead the company to greater and better times, the one who will make most profits for the shareholders.

Nobody in the company however will have any doubt that he is therefore his own self interest. The top job gives him financial rewards. It enables him to have power. It provides him with luxuries in having most things done for him - all he has to do is pontificate about points of principle or strategy, attend meetings and make speeches, usually the same speeches, and sometimes give interviews. The idea that the prospective CEO wants the job because he wants to act in the best interests of the shareholders is laughable. They are merely an inconvenience that needs to be satisfied so that he can get on with what truly matters to him – getting as much of the corporate profits into his own pocket. Any candidate who suggests that he wants the job for altruistic reasons would be immediately removed from the list. That suggestion would be greeted with universal skepticism by his colleagues.

The appointing committee will ask what he can do for the company. It is realistic and regards the matter as one of mutual interest. He delivers better profits, and in return gets the large rewards. However the appointing committee is made up not of the shareholders but of people in the same position as the CEO. They are kindred spirits.

Why should things be any different in governmental politics. The politician who wants to be prime minister or president wants the job for himself. He does so for all the reasons that a CEO would want it, except that the remuneration package is less of a priority and power is a greater one. Does anybody remember the scramble during the 2000 US presidential election when either candidate could have won depending on whether votes were counted or not. Can anybody who witnessed the effort that took place in deciding whether Bush or Gore had won have any doubt that these two men wanted to win for their own purposes. They like to give the electors the impression that they want to win in order to serve. Nothing can be further from the truth. They simply want the top job just as a CEO wants the top job. They want it for themselves. They want the prestige, the publicity, the power, the position. Certainly they have to pay their dues and they reward their supporters. They after all make many promises to get elected.

It is amusing to see people's reaction to the position of the queen of the UK. Her supporters like to think that she does not want the job. She would rather do something else. She only does it because of her overwhelming sense of duty. It is as if her successors must by definition be worse than her.

In fact the history of the British royal family is one of fratricide, matricide, patricide. They have killed and plotted to get their share of power by doing some of the most egregious things to members of their family. Yet people are deluded. They see what they want to see.

And why is it that so many people do not see that politicians want their jobs for their own self interest and esteem – their ambition. The answer is simple. They believe that by voting for one candidate or another they will benefit themselves financially. This sounds like a good deal. Just turn up at a voting station for a few minutes every 4 or 5 years or so and if the candidate that you are backing wins he will transfer wealth from the other side to you. Not a bad deal. That is why people vote. That is why they say things like "George Bush is the finest leader America has ever had". They simply think they will benefit from a transfer of wealth.

Modern politics is about redistribution of wealth. Wars still go on but they are no longer wars for profit. They tend to be wars of principle carried out frequently so that the political leaders can be re-elected – assuming that they win the particular war. Modern politics is about the economy. People believe – rightly – that governments are able to re-distribute wealth. As a result there is tension to take wealth from the other side, but since there are two sides and redistribution by law tends to be somewhat indiscriminate no government has been willing to make material redistributions. The amount of redistribution of wealth through taxation is now very limited. The status quo tends to be maintained.

Yet governments either do not know or understand or if they are they are unwilling to point out to people that vast sums of wealth are redistributed in the private sector daily.

Politicians deal in words. They hold rallies and they make set speeches. Here in Britain the political leader and his government are subjected to questions in parliament. However the persons questioned need not respond. They merely address the issues that please them and there is no recourse. In fairness that happens also in courts of law where a witness may not answer the question he is asked at all. The judge will usually turn to the advocate asking the question and comment wryly "you have asked the question a number of different ways and that is the answer you keep getting , move on". In other words the evasive answer creates an inference. Politicians are just more expert than most witnesses in courts of law. They are after all professionals who have armies of advisers who prepare them with answers to the questions that they may get thrown at them.

The problem is the public. The majority do not understand the process, and are also partial. When questioned in an interview politicians adopt the same formula. I remember a sketch in Yes Minister in which a civil servant was late and apologised. His excuse was that he was delayed by the press. "You spoke to the press" the minister said astonished. "And what did you tell them". "I answered their questions" he said. The Minister was horrified. "You did what". "That's not how you deal with the press. You tell them "That's not the question, the real question is and then you tell them the question you want them to ask and answer that". That is exactly what politicians do. And we apparently accept that, although of course we notice it.

Only fools believe what politicians say. Judge them by their actions not their words. Words are cheap. Yet they are judged by their words not only by the public but also the press who ought to know better. The press of course prefer an easy life and if they merely repeat what the politicians say they are more likely to have an easy life. So they act as the mouthpieces of the politicians, particularly the government.

When asking a politician a question about his principles and beliefs journalists in particular should ask "could you please give me one example of an action that corroborates what you have just alleged" or some such question that asks for evidence of actions that support the words and claims.

I recall listening to Dick Cheyne who was being interviewed about the Iraq war and how he reviewed intelligence material. We all know now that the intelligence material that was used to justify the war was wrong. Human nature being what it is the chances were that intelligence went both ways. Naturally they selected the reports that supported the war and ignored the ones that said that Sadam Hussein was no threat. Cheyne put pressure on people in the intelligence services to produce reports that supported the war. He justified his actions by saying that going to war was serious and he subjected to very rigorous questions the intelligence officers who made reports. The impression he created was of a person who did not want to take a step towards war without being absolutely sure. In fact his actions were exactly the opposite. He did everything possible to go to war. Yet the analysis by the press and other pundits was tepid.

The interviewer left Cheyne's answer at that. A more diligent interviewer should have asked "please give me one example of an intelligence report that indicated that Sadam was a threat that you threw out as unreliable, and one that went the other way and your reasons for rejecting either". Cheyne would have been unable to give a reply and would have responded with a completely unrelated answer. That at least would have proved his guilt. Of course Cheyne would have claimed national security as a defense for not answering the question.

Has anybody noticed how often politicians start an answer to a question with the word "what". What is a word that is used to ask a question. Our politicians however have turned it into an affirmative statement. So common is the use of this form of answer that ordinary people now use it indiscriminately. The words "what" and "is" are introduced into an affirmative statement that does just as well or rather better without them. Thus we have "what we must do is ..." When "we must do ..." is much clearer and simpler. "What we are trying to achieve is ..." When "we are trying to achieve ..." Is far easier to understand and clearer. It is now so commonplace that most people use this corrupt form of unnecessary words. Why is it so beloved of politicians such as Tony Blair, who is one of the worst offenders. It is a way of combining a question with an answer. Thus when a politician does not want to answer a particular question because the true answer is embarrassing or will reveal that he lied or was behaving corruptly, he will use the word "what" to start to affirm something. The implication is that he is really answering the question. Thus "what are you trying to achieve" is answered "what we are trying to achieve is". But if the politician is not asked "what are you trying to achieve" but "when did you find out about the money not reaching the persons for whom it was intended" will be answered with "what we are trying to achieve is" thereby implying that the questions was "what were you trying to achieve". Always beware a politician who starts an answer to a question with the word "what". He is trying to redefine the question and to pretend he is answering it. If he was really trying to answer a question honestly he would omit the words "what" and "is" and get on with it.

27.   THE EEC, MONETARY UNION AND SOVEREIGNTY

Many years ago I had lunch with a distinguished member of the financial community in London. It was a time when Britain had just been bounced out of the ERM. That was the mechanism by which the £ was linked to other currencies within the EU. My lunch partner repeated the mantra about how it was impossible for Britain to join the Euro because there was no convergence between the European and British economies. This smokescreen is one of those tricks that are used by the articulate educated classes to mislead people. A new phrase is used. It makes superficial sense. People accept it as if it is the holy grail and it becomes received wisdom. If asked why this particular mantra has gained such credibility, the answer one will receive is that it is obvious. Of course it is not obvious at all. Like other similar ways of persuading the masses to accept something as truth merely through repetition this mantra has only to be examined with rudimentary care to discover that it is nonsense.

Superficially of course it sounds like common sense that two countries that have disparate economies should have different currencies. But that ignores the real function of money, which I have addressed in an earlier chapter. But let me get back to my story, and I will return to the analysis of the Euro later. I decided to be provocative to my lunch host and said that I cared little about convergence and sovereignty, all I knew was that these Europeans were either beaten or saved in the war by us and therefore we should lead such an enterprise. My host readily admitted that that was exactly how he felt. The veneer came off and the truth emerged. It was sheer prejudice. He did not object to a single currency if it was the £ sterling. He merely objected to the economic tune for the UK being determined by a committee in Brussels even though such a committee would include representatives of the UK.

Before considering the case for and against the Euro analytically it is worth addressing the prejudicial aspects. Why are so many people in the UK opposed to the Euro. Would they still be opposed if they became wealthier as a result? Perhaps they would. They would rather be poorer and more British than richer and less British. But would they? I doubt it. The argument seems to be that they want this vital part of the British way of life – our economy - to be governed by a British person. The fact that we have a German queen and that the head of the English football team was once a Swede does not seem to worry people too much. Now we have a Canadian governor of the Bank of England. Perhaps that is more acceptable because at least he is not a German, like our queen.

The fact that these foreigners who run vital parts of our country is ignored. I merely make the point that it is results that matter surely rather than whether the decisions that led to the results were made by a person who was British or not. I doubt that anybody who sees economic policies adopted that are advocated by a Russian, American or Austria economist would care two hoots about the nationality of the individual. I guess the implication behind the objection to a foreigner is that he could not be trusted. Yet many of our major companies are run by foreigners. It makes no sense. The reality must therefore be irrational.

The fact that some policies about privatisation were first carried out in Chile under the guidance of an economist from Chicago is not considered wrong because of their origins. The ideological and emotional case against the Euro is I am sure overstated and will not stand up to practical scrutiny. People make money by investing in foreign currencies. They may be patriotic but they know where their interests lie. The Falkland Islanders are British but they do not want to and will not pay British taxes. If they had a choice to pay taxes like the rest of us pay or become part of Argentina I wonder what they would choose. After all they left this country and went to live in a far off cold desolate land to avoid British taxes. Not a very patriotic act. Patriotism and emotions about sovereignty are only as deep as the pockets of those who claim it is so important.

Many of the so called "brightest and best" in the UK threaten to leave the country if they are taxed more. That is not the act of a patriot. If your country needs you, you should be prepared to do whatever you can to help. Yet no such criticism is leveled against these putative absconders.

There is a more serious case against the Euro. It is based on interest rates. The skeptics claim is that different countries have different rates of inflation and since inflation can only be controlled by interest rates it is essential that each country that has a different rate of inflation has a different currency so that interest rates that are appropriate to that situation are applied there.

I have discussed this matter in a previous chapter and there must be doubts whether raising interest rates reduces inflation or vice versa. However for the purposes of this chapter we must assume that it is the correct antidote.

We should further assume that lowering interest rates could even increase economic activity, a subject that I addressed in an earlier chapter.

The argument of the Euro skeptics is therefore that if the UK is experiencing inflation whereas other European countries are not then the UK should have a different rate of interest than the rest of Europe. Likewise if the UK was in an economic downturn while the rest of Europe was not the UK should have a lower rate of interest than the rest of Europe in order to enable it to recover.

Of course that argument applies in the US or Australia, or indeed for parts of the UK. Russia or India are even more extreme examples, and now China and Brazil, which have two clearly different economies could be added to the list.

For many years we in the UK have talked about the North / South divide. The North is doing badly economically whilst the South is doing well. Should the North not have its own currency and interest rates.

Somehow we manage and so do other countries.

There is no reason why Europe should not be treated in the same way.

Of course the reality is that manipulating interest rates has no real effect upon economic activity. It is the perception of profitability, which might involve the perception of future inflation that affects economic activity. It is hard work and not monetary manipulation that affects economic activity.

At one time Britain ran an empire that stretched from Canada to Africa, to India and Australia. Each of the member countries including economies so disparate as India and Nigeria, Australia and Cyprus, had the same currency, the £ Sterling. None of them complained. None of them were prejudiced by having the same currency. There was no runaway inflation in any of these countries.

But then we controlled that particular single currency, and furthermore we had stable and honest money because we were on the gold standard. Things are different now.

In the Euro zone in order to raise interest rates or print money one must have the good of the majority in mind, and in some cases unanimity. The Euro zone has more honest money. Politicians of one country cannot simply devalue a currency or cause hyper inflation in their currency. They cannot just print money and pay their creditors with useless pieces of devalued paper.

That makes the Euro currency more stable, more like the gold standard.

Is it really a good thing to have a government that can defraud creditors by paying them with useless currency. They will only do that once. Is it such a bad thing that members of the Euro zone cannot just print money and devalue a currency. Is it such a bad thing that members of the Euro zone cannot redistribute wealth with such ease as the UK can.

The value of the Euro has remained strong despite the problems with Ireland, Greece and Italy.

Their insolvency has been blamed upon their membership of the Euro. Yet those who blame them advocate that they could easily get out of their problems if they had their own currency by simply paying creditors with devalued money. Is that really a good solution. Paying with devalued money is the same as paying only a percentage of one's debts. That is what happens in insolvency.

Anybody would think that insolvencies do not happen in those countries that borrow in their national currency. That of course is nonsense.

It is also possible for UK companies and indeed the UK government to borrow in Euros.

Insolvency is nothing to do with the particular currency in which one's debts are denominated. It is simply borrowing more than one can repay.

I am not pro the Euro. I am neutral on it and that is the only legitimate conclusion I can reach on the subject. I am marginally in favour because of the exchange costs that we incur whenever we go abroad. Moreover having the same currency makes a market more competitive. It makes prices easier to measure and compare. It makes the computer vendors in Ireland susceptible to the price pressures from European producers and forces them to keep their prices low.

The recent economic collapse of many Western economies under a massive burden of debt has resurrected arguments against the Euro. We are told for example that Greece should be outside the Euro. If it still had the Drachma it would simply be able to devalue it and hey presto its troubles would be over. This is facile nonsense.

Devaluing a currency is the equivalent of defaulting on its debt. If I was entitled to receive 100 drachma and could buy $10 with it when I lent the money but when I received repayment and as a result of devaluation I was only able to buy $5 with the 100 drachma I received I would consider that the borrower had defaulted.

If I knew that such devaluation was a possibility I would either not have lent the money or done so at a much higher rate of interest.

And what would be the consequence of such a notional default. Would anybody lend to a borrower in Greece again.

No the Euro is merely a measurement of value. The more constant it is the better because it enables true values to be recognised and proper calculations of risk to be made. It does not matter what currency is used to measure value as long as it is constant. The more constant it is the better it is.

The most recent country to suffer in the Euro zone has been Cyprus. What happened in Cyprus is a good example of irrational reaction by so called experts. The commentators are united in arguing that the problem with Cyprus is the result of the Euro and it may lead to the demise of the Euro.

Yet as a politician interviewed on the matter said, it is nothing to do with the Euro. There are countries inside the Euro that have economic problems, and there are countries outside the Euro that have economic problems. There are countries inside the Euro that are doing well and there are countries outside the Euro that are doing well.

A closer analysis of what happened in Cyprus would be helpful to show the failure of logic by our so called experts. The commentators frequently and negligently say that Cyprus is insolvent. This is in fact not the case. What happened in Cyprus is nothing to do with government insolvency as happened in Greece. What happened in Cyprus is what happened in the UK and US and indeed other countries outside the Euro Zone. It was a banking crisis. Two of the largest banks in Cyprus were insolvent – just as the largest banks in the UK and US were insolvent in 2007/08.

The banks could either have been left to fail leaving depositors with a fraction of what they had deposited or they could be bailed out leaving the bill with the taxpayers.

Unlike the UK and US the Cyprus government did not have enough fire power to bail out these banks. It was nothing to do with the Euro. It was because the size of the banks was several times one year's GDP of Cyprus. How did these two banks get to be so large. This of course happened in the UK with RBS and the US with Citibank. It also happened in Iceland. In the UK and US the taxpayer paid the price. In Iceland the failed banks were allowed to fail.

The Cyprus banks grew to such a size because of deposits from Russians and their decision to attract more and more deposits by offering unsustainably high interest rates, like the Iceland banks.

For reasons best known to the Cyprus government they decided to ask for the help of the ECB. They could have merely left the banks to fail as did the Icelanders.

When an entity is insolvent the question is how is the pain to be shared. The US and UK decided it had to be shared collectively as in a socialist state. In Iceland it was decided that the creditors should take the paid. In Cyprus it was decided that the depositors should share the pain with other Euro zone members. None of that means that the Euro caused the problem. The problem was caused by the old principle of liabilities exceeding the value of assets. That is the definition of insolvency. It has always been.

The Cyprus banks could have borrowed in any currency. They probably did so. They could have used their own currency and still have been in the same situation. They simply took on debts that were not matched by their assets. The consequences were inevitable. The Euro neither enabled them to borrow these large sums not compelled them to do so.

Indeed it is at least arguable that the banks grew and grew because they offered facilities for tax avoidance or evasion or even money laundering. That approach to business, particularly the low tax rates, is arguably the real problem since Ireland also collapsed financially. It is not of course inevitable that a country with low tax rates will fail. It is however a warning that there are no quick fixes. There are no panaceas. Low tax rates that give rise to rapid apparent growth often lead to problems. There is no substitute for hard work and slow but steady progress. Any economy that grows too fast will probably cause imbalances that will destroy it sooner or later.

A good economy is a stable economy not one that grows too quickly. Rapid economic growth in advanced countries is either illusory or the result of wealth redistribution and when the person or country that has to pay the price is asked to pay it the inevitable reaction is that they do not want to and do not like it. They right ask "why me". The apparent growth then has to be unwound and other innocent parties suffer, usually closer to home.

28.   MARKETING AND ADVERTISING

Although I have written about professionals I have decided to write a separate chapter about this particular breed of professionals simply because their profession involves the manipulation of people's minds. They are the master brain washers. Their job is to make people do what they would not otherwise do. They are employed by companies wishing to increase their sales as well as by politicians who wish to be elected. They are professional brain washers.

These people unashamedly have meetings at which they discuss how to make us ordinary people do what we would not otherwise want to do. They discuss how to change our minds. In particular they discuss ways of making us part with our money. In many cases they work on ways of persuading us to pay more, far far more, for a product than it is really worth. The basis for their profession is that a sufficient number if not most of us, are so incredibly stupid that we can be led to do what they want us to do. And of course what they want us to do most of all is to pay them money.

If a highway robber were to try to take our money we would complain. If we are conned into parting with our money some people will say that we only have ourselves to blame. The professional marketing executive however does this every day and nobody complains. Certainly there are sometimes complaints about false advertising but these are few and far between. Generally marketing is subtle, assumes we are thick and will part with our money much of which finds its way into their pockets. And of course they are right. We are that stupid. The proof is the wealth of these people.

Marketing executive believe, apparently correctly that we are influenced by certain colours. They believe we are influenced into buying more petrol by showing us a picture of a tiger running along a beach. They believe that we will buy useless creams to make our sagging muscles firm again as if we were 20 years old again. To back up their claim they show us a picture of a 20 year old claiming that she (it is usually a woman) is 50 years old. The picture may be hazy and blurred but the model is glamorous. We fall for it although these expensive creams do nothing at all.

Advertising is generally used to take customers away from one supplier in favour of another. They try to make you believe that the other product is better. They use all sorts of tricks at the basis of which is the assumption that we are fools, and in many cases they are right. Their strategy will only succeed if we really are fools.

Advertisers however are very slippery. It is often difficult to find out whether an advertising campaign has succeeded. There are all sorts of well known statements that describe this problem such as the one from an alleged MD of a major company who claims that he knows that 50% of his advertising budget is a waste of money but he does not know which 50%.

The truth is that it is impossible to tell whether an advertising campaign has worked. I remember one business in the 1970s in the UK who never advertised but whose sales were increasing annually. He was constantly being pestered by advertisers to use their services. Why should I, he asked. Because your sales will increase came back the inevitable reply. But my sales are increasing. Ah but if you advertised they will increase even more. One year he relented, and did advertise. His sales dropped. When he complained the advertiser said that if he had not advertised his sales would have fallen more. It's like punching a snow flake.

Yet large companies fall for it time and again. As a general rule I never listen to what a supplier says about his product. Many people take a different view. They will ask a supplier what the product is like, as if they would say if it was rubbish.

The advertising brochures that one is given at car show rooms are a good example. They make the car look wonderful and those who drive it wonderful too, just like we would like to be. The implication is that if we drive a car like that we too will look wonderful. And people really believe that rubbish. If they do not then the advertising budget is a waste of money.

We know that there are three motivating forces, greed, sex and fear. Advertisers tend to focus on greed and sex to persuade us to part with money that is better off in our pockets. Of course they use flattery to persuade us that we should give them and their clients our money. They are very able brain washers. You should beware of their tricks. Here are some examples.

Once upon a time, long long ago, music involved the production of beautiful melody. Nobody knew what the person singing or playing looked like. People like Steve Wonder was blind but had a beautiful voice. People listened to his wonderful voice. Luciano Pavarotti had the most wonderful voice and people loved listening to him. No matter what you looked like the public wanted to hear music. Nowadays we have the spice girls and similar bands. In fact there are many girl bands. The members are beautiful and sexy. They dress in the most suggestive clothes and reveal as much as possible. Most of them are tone deaf. Yet people, our young in particular flock to their concerts and listen to their tone deaf monotones. It is utter rubbish. Yet these "musicians" are multi billionaires. Mozart will be turning in his grave. He died a pauper. Yet these tone deaf people selling sex are billionaires. That is what advertisers do. It is true that they play on the simplicity of minds of the young but the old are vulnerable to this kind of pressure too.

Have you ever seen a new car model being launched at a car show. The car usually has draped around it some sexy half naked model who sprawls over it. People apparently will buy that car because of the naked woman. I hope it is nonsense but it happens often enough to make it credible that people fall for this fantasy trick.

Try to sell some fancy cereal and the picture of some sexy woman appears. Apparently we will choose a particular brand over another because one is associated in our minds with a sexy model.

If course the causal connection cannot be established. When asked the advertisers say that these images act on our sub conscious. We identify the brands with these pleasing images and we buy the product. Doubtless other competing brands do the same. So nothing is gained in the end. Money is just paid to the advertisers. Large sums of money for them to buy their yachts and villas in the South of France. And who is paying for it. We are of course. We just do not know it. They are stealing from us and we are unaware of it. Are we fools or what?

Greed is another way of attracting customers. Invest in this fund and you will make a fortune we are told. Stories of people who have made a fortune are told. You will save money if you buy from a particular supermarket we are told as if cutting costs is the aim of the major grocers. They shamefacedly claim that their aim is to keep prices low. If I was managing director of a major supermarket, or indeed a small shop, I would want to charge as high a price as possible. What they really mean is that they want you to buy from them rather than from their competitors and to do so have had to lower their prices but they will only lower them by the minimum amount possible to attract you to their shop. Then they will sting you with highly priced goods that are not on the list of special offers. And we fall for this nonsense time and again - apparently.

Fashion is the big trick of the advertisers. People seem unable to distinguish between different and better. Just because something is different it must be better. The marketing expert will place some uncomfortable item of apparel on the feet or shoulders of a glamorous model. It may be something entirely impractical, indeed hideous. Nevertheless our ladies - it is mostly the ladies - will buy it. All the marketing people need to do is to say that this is popular and suddenly it becomes popular. People will ditch their old clothes and insists on new ones despite the fact that the old ones are in perfect order. New perfumes are introduced and people will pay a fortune to smell a particular way. People walk around beauty departments of shopping malls smelling these aromas, deciding on whom to bestow their hard earned cash. The margin made by these companies is huge. They do nothing that is worth the money they receive and are merely redistributing our hard earned wealth.

29.   SOCIALISED MEDICINE

Now that the US has joined the rest of the developed Western world in providing medical care for all its citizens irrespective of ability to pay one can say that all civilized countries have a national health service.

There are different kinds of arrangements in place in different countries but all at their core have as a principle the right of all citizens – or residents – to health care in times of need.

The US, contrary to popular belief, has had a national health service since the 1960s but it was limited to care for the indigent and for retirees who had paid taxes for a certain period of time. Since most medical care is on the aged a substantial number of its citizens were covered by state funding for their medical care.

Is health care a human right? That is the question that has been decided by those nations that provide their citizens with a national health service have had to address. The opponents of state funding for health generally do so on the basis of market forces principles and choice.

National funding for health inevitably introduces what is often called rationing because the demand for health care is unlimited.

In the UK where there has been a national health service since the 1940s it has always been possible to have considerably more choice and to provide for one's health privately and there is a very profitable health insurance industry and private hospital sector.

Market forces are meant to determine the price of a product. As I explained in an earlier chapter market forces can only apply properly if both the demand and supply for a particular product or service have sufficient elasticity. Thus for example there is no elasticity of demand for water. If the water company decides to charge me £100 for every pint of water I consume I have no choice. Water therefore is not amenable to the forces of demand. It is probably not particularly amenable at least in its natural state to the forces of supply.

Medicine also is not amenable to the forces of demand. If my doctor tells me that I need a particular operation to save my life I have no choice no matter how much it might cost me.

There is another aspect of market forces about which it is important to have a critical approach. Market forces operate only where buyer and seller but particularly the buyer, have perfect information. If the buyer is ignorant market forces are of little relevance. The ignorant buyer simply does not know how much a medical procedure should cost or whether it is really necessary and whether there really are alternatives.

For these two reasons it is foolish to argue that medical care should be a market commodity like buying and selling tomatoes.

There is however another principle that is important and that is the vocation principle. Those who favour keeping the government out of medicine do so on the basis of the assumption that doctors in particular but other medical professionals in general are only in it for the money. This is probably a calumny to many health service professionals who really have a vocation. There is no point in arguing that many health professionals are really in it only for the money. These would probably have lied at interviews when asked why they wanted to become a doctor or join a particular hospital because money is not an acceptable basis on which people generally hire staff, particularly in medicine. There are however numerous dedicated professionals who really do have a vocation.

In the 1970s in Britain when there was a so called "brain drain" of mainly doctors going to the US the vast majority of doctors stayed in the UK and paid the rather higher amounts of tax and received the rather lower salaries that were paid here. These doctors were dedicated and had vocations. It turned out that they were probably better than their colleagues who went to the US. Medical care and the standard of knowledge in the UK was amongst the best in the world and there is no evidence that medical standards in the UK fell as a result of that brain drain.

I usually ask people who enquire about medical care in the UK; "would you rather be treated by a doctor who wants your money or one who gets paid no matter what". That usually settles the argument.

Doctors practicing privately do have a dilemma. In the UK there is no clear boundary between health service doctors and private ones. The practitioners are the same. They practice in the health service and privately.

There is a problem in this respect that I have mentioned elsewhere. These same doctors when approached in their government jobs tell the patient that there is a long waiting list for the particular treatment that the patient requires but if he goes privately and pays that same doctor he could have the operation in a few days. Clearly the resources are nationally available. There is a serious conflict of interest in this approach.

The proper solution to this problem is for a clear demarcation to exist between private and social medicine. A doctor should not be allowed to moonlight. He should make his choice. He either wants to practice privately or in the government service.

Private health does lead to unnecessary procedures which leads to insurers doing their best to gainsay the doctors in order to control the expenditure on medical services.

The US spends more than any other country in the world on health. Yet US citizens do not live longer. More expenditure on health does not lead to better or longer lives.

Medical care is also frequently unbalanced. The first million dollars that is spend on health will save lots of lives and give the beneficiaries a long and healthy life. The last million dollars in an

357

advanced country like the US arguably prolongs life uselessly. Vast sums are spent keeping old people alive on machines for a few more weeks whilst a small amount of money spent on inoculating children in Africa would probably result in considerably good for very low cost.

Medical advances are often achieved without any proper regard to the quality of life. Doctors experiment and spend fortunes on something that might have little benefit.

Drugs companies frequently introduce drugs that turn out to be harmful. There is therefore an army of controllers to ensure that they do not do so.

The constant tension between patients with money and patients without for the attention of health professionals that are in limited supply gives rise to problems that a national health service, properly regulated would avoid. There is no reason why a wealthy person of 75 should get a heart transplant whilst a poor person of 25 should not. Money should not be allowed to make such decisions.

Cuba has one of the most oversupplied health services in the world. There are many doctors and many hospitals. All are free at the point of delivery. Medical personnel receive small salaries. They are not motivated by money and there is no evidence that Cubans are less healthy than their US counterparts. Indeed rationing ensures that there are few overweight Cubans.

Medical care has no place in the market. It is unseemly to have something so important exposed to the principles that govern other ordinary commodities.

30.   CELEBRITIES

The creation of the celebrity culture is a very good way to demonstrate how modern economies have changed over the past 30 or 40 years and the principles set out in this book. It is a very good example of redistribution of wealth and the consequences of paying people larger and larger wages for doing the same job and not having proper regard for market forces.

Celebrities at one time were people with exceptional talent who entertained us. They were film stars and musicians and to a lesser extent sports stars. These celebrities still exist today but they have been joined by an ever increasing army of celebrities who have no particular talent. Indeed the modern day celebrity is just an ordinary person doing an ordinary job. The classical celebrities lived lavish life styles even 100 years ago. However they were few in number. They were the glamorous Hollywood movie stars. There were many other people in the movie business but many of them had a hard time making ends meet.

In recent times the incomes of film stars as well as their number has increased in multiples. Whereas 50 years ago a movie star would own a large house, an expensive car and possibly a yacht, now they have several homes, several cars, a yacht and a plane. They have apartments or villas in New York, the South of France, Cloisters and San Francisco. They have penthouses or mansions in Sydney, London and Paris. They have large boats and small boats. They have fast cars and big cars. They have so much money they do not know what to do with it. They cannot spend it all so the rest is invested in the stock market, property investments, old masters or lies around in a bank deposit account.

The number of stars – why is it that anybody who appears in a movie is called a star – has increased exponentially. So have the number of shows. That is because the number of outlets has increased as a result of TV. The most average comedy show produces stars. There are series that go on for years with very ordinary actors, all of whom make a fortune. Viewers watch TV and accept whatever is on. They are not discriminating. They watch TV because it is their time for watching TV and there is nothing else to do. What they watch when they watch TV is not necessarily good it might be the least bad but they have to watch something because it is their leisure time. You therefore find that when there is a good show on TV there are many others on competing channels, and when there is nothing, well there is nothing good on any channel. The TV companies do not want to waste time with good programmes when other channels are not showing anything good.

Sports stars too have seen stratospheric increases in wages since they became professionals so that nowadays the top performers rival the top film stars in wealth. However their numbers have not really increased materially. The football league clubs are roughly the same in number as they were 100 years ago and they play roughly the same number of matches in front of live audiences that are roughly the same size as they always were.

A recent innovation however has been the increase in the number of celebrities. TV news readers are now celebrities and are paid fortunes for doing what most people do for nothing and perhaps would gladly do on TV just for the privilege of being on TV. Cooks who are no better than our grandmothers at cooking a great meal are now celebrities and are paid fortunes for doing what most people do regularly. There are even celebrities who will teach us how to boil an egg and they are paid fortunes for their advice and commentary. There are models whose main skill seems to be in walking, albeit in a rather peculiar way. There are celebrity estate agents who earn a fortune doing what their counterparts around the country do every day of the week. There are even celebrity cleaners. Doubtless sooner or later every kind of activity will have a celebrity no matter how unskilled one has to be. The term has come to mean "recognizable".

There are game show hosts whose skill seems to be in asking questions written down for them and then awarding points for the answer that is also written down for them. This is a skill that most of us possess and many of us play such games at home. Yet those who do it on TV are paid fortunes for doing a very ordinary and unskilled job.

Then there are the ubiquitous talent shows. Here at least the participants are showing a particular talent.

All the new shows – reality TV, talent shows and game shows - have one thing in common, they show ordinary people on TV. The viewers seem to be fascinated in seeing ordinary people like themselves appearing on TV. They want to see ordinary people.

The ordinary people who are the real stars of these shows receive nothing for their participation, except that talent shows can propel a winner into real celebrity status. It is the hosts, whether they are estate agents or questioners in a quiz game, who are the celebrities. It is they who receive fortunes for doing an unskilled job that many if not most of us could do.

The fascination with appearing on TV can be seen when one views TV cameras at sports matches. Whenever the camera shows spectators who then see themselves on the big screen they get very excited. This reaction would suggest that there is an unlimited number of people who would gladly appear on TV for nothing.

This eagerness to appear on TV and for ordinary people to watch other ordinary people on TV has somehow led to the creation of celebrity judges and celebrity hosts some of whom have become billionaires.

The ordinary people who appear on TV and are the real stars of the show receive nothing for their services. It is the hosts and judges and other participants who appear week after week that achieve the status of "recognition" and therefore become celebrities.

The pay of these ordinary people doing something relatively unskilled including expressing a view as to whether one likes a particular contestant or not – something that anybody who buys a particular CD does for nothing, and indeed puts his money on the line to show what he really thinks –now rivals and in many cases outstrips that of exceptional classical celebrities. How has this phenomenon occurred?

Clearly there are differences between the two kinds of celebrities. It is fair to distinguish between the skilled and unskilled celebrities, the former being the ones who have a particular talent and the latter doing rather ordinary jobs that we all do – like cooking, cleaning and buying houses - or can do with a minimum of training – being a quiz master.

The pay of skilled celebrities has rocketed recently. Footballers now receive multiples of what their predecessors received 50 years ago and so do movie stars and other skilled entertainers.

The question that concerns us for the purposes of this book is how can these vast income of both the skilled and unskilled celebrities be justified. How are they determined and what are the consequences for the economy of these large payments.

In a market economy the wages of both kinds of celebrities should be determined by market forces. The wage for any service provider is determined by the interaction of supply and demand. If there are more celebrities able and willing to do a particular job their wages should go down and vice versa. If there are more viewers willing and able to see these celebrities in action their wages should go up and vice versa.

The service that a celebrity provides, whether he is a footballer, film star, a TV news presenter or one of the unskilled modern celebrities who do ordinary things consists of entertainment to members of the public who pay to view the celebrity in action.

The sums that the celebrities receive for their services are theoretically – at least in a market economy - determined by the interaction of demand and supply for these services.

We like to think of a market as being similar to the one where we buy food and other goods that one sees in towns and cities around the world. In such markets the consumer knows and understands what he is buying. He compares prices. There are many vendors selling the same products so the consumer buys and pays the lowest price for the product he considers best suited to his needs after comparing the goods on offer. Suppliers compete with others and keep their prices as high as possible for their benefit but low enough to sell their products. There is a rather fanciful belief in the supporters of the market system that markets always tend to produce the lowest prices and indeed that those who participate in markets are supporters of market forces.

Neither of these assumptions are true. Both buyers and sellers have opposite interests. Buyers do not like market forces when they push prices up and sellers do not like market forces when they push prices down. Markets are just as able to push prices up as down.

One important aspect of such markets is that day after day and year after year the same or roughly the same goods are sold. The buyer gets used to paying the particular price and knows by comparison what the price of a chicken is relative to the price of tomatoes or a kilo of beef.

How does the market in celebrity services work? It operates in a way that is entirely different from what happens in an open market. It is considerably more complicated than that. The consumer is the viewer. The viewer sees the celebrities on TV or the cinema and sometimes in live events.

When he views the celebrity live he pays a price for the ticket that is determined by market forces roughly similar to what operates in an open market. However the celebrity frequently does not perform on his or her own. He is part of a production, whether on stage or at a football match. It is a collaborative effort. The price paid by the viewer has to be shared, in the case of a theatre performance between all the production staff, the owners of the theatre and the performers and in the case of a football match between the members of the team and the clubs.

Sometimes the performer is an outstanding solo singer. He will of course have accompaniment from a band and other supporting staff but there is no doubt who is the one who the paying public are paying to see. Indeed the supporting staff can probably be replaced with ease by the star and they are employed by him or her.

At football matches or opera for example the situation is different. The effort is far more collaborative. Thus for example the star of a football team might receive £200,000 a week whereas the groundsman might receive £500 and the team physiotherapist might receive £1,000. Another less famous playing member of the team might receive £50,000.

Indeed without the supporting staff the show or game simply cannot go on. In such cases how does the share of the proceeds take place?

There is indeed a market that determines how much a football star like Messi might earn but it is a very small and arguably rigged market. It is certainly not a market like the open market where we buy food and other goods that are displayed for sale day after day and year after year. Indeed the particular object – the services of the celebrity in this case – is unique and might only ever appear on sale once in a lifetime, just like an old master.

The clubs that are able to buy the top players are frequently owned and backed by billionaires who have so much money that they do not know or care what they are paying. The clubs are their hobbies. It is the same with expensive real estate. The market for ordinary real estate might be in a recession but a billionaire might pay a huge sum for a penthouse in Paris. He will pay whatever it takes just because he wants it and can afford it, not because that is its market price. Market value, or rather value for money does not enter into their consideration. They simply want the best footballer and will pay anything not because that is what the footballer is worth but because they can afford anything. The market is as false as the market for old masters. That is how the "market value" of the top footballers is determined.

With movie stars and other performers the situation is somewhat different. The shows are generally produced by somebody who is not using his own money. The producer makes an assessment that if he pays a small fortune for a particularly well known actor or musician the public will come and view the performance. The potential profitability of the show is important, whereas it is not to a billionaire football club owner.

The assessment of profitability might be correct or not. The celebrity who is chosen to be the lead whether in a live opera or film or theatre production might make or break the show. However the amount of the proceeds received from the viewers is divided very subjectively. The producer negotiates with the celebrity who has pulling power and decides whether he can afford the price. The rest goes to the supporting staff who can be bought off cheaply because there are so many around just waiting to be employed on the stage or cinema and will work for practically nothing.

Of course the consumer gets no say in how the price that he pays for viewing a live show is divided. He might decide that the lead artist or player in a football game is worth twice or three times the average. Yet the producer or football manager might pay him 200 or 1,000 times the average of all the collaborators who brought the show to the viewer.

There is a final control when one views a show or game live and that is the price paid by the viewer. If the price per seat is too high the celebrity might not be affordable. That sets a limit on the salary that he might receive.

When one views a football match or tennis match one might get as much pleasure in viewing a player ranked 100 as one gets viewing a player ranked number one. Indeed there are many instances in which a top team with celebrity players has lost to a team ranked far below them and even lower down in terms of incomes of the players. One sees top tennis players who have an entourage of professionals advising them what to eat and how to train and get fit struggling against and being beaten by outsiders who have no such facilities. Indeed even in terms of fitness the amateurs might rival the top professionals. Yet the pay of the top professionals is several multiples of what the lower ranked player earns.

The public might be very willing to pay half the price to see a 100 ranked player instead of the top ranked player. The 100 ranked player will receive far more than he received. In short the viewers watching a tennis match between a top ranked and 100 ranked player might choose to pay the top ranked player 2 times what the lower ranked player receives. Yet that is not how the proceeds of the sale of the ticket are divided. The top ranked player receives 10,000 times what the 100 ranked player receives. The view of the person who pays the price are ignored. The matter is left entirely to the discretion of the owner of the tournament or producer.

In short the person – the consumer – who pays the bill gets no say in how his money is divided. He either takes it or leaves it. The fact that he might be far happier with a second rate team at 10% of the price of the ticket is irrelevant. He does not have the choice. The choice is made for him. He can take it or leave it.

There are many stories about promoters or movie stars or musicians sending talented musicians away because in their opinion that is not what the public want, or because what they are offering will never sell, only to proved very wrong. How many talented performers have been prevented from entertaining the viewers because of the uninformed and wrong prejudices of a promoter?

Of course the explosion of exposure to TV has created more problems. The matter is taken away from the live viewer who has a choice to pay the price for the seat or not. I shall discuss the dynamics of TV in more detail later. At this stage it is sufficient to say that the calculation of relative worth of performers is even more complicated when viewers pay to see celebrities on TV.

Whereas the relative value of celebrities in a collaborative venture cannot be easily determined it should not be left to the whims of an individual in a small rigged market. There must be better ways of determining relative value.

Fortunately at least in the case of the skilled celebrities one can look at the changes from one year to the other in order to consider whether the changes in pay are justified.

One can for example compare with relative ease the price for the services of a celebrity today with his price at some earlier time and determine whether and if so to what extent any increased were justified by the change in the demand and supply for his services.

Starting with the supply side one should ask what a celebrity did one year compared to the previous year or earlier time, to be worth the increase in wages that he or she received. It is after all the vast increases in the pay of these skilled celebrities that has caused alarm and imbalances and might cause economic problems in the future.

A good place to start is with an analysis of the incomes of sportsmen and women. Has their productivity increased? The length of football matches is the same now as it was 100 years ago. The famous Pele is probably a better player than the footballer now who earns multiples of what he was paid. Golf records stand despite the equipment that allows golfers to strike the ball further. Tennis matches are of the same duration as before. There is no evidence that sportspeople do more or are more efficient. They are probably fitter as a result of hiring an army of professionals to help with their diet and training but the evidence in terms of performance is not of any great improvement.

Boxing matches are as long and there is probably nobody who would say that today's boxers are better than Ali. Yet today's boxers earn far more.

Ballet dancers of today are not any better than Nureyev. Moreover the shows that they perform are the same as they were in Nureyev's time. The list of comparisons can go on and on.

Clearly the output of sports people is not really any greater than it was. So how are these increases in real earnings justified?

Perhaps they can be justified on the grounds that more people view the vents live. There is no such evidence. The grounds – just like cinemas and theatres - are largely the same size as they have ever been and they are just as full as they were 50 years ago. The enjoyment of the public in terms of hours spent being entertained live is therefore roughly the same. So what is the justification for all the additional money that the celebrities are being paid.

Clearly it is not additional efficiency or productivity, the beloved term that is used in industry to justify increases in wages by trade unions or industrialists.

The answer is of course TV. Satellite TV has made entertainment available to the masses. Although the average football ground can only accommodate 50,000 viewers the TV rights make particular football matches available at the other end of the world. People in China or South Africa are now able to watch Manchester United play Chelsea because of satellite TV.

The TV companies incurred large capital expenditure in order to achieve their objective of bringing sporting events to the masses.

They had to recoup their expenditure. They did this by selling subscriptions to viewers and from advertising. The sports clubs and events organisers decided that they were entitled to a share of the income of the TV companies. The sportsmen and women likewise demanded their share, which increased as more and more viewers took up subscriptions for sporting channels. It was pure wage inflation. No additional output existed in terms of the efforts of the players. What they did merely came to be shown in living rooms around the world.

It was not the efforts of the players and their acolytes that caused this undoubted benefit to viewers. They just did what they had always done. Yet they were able to participate in and add to the cost of the TV companies who had to take the vast sums paid to these celebrities before they could recoup their investment.

Why did the celebrities charge so much for being viewed all over the world. The simple answer is because they could. The TV companies had to gain access to the sports events and were charged for the privilege. No significant or proportionate additional wealth was created by the players or the sports clubs, the additional wealth was produced by the TV companies, which incurred substantial capital expenditure in their enterprise. The demands of the sports companies merely added to the cost of the TV companies, which of course was passed on to the viewers.

The TV companies also obtained additional revenues from advertising. Whether the advertising worked or not is irrelevant because in most cases modern advertising involves competition for market share. One company advertises to take market share from its competitor. The advertising either is a waste of money or not. If it works the competitor retaliates by advertising and the status quo is returned. Nothing is achieved except that the costs of both companies increased and the income from sale of the end product has to be shared with the advertisers. Somebody in the production process has to get less.

Nevertheless from the point of view of the TV companies advertising is an additional source of revenue. Its cost is borne by the consumer of the end product or alternatively it has to be recouped from the other parties who are involved in the production of the end product.

We are still in the early stages of the TV satellite revolution. There was no way of telling how much money the TV companies would earn. They made estimates and on the basis of those estimates they competed with other TV companies for the rights to screen sports matches. Some market forces were in play but the competitors were small in number and the market small. Some of the TV companies have gone into insolvency because they overpaid. Some football clubs are insolvent because what they paid to their players was excessive. It will be sorted out in due course but in the meantime the price on sale of the end product has to be shared not only with the advertising executives but the footballers and the TV companies and their executives. We have yet to find out whether these people have been overpaid. In all probability they have been because to the extent that no additional end products have been produced and sold the increasing payments to sports people has to be offset by a reduced living standard elsewhere. The corresponding part of the transaction – payment – remains outstanding.

Superficially it would appear to be entirely reasonable to conclude that by bringing football matches to the masses a great good has been done for all and it is legitimate that the footballers should receive large increases in their incomes although their output or productivity has remained largely the same. The masses are willing to pay. The TV companies have created the new facility and are willing to pay the football clubs which in turn are willing to pay the footballers vast increases in their income.

So long as the TV companies and football clubs are solvent everybody should be happy.

There have been some TV companies and football clubs that became insolvent because the sums that they paid to clubs and to footballers have been excessive. However that is the normal consequence of doing business. It is what entrepreneurs do. They take risks and sometimes they overpay or their calculations turn out to be badly wrong. I make no criticism of these miscalculations.

However an economist who merely looks at the increases in incomes of footballers and football clubs without looking at the real source and consequences of such changes in income and who does not question whether any additional wealth is being created is failing in his duty.

Wealth creation and GDP increases are usually calculated either by calculating what has been produced or what has been consumed, comparing one year with another. The output is equal to the input for GDP purposes because everything that is consumed is – quite properly – assumed to have been produced.

In the case of the skilled celebrities an important dilemma faces the economist.   The output of the celebrities – the hours spent by the performers – has as I have shown remained the same. The consumption however has increased as more and more viewers get to see their favourite sports teams or sports stars playing their games. This has been occasioned by the introduction of satellite TV. In the process the price paid by the TV companies for the right to screen sports events has increased substantially with consequential stratospheric increase of the wages of these skilled celebrities.

We are here faced with a dilemma. Whereas the output of the producers has remained the same the consumption has increased. This is a unique phenomenon. The value of the output has simply increased substantially. Can that really be described as increased GDP or is it merely inflation.

Nobody has even considered that this is a possibility. Of course the capital expenditure paid by the TV companies does constitute additional wealth. The fact that the masses can now see their favourite teams and sports events on TV when they were previously unable to do so is clearly a benefit. However that is not our concern. We are concerned mainly with the increase in pay of the celebrities for doing what they have always done before. The cost to the football clubs for inserting a TV camera or two on their grounds was insignificant. Yet the rewards that they received has been astronomical. Can that really constitute increased GDP, which is how our economists have classified it.

Why is that important. So what if a few cameras in a football ground gives rise to vast additional amounts of revenue to the football club? The matter requires additional analysis.

In particular it is important to consider the point of view of the consumer and his ability to pay for the privilege of viewing his favourite team on TV. A proper analysis of what occurred when satellite TV was introduced is essential in considering its effect upon the economy.

With mechanization we assumed that we would have more leisure time but the opposite seems to have happened. Even if the number of hours spent working had decreased there was always a maximum amount of time per day in which the average consumer could spend being entertained. The number of hours per day has not increased.

In economic terms the explosion in viewing of sporting events suffers from the problem of reciprocity that I discussed earlier. If the TV companies sold their product to those involved in the internet revolution and received in return internet access no difficulties would arise. It would be – eventually once the money had changed hands from the buyer of the TV subscription to the supplier of the internet and vice versa - a pure barter transaction in which those involved in the internet provided internet services to those involved in screening sporting events via satellite TV and vice versa.

372

Unfortunately that would involve a very small number of transactions and the capital expenditure involved by both the internet and the TV companies could not be justified.

Satellite TV and later the internet had to be made available to the masses, who unfortunately in most cases have nothing to offer in return. For a while they borrowed in order to pay for viewing their favourite team or sports personnel playing. Now the borrowing is at an end because no more can be supported. The viewers have two options – to default on their borrowings, and watch no more TV or to reduce their expenditure on other forms of entertainment, such as going to pubs and restaurants or other forms of discretionary spending. Sooner or later the apparent growth created by the viewing of sports events on TV will turn into a zero sum gain as the economy rebalances and the subscribers to the TV companies withhold their payments from pubs and restaurants and other business that benefit from their discretionary spending.

The excessive wages of the footballers and the multitude of celebrities will therefore be paid for sooner or later by the collapse of pubs and restaurants, and perhaps car and travel companies and other suppliers of discretionary goods and services. The effects of the absence of reciprocity might be felt elsewhere in other continents. One thing is certain and that is that there will be consequences. For every additional £ received by the footballers and other skilled celebrities there will be a corresponding £ suffered either by another business or person. That is the inevitable consequence of inflation in wages for producing nothing more than one did before receiving a substantial wage increase.

The large rewards that are paid to the new army of unskilled celebrities who do ordinary things like cooking or identifying the function of a room in a house, are also difficult to explain logically or in terms of value or indeed market forces.

How can their astronomical salaries be justified and who pays for them and how. The answer to the latter question is difficult to determine but one can say for certain that unless they produce additional wealth their efforts and particularly the vast sums that they are paid constitute merely inflation and the effects of their vast payments will be felt elsewhere, possibly in Africa or India or even at home. For every additional £ paid to somebody in a zero sum gain activity there will be a £ less paid to some other person sooner or later here or elsewhere.

How is the analysis above relative to the new breed of celebrities that I have called unskilled celebrities?

I have called them unskilled celebrities because their work is done and can be done either better or worse by us all in some cases without but in other cases with a minimum of training.

Take a presenter master on a quiz show. They are paid huge sums to ask questions that are presented to them with answers. This not a particularly skilled job and the viewer wants to see the public and is minimally concerned with the confidence or otherwise of the presenter.

Yet no effort is made to introduce other presenters who might charge a fraction of the sum that is paid to the unskilled celebrity in this case. Market forces are purposefully excluded. The attitude seems to be that the number of viewers is satisfactory and one should therefore leave it at that. Only profitability is important. Of course that is the wrong attitude. The profitability of the shareholders could be much higher if a lower paid presenter was found. The answer is "why change a winning combination?". That of course means that market forces should be excluded and the duty of the executives to maximize the profits of shareholders should be ignored. So long as the shareholder gets enough that is the end of the matter.

It is the same with for example estate agents. The TV estate agents earn small fortunes. Economic theory is that so long as there is a large queue of equally competent estate agents able and willing to do their work of showing persons around a house in front a TV camera and pointing out the bathroom and the living room, the sums paid to these TV estate agents should be only marginally higher than what is paid to other estate agents. This particular principle seems to have been entirely ignored in determining how much to pay TV estate agents. Their income seems to have been determined on the basis of the number of viewers who tune in to the particular channel and if it is sufficient to make a profit to leave it alone. The fact that the same number of viewers would turn on to the channel even if other agents were doing the job for a fraction of what is paid to the established celebrity estate agents one should leave it alone. The market should be excluded. If it works sufficiently well the market can be ignored.

TV newsreaders are paid fortunes apparently because people watch them although there are large numbers who would be willing and able to do the same job for considerably less. Yet there is no evidence that people would not watch other less well paid presenters. There is no attempt to use market forces by asking the celebrity to take a pay cut because he or she can be easily replaced by a multitude of new readers. The argument seems to be the circuitous one that people are viewing that particular presenter and therefore he or she is the reason why they are watching and the viewers would go elsewhere if some other presenter read the news. Yet there is no such evidence that this is the case. In consequence these presenters are paid large sums that are determined by their ever increasing and self perpetuating status.

One innovation in news reading and presenting current affairs programmes has been using two presenters rather than one. It is always a male and female. They alternate in reading news items or presenting some item. One would have thought that as a result they would have to share what is paid to a news reader or presenter who acts on his or her own. Yet although there are two people doing the job of one the news readers or presenters are paid the same as if they were indeed doing the job on their own. This does not happen on the shop floor.

The theory behind this novel approach to news reading and presenting seems to be that men prefer to watch women and women prefer to watch men. Somehow it is explained in terms of sex. Certainly there is evidence that people like to watch attractive photogenic people. That does not justify the increases in wages since there are any number of photogenic people around who could do the job. There is also evidence that many viewers watching a current affairs programme care little about the image of the presenter and more about his or her intellect. There is also no evidence that viewers will desert those TV channels that use one news reader in favour of one that uses two photogenic readers of different sex. Yet this apparent inefficiency persists.

Other TV companies experiment with presenters standing up instead of sitting down the sole purpose of which seems to be to enable the viewer to see the presenter's legs.

Forty years ago there was one news TV channel, the BBC. Then there was ITV. Now there is Sky, CNN and many others.

Since it is the same news that is being presented on different TV programmes it is logical to infer that the number of viewers of news on Tv channels today is smaller and not greater than it was then there was one TV channel showing the news.

If there are fewer viewers surely the presenters should earn less. Yet the opposite has happened. The laws of economics and supply and demand have been stood on their head. You now get paid for doing less or for, in this case, having less viewers. If this is inflation the consequences will be felt sooner or later elsewhere. The additional pay for doing less will result in somebody in Sub Saharan Africa suffering the consequences.

www.ingramcontent.com/pod-product-compliance
Lightning Source LLC
Chambersburg PA
CBHW051439170526
45166CB00001B/41